BETWEEN THE STITCHING

*Discovering Yourself After
Losing Yourself*

Taylor Higgins

ISBN: 9781980810285

Cover Photograph, Eric Snyder Photography
Photograph of the Author, Creative Sparks Imagery

Printed in the United States of America

First Edition: July, 2018

First Printing: July, 2018

*To my beautiful parents, for supporting me as I carve
my name into this world.*

*And to my dearest brother, Sean, for ensuring the tools in
which I choose to carve with are always sharpened.*

A NOTE FROM THE AUTHOR

I never thought much about the game of baseball. Writing has been a life-long passion of mine, but never did I think I'd combine my love for arranging words with this particular sport. Welcome to my journey. With an open and honest heart, I invite you inside to join me during some of the most influential years of my life thus far.

My goal here was never to sabotage marriages, blast the game of baseball, or assassinate individual characters. I wrote this book to help mend the broken organ inside my chest. This story was my sole outlet to vent about real tragedies I'd endured. I am simply telling my truth. If you find yourself affected by my tellings in an unfortunate manner, evaluate your past. Being a decent human being keeps you out of the line of fire. Being a *good* human being keeps you out of non-fiction novels. These pages saved my life. To a universe full of fellow battered souls, heal with me through relation. — T

1

I attract broken people; lovers with misaligned framework and friendships with precarious foundations. For such an organic soul, I've always found this to be undeserved. Why must I be handed these defective individuals who have only mere fragments of themselves to offer? More importantly, why do I feel obligated to sweep these shattered particles into my dustpan and adhere them back to the damaged bodies they belong to?

Sometimes the people we love are unable to comprehend how we feel. I'd supply my own oxygen to those who can already breathe for the sake of hearing the crack of a smile. Not everyone operates this way. My mind goes to combat with my heart when someone needs saving and I've always allowed this to be the demolisher of all tranquility. Why barter for love with someone who has nothing to exchange with you?

Have you been introduced to the kind of torture that brings agony to your insides? Though I've made acquaintances with disappointment many times before, my first formal introduction to heartbreak was on a Sunday in July. I was kneeling on my bedroom floor, kneeling because my strength was suffering, with hands supporting my head that had collapsed into my palms. I couldn't find my way to my feet even if I tried. My cries were loud because my house was empty and I let each wail roam the hallways freely. I'd call his phone, for it was in those few short moments of ringing that I'd find solace; I'd find my breath. My sobs were momentarily nonexistent in case of the rare chance he decided to answer my phone call. I needed him to survive. I'd lift my gaze just enough to meet my unfortunate reflection in the mirror across the room. The skin on my face was blotchy and red; eyes bloodshot, lids swollen. I was drenched in my own tears and as I stared into my pathetic, green-eyed reflection I thought, *"How in the world did you end up like this?"*

That same night, for pleasure, I created a list of those who would attend my funeral if I were to die. Who would weep with folded heads and praying hands before my still, premature body as I was left out for display in a wooden box? Intentional suicide was never my mission. I knew my life had beautiful potential and I had no desire to cut it short. But he was killing me, from the inside out, and he knew it. I think he began to enjoy it. I believed I wouldn't live to see year twenty and the long list of people who would come to mourn my sudden departure gave me hope that he would recognize my importance one day.

So, how does one allow thyself to bask in such misery?

The attendance of love fuels emotions and generates actions. We operate upon our ability to give and receive love. There is nothing in this world more powerful than love. But when love fails us, or when it exits our life without appropriate reasoning, how are we expected to adjust and conquer such an influential emotion?

You may have to come apart on your bedroom floor on a random Sunday in July just to shake hands with the person you were meant to become all along.

Thick, heavy rain pelted the windshield of my BMW like hail as I sat atop the hill that overlooked Hadlock Field. It was June but the weather in Portland, Maine that night reminded me something of southern Florida's unpredictable showers; out of the blue and out of control.

Hadlock Field was home to the Portland Sea Dogs, a minor league, Double-A, baseball team affiliated with the Boston Red Sox. For those who are unfamiliar, this simply means if you earn your way from Double-A to Triple-A ball, you might have a shot at a shot at the ultimate goal— a major league debut.

One might ask, what was an eighteen-year-old pageant girl from Massachusetts doing at Hadlock Field, dressed to the nines only to be rained on and forced to watch a minor league baseball game alone from her car? I was there for a guy. A player, rather. *A Sea Dog.*

"Your Centerfielder... Number Eleven... Skyler Williams!" The announcer's voice echoed off the replica of the Green Monster in the outfield as I adjusted myself in the seat of

my car to get a better look at my sole purpose for being here. The poncho-wearing crowd of not even twenty people applauded weakly as he wiggled to the plate and prepared himself for the pitch. Typically baseball didn't excite me, nor did I watch many [any] games, but number eleven had my undivided attention as soon as he entered the batter's box. I held my breath at the crack of his bat and watched a pop fly land directly in the shortstops glove. *Shit.*

The umpires allowed the game to continue on regard-less of the weather and just long enough for it to count as a full game to avoid making it up. I couldn't wait for it to end. I'd never met number eleven before. Well, techni-cally, I had. It was in passing at a charity event but it was his Facebook message later that night that sealed the deal. After a thorough investigation of the life Mr. Williams chose to portray on the internet and weeks of constant, flirtatious messages, tonight would be the first time we'd spend time together. Alas, I saw the most beautiful thing I'd seen all night before my very eyes. The grounds' crew rushed onto the field to cover the infield with a tarp and the players dispersed into the locker rooms. The game was over and the Sea Dogs ended with a loss.

My phone began vibrating in the cup holder before the diamond of dirt was fully covered. It was Skyler.

"Hello there!" I sang into the phone.

"Please tell me you came."

"I'm here! In my car. Didn't feel like getting soaked. I saw the game too!"

"I'm sorry you drove up here for a rainy game."

"Oh, I didn't drive up here to enjoy the outdoors. Or for a baseball game, really. I came to see you."

Skyler giggled into the phone.

"I'm gonna take a quick shower. I'll meet you in the parking lot in a few."

All of a sudden I was nervous. I examined my make-up in the rearview mirror with the same lighting that illuminated Skyler's game and drenched myself in perfume for the sixth time, soaking my chest and neck so I would smell scrumptious during our greeting hug. I made sure my brows remained even and my overdrawn lip liner was still intact. I began chewing a brand new piece of gum and propped my boobs up perfectly in my black crop top. I was ready.

I watched a small crowd form at the gate surrounding the clubhouse where I'd assumed players would begin making their exit. Some wore ponchos which led me to believe they contributed to the undersized audience behind home plate. They gripped broken bats and worn pairs of cleats, and with wide eyes and bated breath, uncapped their markers as shadows appeared from the clubhouse doors. Dedication, I tell you. Some players stopped to scribble on the random assortment of paraphernalia, but most didn't even make eye contact with the shouting pack of faithfuls. As I analyzed the desperation within the fans, a man appeared from the darkness of the lot and tapped on my window. My body jerked.

"You scared me!" I cried.

"I tried to avoid the crowd. I came out a side door. I apologize for sneaking up on you like that."

I smiled like an idiot as our eyes made official contact. They were some shade of light blue, and they too were lit up by the stadium's flood lighting. His voice was sweet and his accent; a southern one.

"What?" he laughed. "Why are you looking at me like that?"

He gazed shyly at the ground as if my stares were too much for him to handle but he couldn't help but smile like a fool, too.

"It is so nice to finally meet you Skyler."

"I don't normally laugh this much, I promise. I'm just really happy to be looking at you right now. You are. Wow. You are beautiful."

I was beaming. Really, I mean you could probably see teeth for days. And in that moment I knew this man named Skyler would change my life forever.

"You're getting soaked. Let's get out of here," I said.

"Most restaurants in Portland close early. Come hang at my place? It's just up the road. You can follow me there. My truck is parked across the lot."

I followed his red, lifted, Chevrolet truck with large tires and a peach embroidered Georgia license plate for what seemed like forever down the barren back roads of Maine. The roads were long and winding with a street light every few miles. The farther we drove, the more static took over the radio and the fog, my view.

The sky was clear, forgiving all thundershowers from earlier, and the moon was glowing. When his truck entered the driveway to a house, it was obvious that it was a very big house.

"You see the deer on the ridge line?" Skyler said as his feet found the ground after free falling from his massive choice of transportation.

"Kind of. It's really foggy out here. And quiet."

I slammed the door to my car.

"Reminds me of home, Georgia. I love to deer hunt you know."

"It's peaceful, I'll say that." I lived twenty minutes outside of Boston and my city-slicking-self was used to bright skylines, angry drivers, overcrowded sidewalks, loud noises, and people who talked too fast. I knew nothing about deer hunting.

I followed him through the door next to the triple car garage and up a dark staircase, landing me in a marble foyer. It was rustic yet modern, wooden but chic. It was exceptional.

"This is your place?" I questioned.

Skyler smiled as he unlocked two massive, pine doors and lead me into a grand living room.

"Right this way, milady."

Tufted couches, wool rugs, pool tables, a full-length bar, and a stoned fireplace.

"What are you drinking?" he asked me from behind the bar.

"Um. I'll have whatever you're having."

He handed me a beer as I found a seat on the fancy leather. Laying out a coaster for himself, Skyler dropped his beer and headed towards the fireplace where a simple switch would ignite a flame. I admired my surroundings as I waited for his return and, in doing so, noticed neat arrangements of photographs with children throughout the room. The children were the same in every picture.

"Do you have kids?" I joked.

Skyler stared back in great confusion.

"I'm kidding. What's with the pictures?"

I pointed to the collage of redheaded babies on the mantle.

"I live with a host family. It's basically a family that volunteers their house for a player during season. I lucked out, not many guys get host families. I feel bad for the Dominican guys. They come over here with no car, no housing, and barely speak English."

"How'd you get so lucky?"

"With you or are we still talking about host families?"

I laughed awkwardly as anyone receiving a compliment from an attractive stranger would.

"This is my second season in Portland. I just happened to get lucky last year and they invited me back."

"Well, where do the other guys that aren't so lucky stay?"

"Five or so of them will go in on the cheapest apartment they can find. Some guys will cram into a hotel room together. It all depends. Air mattresses are our saviors."

I sat for a moment to digest these tragic conditions. The fire crackled softly as he joined me on the couch.

"That's not fair." The words practically burst from my mouth.

"*That* is minor league baseball."

Skyler tossed his head back and gulped down a hefty sip of beer. He scooted closer to me on the couch; our kneecaps now kissing.

"You are so beautiful, Taylor Higgins. Really. I catch myself staring."

I lifted the can of Bud Light to my lips as if it would hide my second toothy grin of the evening. I accidentally clanked the can on my front teeth and, without sipping, allowed my lips to rest on the aluminum edge as I gazed into the eyes of someone who already made me feel so loved.

Skyler placed his hand on my inner thigh.

"Spend the night. It's late and the weather hasn't been good."

Surprised at the request, I shrugged my shoulders. His words reeked of beer but his eyes and the tone in which he spoke were the ones that told me to stay.

"I guess I could stay."

He smiled and began massaging my thigh in a slow, rhythmic pattern with one hand. This was no longer casual drinking. Placing his beer on the table once more, he then removed mine from my grasp. Side by side they sat, as did we. My body was tense in the most ultimate way possible. Skyler leaned in as if we were about to share our first kiss but quickly rerouted to my ear. As his grip around my thigh grew tighter, his breathing equaled the intensity. He exhaled as if he were being pleasured though I hadn't even laid a finger on him yet.

Skyler's tongue found the tip of my ear and as he tasted from cartilage to lobe, I too began breathing heavily. With a sudden crunch, his teeth secured a grip around my earring. My body convulsed.

"I wanna know everything about you, Taylor," he whispered.

"I want to tell you everything."

He slid his hand underneath my hair where his palm would firmly swallow my neck bone. The pressure was enough to force my head to his face. Our noses pressed together; lips practically touching. Two very different worlds would soon formally collide at the meeting of our mouths. Was it passion? Was it lust? I watched Skyler squirm; hips practically thrusting in place.

My hand found his belt buckle.

"Are you sure?" he asked.

With strong desire in my eyes, I nodded. Skyler hurriedly undressed me; we managed to keep our lips attached the entire time. And when all I was left with was bare, naked skin, I leaned my vulnerable body backwards to study the man before me as he stripped himself. His silhouette was black against the roaring fire behind him.

I was completely naked on a stranger's couch, with a stranger, yet raising the tip of my finger to my mouth was the only suitable thing I could think to do. I bit and

I sucked as I listened to the unbuckling of his belt. The soft leather was flexible and swam freely through each loop on his jeans as he yanked it to the floor. I anticipated the way he would feel inside me. I was curious about the way his flesh would feel against mine for the first time. I wanted to smell his skin.

Skyler Williams dove into my collar bone. He soaked me with saliva only to use it as lubricant while massaging my breasts. His eyes examined every inch of my body; his hands followed where his eyes went. The chain worn around his neck, a cross, trailed his hands, running cold down my body. Impulsively, I tossed my head backwards. Enough to bring my gaze to the ceiling though I still wanted to watch him. With an arched back and white knuckles, I held onto his biceps as the evening unfolded between my legs.

Then, without hesitation, Skyler lifted my body to the nearby pool table. My nails clung to him, toes curled, as he thrusted into me. I slapped my hand over my mouth in hopes of silencing the moans; I didn't want to wake this so called "host family". I studied the room as we had intercourse for the first time. The dollhouse, toy trucks, an easel for painting. Could this be any more inappropriate? What if we wake them?

Skyler slipped a finger into my mouth as soon as he saw an opportunity to do so. My lips suctioned around this finger. I began to suck. Slowly. I demonstrated my mouth's capabilities. The low sounds we both made confirmed these newfound pleasures. Moments later, Skyler went into a fit of uncontrollable spasms on top of my body. I couldn't tell if it was pain or pleasure at this point.

"Did you just..?" I asked as I looked down at his penis. A white-ish, gooey liquid lay puddled on my stomach.

"I'm sorry. I just. You felt so good."

"Don't even worry," I said reassuringly. "That foreplay will getcha."

What I really wanted to say was, "But it wasn't even ten full seconds?"

"Did you?"

"Cum?" I asked.

He nodded. He looked as if he had failed me.

"Oh my god yes," I lied. Obviously."

The sun woke me bright and early the following morning in a bed with a sleepy Skyler by my side. For whatever reason, it felt as if I had been waking up next to him for years. We had been speaking via phone for quite some time, but this, this was unexplainably natural. There were no blinds on the floor-to-ceiling windows but instead, a fleece blanket draped over a curtain rod to barely hide the rays of light. Two plastic storage bins filled with wrinkled clothing and a suitcase of what looked like dirty laundry sat on the floor on my side of the bed. He had a closet, and the door was ajar, but the closet was empty. And my favorite detail of all; no air conditioning. Just a big, noisy fan to keep us from overheating in the June sun.

"Morning," I said with a raspy voice as I nudged his body. His eyes opened and a grin appeared upon his face. I had to pee but I didn't want him to hear my morning stream echoing off the bathroom tile quite yet. Peeing is weird at first.

"Mornin'," he whispered back, speaking away from me to hide his morning breath.

I gently attempted to wipe a cluster of crust from his eyelid.

"You know who you remind me of?"

I honed in on his pupils, hanging on the words to come. I waited for names like Carrie Underwood or Kendra Wilkinson.

"Who?!"

"My ex-fiancé. God, y'all might as well be twins."

I mean really, what a way to dampen the mood. Good morning to you, too.

"Interesting. Was not expecting that."

"Yes. My college girlfriend. I'm telling you, identical!"

Skyler flashed me a picture of a blonde girl on his phone who, unfortunately, looked incredibly similar to me. Who, unfortunately, remained in Skyler's photo gallery.

"Well what happened?" I asked. "Why aren't you together anymore?"

"Takes a special person to live the baseball life. I'm always traveling and I barely make enough money to support myself, never mind another person too. We spent more time apart than we did together and she didn't want to live like that anymore. She wanted to buy a house and start a family. She wanted a life partner. I couldn't give that to her at the time. It broke us. And it broke me that she couldn't support my dream."

"That's unfortunate. Or... maybe it isn't." I planted a kiss on his lips in hopes of changing the subject.

"It was sad but it has been years now. She hooked up with a random dude and he gave her the kid she always wanted. Maybe all of that happened so I would end up here in this moment with you. Ever think of that?"

"Maybe," I smirked.

Skyler jumped out of bed after looking at the time on his phone. Another day given to baseball would soon begin. I watched him dig through the bin of wrinkled clothing in search of some clean items.

"Nothing like living out of bags and bins year round," he said. "I really need to do laundry."

"I still can't get over the fact that you play seven games a week without a day off."

"That's the minor league grind."

"Can you call in sick today?" I asked with puppy dog eyes.

I was kidding. Kind of. But Skyler looked at me as if I were insane. He brushed his teeth, gelled his hair, and put minimal items into a bag. Today the Sea Dogs were being chartered by bus to Harrisburg, Pennsylvania for a series against the Senators. One bus means you and your bag share one single seat. Triple A bus rides allow for two buses and the relevant players get both seats to themselves. Imagine calling two bus seats a luxury?

"I leave for National's next week you know," I said. "I want to see you before I leave."

I was crowned Miss Teen Massachusetts this past April, which is why we briefly met during a charity event, and I would represent the state of Massachusetts at the National pageant in Washington D.C. during the first week of July.

"We will be home next Friday. Come spend the night?"

"My flight leaves at six the next morning. *Leaves!* I don't think that will work."

"I don't know then. That's really the only way. Otherwise, we'll just have to wait two weeks. We can do that."

"Two weeks! I can't wait two weeks. I'll see you Friday night. I'll sleep on the plane." We said the sweetest of goodbyes in the host family's driveway as I wished him well for the very first time on his road trip. I'd known Skyler's physical presence less than twenty-four hours yet I'd confidently realized I would forever dread our farewells. He had awakened something inside me at such a young age. I was excited for our time together and I was eager to give him my heart. I craved our connection at all hours of the day. Skyler, at twenty-six years old, made me feel sad that I hadn't met him sooner in life. That I'd missed most of his twenties. That I'd lost out on memories we could have made sooner if only our paths would have crossed at an earlier time. Now, all I wanted from Skyler Williams from Georgia was *more* of Skyler Williams from Georgia.

2

Awaiting the return of a baseball player after we'd been forced to be apart for so long, was a mind game of its own. Anticipation turns into a form of torture, and this particular lifestyle had the ability to make an average week feel like a decade. I discovered the importance of "live streaming" minor league baseball games. I'd crawl into bed with my laptop and watch a grainy, often times blurry, version of a baseball game just to catch a glimpse of number eleven's face and of course, always sending him a snap of my computer screen to prove I cared enough to watch it. If this was his life, it would be mine too. I gained interest in the game itself.

His performance at the plate and in the outfield became ridiculously important to me and I wanted to be a part of his good nights and his bad nights as they happened, even if we were in different states. Post game nights consisted of a late night phone conversation once he got back to his hotel. We'd chat about our days, his game, and how this particular hotel lobby had the warmest cookies in the league, until we'd both start to fade. We would lay in separate beds with our eyes closed, hundreds and hundreds of miles apart, holding phones against our ears just to listen to the sound of each other's presence, the sound of breath. I didn't know a thing about the baseball life, but I so badly wanted to be a part of Skyler's life.

If I'm being honest, the love Skyler and I grew into, was like no other. We harbored on the thought that our individual selves had been created only to find one another. That our lives hadn't begun until just now.

Two weeks after our first encounter, Skyler told me he was in love with me. He sent me flowers when he was away, cards with poems inside, and pictures of houses he dreamed of buying with me one day. He sent me horoscopes that related to us as a pair and pictures of gorgeous, blonde children that resembled me, the girl he labeled as his "future". He suggested we begin our search for engagement rings and offered ideas of potential venues for our wedding day. He was the one. It happened that fast.

I spent my week preparing for National's before driving to Portland the following Friday as promised. I packed until I was over packed and until our sleep countdown was over. *Three more sleeps! Two more sleeps! One more sleep!* And though we would soon begin another countdown, it wasn't for us to think about this particular Friday.

As I watched the sun set over a five past seven first pitch at Hadlock Field, I thought about one thing and one thing only: setting my alarm that night. The alarm that would wake me from the minimal amount of sleep I knew I'd be getting, and would once again force me away from Skyler for an uncontrollable period of time. Time, god damnit. There's never enough of it. Except during baseball games. Then it becomes infinite.

Three and a half hours and nine innings later, the Sea Dogs picked up a win. A win, in my book, meant I'd be dealing with a happy Skyler. He also got on base during each at bat tonight, so yes, there would definitely be a happy Skyler.

"Finally got to see a game from the stands," Skyler said as he exited the clubhouse doors. I was waiting for him to come out. Once my brain registered that it was in fact his voice coming from the muscular shadow, I ran directly into his arms. His hair was still wet from his shower and his body smelled of cheap locker room soap. He picked me up and held me as I wrapped my legs around his body.

"I missed you. I really did," I said into his ear. My head was on his shoulder.

"I missed you too pretty girl."

We pushed passed the tiny crowd of straggling fans awaiting autographs at the gate. For the first time, I made eye contact with these devoted individuals. They looked... well we were in Maine, I'll leave it at that.

"I don't want to go to D.C.," I said as I ran my fingers through his hair. We were in bed at his host family's house. Skyler didn't have a TV in his room so we sat in darkness and listened to the sound of the industrial fan.

"You'll be back before you know it Tay. You're gonna do great."

"I know. I just. I'll miss you. That's all. I feel like that's all I do. Miss you."

"That's baseball, baby. I told you. It ain't easy. We will be fine."

Nobody was forcing me to enter into this lifestyle. Nobody was forcing me into the sweltering heat to watch a game two hours from my home only to turn around and get on a plane. I knew I'd spend my time missing someone who couldn't control the things that made me sad, I'd already accepted that. People hear the title *professional baseball player* and immediately assume money and fame. Skyler, as a professional baseball player, earns a salary of less than ten-thousand-dollars per season. He is only paid during season, leaving him to fend for himself during the baseball-less months. From my understanding, players survive in the off-season from teaching baseball lessons, picking up a part-time position at Dick's Sporting Goods, and if their ego allows it, filing for unemployment. Though you are essentially an attachment to a major league club, there is absolutely nothing glamorous about minor league baseball.

But you had sex with him the first night you met him, you whore! How is that love? It's 2018. You know when you know, people. Minor league baseball, however, is a force. If you understand this and choose to accompany someone through the minors anyway, you have real love on your hands. Minor league ball will strip you of everything you have: Money, confidence, morals, health, strength, courage, faith. It is a business. If you can consistently produce, you will stay. If you slip up, you will be replaced. If you're looking for door knob diamonds and vacations in Bali, minor league baseball is not the place for you. It is a place to prove that love is unbreakable. Besides ladies, being a cleat chasin', puck sluttin', whatever-you-wanna-call-it kinda chick is about as cool as the fake ID you ordered online when you were sixteen to prove to your local Super Bowl champions you were old enough to hang. I chose him for *him*.

The repulsive sound of my phone's alarm clock woke me at 2:00 AM on the dot. I slowly made my way out of bed and into the bathroom. As I brushed my teeth, my reflection in the mirror spoke volumes. My eyes were so tired. The opportunity of a lifetime awaited me, yet my heart just wasn't in it in that moment. The chance to represent my country was on the horizon and the only place I wanted to be was in Skyler's arms. Wherever that would be.

I leaned over Skyler's sleeping body to kiss him goodbye. Neck, cheeks, and lips.

"My breath stinks," he announced.

"I couldn't actually care less."

"Go kill it in D.C. Enjoy it! You got this Tay. I believe in you."

I wanted to cry. I didn't want to go. Please don't make me go.

The drive from the host family's house to my house in Wilmington was a long, dark one. Three tolls; five dollars, three dollars, and two dollars. These were landmarks to me and helped me determine how much longer I'd be on the road. They were also smashing my spare change collection in my center console. Being a full-time college student meant I was poor and becoming a baseball gypsy required money I quite frankly didn't have. Scraping by would become my new profession. By circumstance, not choice.

I knew exactly where I'd lose a radio station on the road and what channel to switch to as I made my way through southern Maine and New Hampshire. I became familiar with the road's massive potholes, and knew exactly when to switch lanes to avoid them. My gas tank was always on the verge of empty and the mileage on my 2006 BMW was skyrocketing. I did all of these things without blinking. It was my duty to make this work. He had no control of his life so it would be me to sacrifice the time and energy to bring us together.

All state titleholders are required to travel "appearance ready," meaning we should be dressed professionally instead of the typical sweatpants, sweatshirt, and bedhead airport attire. The Miss Teen Massachusetts sash was to be draped across my body at all times in public during travel.

My father, Joe, mumbled, *"Fuckin' douchebag!"* under his breath in the wee hours of the morning while attempting to stuff four suitcases into the car after I arrived home. He then threatened me about being late. I am always late. Inside, my mother, Denise, scolded my fifteen-year-old brother, Sean, for taking his sweet time getting out the door. Even in a burning building, Sean's pace will never change.

Ninety-three south, the interstate that goes directly into Boston, was normally a parking lot. Because we left before the sun came up, we sailed into town in twenty minutes. I continuously nodded off in the back seat, allowing my forehead to bang against the window each time. My orange-like foundation left smudges on the glass. My parents used this as an *I told you not to go to Portland last night* moment. Spare me, rents. I'm in love.

I paraded through a near empty Logan International Airport with the Massachusetts sash draped proudly over my body as instructed. I posed for a few pictures, handed out a few autograph cards, and signed a few personal objects before shoving the sash back into its case. I didn't want the attention. I didn't want to engage with others. I wasn't happy but it was my job to make everyone else happy. *He* should be able to share this with me.

Cameras, compliments, new voices, and well wishes surrounded me. I made so many people smile. Did they know a part of me was missing? Could they sense my inner sadness? I didn't know how to retrieve the same bliss I'd been handing out all day and it was disappointing; exhausting. My heart wasn't with me. My heart was playing centerfield in Portland. I needed to go home.

But I didn't. Day one of National's consisted of registration, contestant meet and greets, and a mandatory dinner. Luckily, they kept us busy. The events, fashion shows, fittings, charities, parades, rehearsals, and interviews reduced the time in which my brain would marinate in the sweet thoughts of Skyler Williams. There was minimal time to use my phone. In fact they told us not to use our phones. But at night. Oh, at night. I missed him until my eyes closed. My body needed him in a way it had never needed anything before.

On the night before the nationally televised pageant, I convinced my mother to book me a direct flight out of D.C. as soon as the show ended and Miss Teen Whoever was crowned. It wouldn't be me because I didn't want it badly enough. After the whole *Do you know how many girls would kill to be in your shoes right now?* lecture, she agreed. I think she felt the ache in my heart. The longing. I had a flight to Portland two hours post pageant, regardless of the outcome. Now I just had to compete.

I snuck in a call to Skyler before the competition.

"How is it going babe?" he asked. I was surprised he asked. Usually I'm the one asking about his day.

"Busy. We've been rehearsing all day. They are very strict with us. My feet are killing me. Heels all day. Brutal. I'm going to need a full body massage after this."

"I can do that for you. You excited?"

"Yeah," I lied. "Guess what? I'm flying to Portland after the show!"

"Tonight?! You changed your flight?"

"Well, I booked a new one."

"Send me your itinerary and I'll be there baby. I can't believe you changed your flight. I'm so excited to see you! Now get out there and perform!"

I wore a red, mermaid dress with crystal beading as I allowed my excitement to see Skyler fuel my onstage performance. I envisioned myself boarding the plane the entire time.

"Taylor Higgins... Eighteen... Massachusetts!" I introduced myself through a microphone to a theater full of people I didn't know. The stage lights were bright and my view, nothing but a pitch black blur. I don't remember much of it honestly.

Not one state from New England placed. Miss Teen Arizona took home the National crown. Alabama was first runner up. Bama said she had been competing in pageants her whole life and I won't lie, I felt like a rookie compared to some girls. Miss Teen Massachusetts was my first pageant ever, National's my second. I took home not a National crown, but an experience high school could never give me. I had been chosen to represent my lifelong home state of Massachusetts, performed during a live broadcast, and interviewed with a panel of ten prominent celebrity judges from around the country. Alone, these experiences would shape my future in more ways than one and for that I was grateful.

I thanked my parents for everything it took to get me there, and then deserted them at the hotel. They were to fly home in the morning with Sean. I took the hotel shuttle to the airport and finally fulfilled my fantasy of boarding a plane to Portland, Maine. I was on my way to find home.

It was the coldest, emptiest flight I'd been on and my body refused to fall asleep. I tossed and turned in my seat; shivering in misery. Then, bang. The wheels of the plane touched the ground and the weight of my body was forced forward. I texted Skyler to inform him of my arrival.

In a state of sleepy confusion, I realized home would never again be measured by sheetrock and beams or two coordinates on a grid. "Home" is the people that make you feel like you are exactly where you are supposed to be at that moment in time. While deplaning, I felt the chill in Portland's midnight air. It wasn't this cold in D.C., but the cold air felt right.

I saw him before he saw me. He was standing at the correct luggage carousel. I dropped everything in my hands; my purse, my crown box, a sweater. And ran. He saw me because my feet sounded like a herd of cattle coming in hot. He was smiling as I attacked. People probably thought I spent the past few months backpacking Nepal and I just got off my international flight. A second full week apart was completed. I didn't want to spend any more time apart. I wanted to travel with him.

"Hi babe," he said as he stroked my back during our longest embrace yet.

"Are you sick?" He had almost no voice.

"Very. I'm sorry. I should have told you. You're going to get so sick. Or should I say *wicked* sick?"

"What kind of sick are you?"

"Everyone on the team has the flu. So maybe I have the flu. I don't know. Sore throat. Fever. Chills. Body aches. Stuff like that."

"Have you seen a doctor?"

"No. I probably should. Let's find your suitcase and get out of here."

We arrived to the host family's house around 1:00 AM. I flopped onto the bed still feeling as though I was onboard a moving plane. I listened to each sound as he rinsed his face in the bathroom sink while anxiously awaiting his chest pressed against my backside. The room went dark and Skyler slid underneath the covers smelling like minty toothpaste, finding his way to me in nothing but the moonlight the makeshift shade let in. He held me tight with one arm over my body. Our hands aligned and our fingers interlaced as I drifted into the most peaceful of sleeps. Tonight, home was this basement.

"Told you we could do it Tay."

In mid July, a wonderful thing happens in the baseball community. The All-Star Game. It is a symbolic game consisting of select players from each team throughout the league. If you are not selected to play in this game - as Skyler wasn't, this simply means you have a few days off. Full, uninterrupted, baseball-free days? Sign me up.

"How will you be spending the break Skyler? Any plans? You know we have the lake house. It's about an hour north. It's all yours if you want it," said his host mom, Holly.

Today was my first day meeting Holly. It was the first time I'd been in her house during the day. It was noon and her teeth were stained with red wine.

"Really?" Skyler questioned. "What do you think Tay?"

"Of course! Take the boat out if you want. You work so hard! Go relax!" She swirled the wine in her glass as she spoke, agitating it before each gulp.

I thought to myself, *"Jesus, lady. It's a Tuesday. Put the bottle down."*

"I wouldn't mind going. Thank you for offering, Holly," I said instead.

Holly moved in to pet Skyler's face.

"I expect a full report on how much fun you had when you get back. We can split another bottle of wine and watch a movie after Jerry and the kids go to sleep. Deal?"

Skyler chuckled and nodded his head. Wait, what? All along I thought host families took in players out of the goodness of their heart. Holly, however, made me feel like she had ulterior motives. I no longer thought she hosted players for free season tickets. But that was just my gut.

"Everything good?" Skyler asked as we drove to dinner in silence. It was two meals and two desserts for twenty-five dollars tonight at Chili's. These types of deals excited us.

"I'm good," I said. Our relationship was still fresh. I didn't want to seem territorial already. Especially over the older woman who provided him shelter.

"You're biting your nails. I know you are thinking about something. Tell me."

"I mean… I didn't know you and Holly watched movies and drank wine together."

"Relax. She's married! She's flirtatious. And kind of a drunk. That's all."

"She wants to fuck you Skyler."

"She's married!"

"Has that stopped people before?"

"She's not even that hot."

"You're an ass. That's irrelevant."

"No it's not. Come on, babe. Stop it."

Skyler grabbed my hand as he drove and kissed the top of it.

"I got my girl. I got all I need right here."

The following day we took my new enemy, Holly, up on her offer to visit the lake house. Just because she flirted with my boyfriend in front of me didn't mean her husband didn't make a shit ton of money and they didn't own a lakefront property. We drove almost two hours after getting lost a couple times with Skyler's teammate, Kyle Creedon, and his wife, Sam. Kyle was a pitcher. He played in just about every minor league organization there was, so I was interested in picking his brain. They were from Texas and sometimes, when they spoke too fast, I couldn't understand what they were saying. But they were really nice people and I was excited about my very first WAG [wives and girlfriends] friend.

When we arrived, the men carried our not-so-overnight bags into the house as we lugged in groceries. I'd never been anywhere as quiet as this particular lake house.

"Ain't got no cable or wifi," Kyle said as he messed with the remote.

"We didn't come here to watch movies hun," Sam said.

Skyler was already down at the dock taking the cover off the boat.

"Go help Skyler, hun. Taylor and I will start dinner."

Kyle obeyed his wife's wishes. I, on the other hand, had zero cooking skills.

"He adores you," Sam said as she unpacked the hamburger buns.

I gave her a strange look, assuming she was still talking about Kyle.

"Skyler I mean. I've known him for a long time. Kyle's been playing with him for the past five years. I knew him back in the Melanie days. That's why I said I can tell he adores you."

"Melanie. Is that his ex-fiancé's name?"

"I'm sorry. Yes. You knew he was engaged before right?"

"Yeah he told me. He also told me I'm her twin. So that's awesome."

Sam laughed.

"You do kinda look like her. You're much prettier though."

"What was she like?" I asked.

"She was a sweet girl. Super quiet, but sweet. She came from money and it was obvious. She always came to visit when the boys played in Salem, Virginia. They were roommates, you know. She'd make the drive in her shiny Lexus and complain about things like humidity in the middle of July. I know they bought a house together right before they split."

"He neglected to tell me about the house part. Why'd they end it?"

"He cheated on her. A lot. But I mean, she was a pain to deal with. I think he was done. And I think she was done too. But neither of them could end it type of thing. They were comfortable and I think she was embarrassed to fail. Restarting can be a scary image."

"He told me she couldn't do the baseball life. And then she got knocked up by a random guy. And now they're living happily ever after somewhere."

"Well who knows. I wasn't trying to stir the pot." Sam quickly changed the subject. "All I know is that he looks at you like you're gold. As he should."

The boys fished from a canoe until the sun faded into the trees. Sam and I bonded over pasta salad and cheap wine in coffee mugs. She was sassy and smart and her energy was infectious. She made me promise one-hundred times I'd visit Texas. I told her, "Only if you visit Boston."

The next morning, I woke with eyes crusted shut. I was sick. I couldn't swallow the saliva in my mouth, never mind water. Against my body's wishes, I'd send myself into great coughing fits. Razor blade pains filled my chest. It hurt to move. I needed antibiotics and I needed them now.

"You alright baby?" Skyler joined me in a seated position on the bed. My coughing antics woke him up.

"I am so sick." I could barely speak. "I need to go to the doctors. How did you live with this?"

"We'll get you right home babe. I'll tell Sam and Kyle and get the car packed."

I felt terrible. Internally, yes. But even more so that I'd cut Skyler's one and only break short. All he wanted to do was fish. I was four hours from my house in Massachusetts and the journey southbound was soon to begin.

I had to wait an entire day before I could see my doctor back home. I wore sweatpants with leggings underneath them, two shirts, a sweatshirt, and my bathrobe to bed. I layered myself underneath five different blankets. I could not get warm yet my fever was rising by the hour.

My mother drove me to my pediatrician's office for my appointment. Yes, pediatrician. I sat on the exam table, braless in a t-shirt, back against the wall. My face was red and I was sweating profusely. The air conditioning vent above me made my cone-titty nipples rise. I stared at the Curious George murals above the infant scale across the room. It was time I graduated to a new doctor.

I left with pneumonia coupled with strep throat. Skyler tore himself up over the fact that he was the one who made me so sick. I told him I knew he was sick and kissed him anyway. That night, he prepared himself for another road trip. I prepared to take antibiotics and rest. My phone rang as I began falling into a drugged sleep.

"How are you feeling my love? I wanted to call you before bed," he said.

"I've had better days," I mumbled into the phone from my pillow.

"I feel so bad."

"I would do it all over again, don't feel bad," I said with pride.

"You know something?"

"Tell me."

"I've been thinking. I really hope we can be like Sam and Kyle someday. Someday soon. Married and so in love."

"Are we just going to skip the whole girlfriend thing?"

"Taylor you are my girlfriend."

"Pretty sure you have to *ask* someone to be your girlfriend."

"I thought you knew. I assumed. I thought. I thought we were on the same page. I'm shocked. I thought you were my girlfriend."

"Technically you never asked. Just saying."

"I didn't think I had to. Wow."

Skyler was genuinely upset by this. I apologized for not assuming the status of our relationship. My apologies seemed to suppress his frustrations and that's all that mattered to me. I just wanted to rest.

Skyler had a five game series on the road in Akron, Ohio. There, the Sea Dogs would face the RubberDucks. I know what you're thinking. Whoever was in charge of naming these minor league teams must have been like, "Let's use the queerest names we can come up with!"

The next day I received flowers at my door.

Beautiful!

I'm so grateful to have met you and to have you be a part of my life. I'm excited for what the future has in store for the two of us! You are my missing puzzle piece in this crazy life I live. Every time I see a white BMW I check to see if it has a Massachusetts tag. Hope this makes you smile because that's when you're the prettiest! P.S. I sprayed my t-shirts with your perfume before I left. I miss you.

I love you!

—Skyler

When I called him to thank him for the arrangement, he insisted I come along on the next away series. "I want you here with me. I'm tired of missing you," he said. The next away series would be one week long, split between Bowie, Maryland and Richmond, Virginia. His family had been planning to make the drive from Georgia to watch each series.

"So you want your girlfriend to meet your family is what you're saying?" I asked.

"More than anything. They will love you."

So, what did I do? I booked a flight to Baltimore of course. Three days in Maryland, three days in Virginia. When I told Sam about these plans, she booked a seat on the exact same flight. Sam, a college graduate with a degree in business management, currently worked part-time at a Forever 21 in Portland to make ends meet. Lord knows, the minor league pay stubs just weren't cutting it. I was surprised she wanted to join but it was great news for Skyler and I.

On road trips, each player is assigned a hotel roommate. Kyle and Skyler requested to room together on this trip, that way one room is paid for by the team and the four of us could split the cost of an additional room. Voila, a cheap way for the ladies to visit all while having our own rooms. #MinorLeagueHacks

"Tell me about your family. Who is coming on the trip?" I sung into the phone late one night after a game.

"My momma, Doreen. She will be your new best friend. My daddy, Shane. He's hysterical. My middle brother, Shia. He's your age. He's... different. You'll see what I mean. Doesn't play sports, wants to be a scientist or something. Stuff like that. And my youngest brother, Sheriden. He's a mini me and he's a really good baseball player. Oh and Mamaw, my momma's momma. She's like a second mother to me."

"You got quite the crew coming. I can't wait."

July twentieth was Skyler's twenty-seventh birthday and with him being in Maine and so far from his family, I felt it was my responsibility to give him the proper birthday celebration. I bought him Rock Revival jeans and some Affliction t-shirts because that seemed to be the standard outfit of choice for ballplayers. Jeans with white piping, Vans, and a G-Shock. That was the clubhouse combination. I was also sick of seeing Skyler rotate through the same three shirts. My mother also baked him a homemade cake.

I drove to Portland, watched his game, and felt as proud as a peacock presenting him with his perfectly wrapped gifts later that night. I noticed a cardboard box sitting on his dresser with a Happy Birthday card on top. Nosy ole' me opened it. Inside read *Happy Birthday, Son!* with a twenty-five dollar gift card to Taco Bell. Because nothing says you're turning twenty-seven like a gift card to Taco Bell. Seeing this made me feel sad for him.

We climbed into bed together; both ready to finish his day with a bang. Literally. We were naked under the sheets. Kissing and touching. Busy removing all articles of clothing. It was hot; wet.

"I love kissing you," he whispered to me.

I kissed him harder. I assumed the host family was home. After all, it was late at night. But Skyler's bedroom was so far from the main area of the house so I wasn't shy when it came to letting my moans roam freely about the cabin if you know what I mean. My naked self crawled atop my boyfriend's naked body. I held a single sheet around my frame as I rode into the night. Suddenly, I heard a noise in Skyler's bathroom. Now the bathroom, which is directly connected to Skyler's room, connects into another adjoining bedroom. That bedroom has an entrance of its own but nobody ever goes in there.

"STOP! Do you hear that?!" I said as I cautiously danced up and down.

"No. Hear what?"

"It sounded like someone was in the bathroom."

"You're hearing things." He grabbed onto my bottom lip with his teeth and released it slowly.

I sat up tall. I dropped the sheet to protect it from our bodily fluids while still riding and preparing to give an unforgettable closer and then, the bathroom door flung open.

"Just emptying the trash can in the bathroom! The only time I can ever get things done is when the kids go to sleep. I wanted to ask about the lake house!"

It was Holly. I fell off of Skyler's body; landing beside him in bed and grabbing blankets to shield our bodies from Holly's view.

"Oh. I'm sorry. I didn't see Taylor's car in the drive-way," she said.

She came into his room late at night expecting him to be alone? To what, have a friendly conversation? Ok.

"And you're still going to try and tell me she doesn't want to fuck you?" I said.

"I have no idea what that was all about."

"This shit is too weird for me." I grabbed one of his t-shirts off the floor and through it over my head.

"Hold on, wait, are we finished?" he asked in a hurry.

"Do you think I feel like having sex after that? You need to figure it out man."

Six days and seven baseball games later I celebrated my nineteenth birthday in Portland and the thought of host mom Holly freshly lingered in my mind. Skyler treated me to breakfast at the Denny's next to the stadium. Room temperature coffee and a sixteen dollar tab had me labeling this as a memorable day.

"I gotta stop at the gas station on the way to the field. I have such a headache," Skyler said as he rested his head in the palm of his hand.

"You didn't drink much of your coffee. It's probably a caffeine headache."

He stirred his pale colored coffee with his spoon. He'd put so much cream and sugar into the coffee that it may have well been a cup of milk at this point.

"A few energy drinks and some Adderall is what I need."

"You take Adderall? Why am I just finding out about this right now?"

"I didn't think it was something I was supposed to tell you. Besides, everyone takes *something*."

"What do you mean by that?"

"Taylor we play games seven days a week with no days off. Eventually your body starts to fall apart on you. So we do what we have to do to keep it together. If they don't test for it and it keeps you on the field, we'll take it. Cept weed. You can't smoke weed in the minors but they don't test for it in the majors. Going to the majors also means you can become a pothead."

"Do you actually need Adderall though? Like do you have ADHD?" I questioned.

"No," he laughed. "Tell any doc you can't focus and they practically throw that shit at you. Like I said, as long as they don't test for it, the organization doesn't care."

I uncomfortably adjusted myself in our booth while fumbling with my overcooked scrambled eggs. Skyler reached into the pocket of his jeans.

"See these?" He presented a handful of tiny, white pills.

"What are those? Why do you have them?"

"Think they're called Tramadol. I don't know. They're painkillers whatever they are. These little things keep me on the field seven days a week, especially this late in the season. My body aches all the time so I call them my *magic pills*. I couldn't play without them."

"They will prescribe painkillers just for body aches? I mean, you're not even technically hurt Skyler. You're just worn out and sore."

He laughed again. "I don't have a prescription for these. They're my Auntie's. She had some procedure done a while ago. Or maybe it was cancer. Who knows. She still complains of pain though just so she can hand the bottles of medication off to my father and I."

"Why does your dad need them?"

"Been doing manual labor all his life. His body is a mess."

I sat in silence for a moment to swallow this new information. It made me look at not only him differently, but his family, his aunt, and most of all— the entire community of baseball. Was it that easy to turn a blind eye on prescription painkillers? *Well, as long as we don't test for it!* What? You're practically holding the door open for drug addiction to what is suppose to be the future of baseball. You can't smoke marijuana in the minors, but other than that, if we don't test for it, help yourself. As if it's some kind of damn free for all. Find your best way to legally use drugs, gentleman!

"How do you get them? The pills?" I asked.

"My mom mails me a new bottle every month. I'm lucky. A lot of the guys have to buy from guys in Triple A or major league players if they have that connection. Guys are always willing to sell."

"That's basically drug dealing." I was pissed now.

"That's basically baseball."

3

Early August came as did my trip to Baltimore to meet the Williams family or, as Skyler referred to them, my "in-laws". I fantasized about meeting the family he spoke so highly of, especially because of how close they were, though my excitement did subside over a handful of pain pills at Denny's. Sam and I shuttled to the team hotel from the airport, a Comfort Inn, which was a pleasant surprise compared to some of the other decrepit motels the teams previously visited.

As I waited for the bus driver to unload my suitcase, I noticed a young boy's bare ass in one of the hotel room windows. *Ugh.* Skyler's brothers were watching us from the window, and that ass belonged to Sheriden.

Our men met us in the lobby and directed us to our separate rooms.

"They can't wait to meet you. My family. My brothers have been waiting in the window looking for the hotel shuttle," Skyler said in the elevator.

"Really! That makes me happy to hear that."

"Here we go," he said as he knocked on a random door.

We were greeted instantly by his mother and grandmother. I was overwhelmed with screams, hugs, and welcoming words.

"How was your flight? It's so nice to finally meet you! Are you hungry?" Mamaw was all over the place with the questions.

"Y'all get up and say hello to Taylor," insisted Skyler's mother to two boys sitting on the sofa bed. The eldest of the pair stuck his hand out.

"Shia. Pleasure."

"Pleasure returned," I replied.

The youngest stayed seated. He couldn't make eye contact with me either.

"I know you," I said to him. He looked at me with wide, disbelieving eyes. "You were the one showing me your butt cheeks in the window."

Everyone laughed, except Sheriden, who tried to hide his dirty, little smirk.

"Where's your dad Skyler?" I asked.

"Sleepin'. Lazy son of a bitch he is!" his mother answered for him.

"I ain't sleepin'! Shut up Doreen!" Skyler's father yelled as he appeared from the back bedroom.

A short man with gray hair looked me up and down and up and down in silence until he finally said, "Well hot damn Skyler! You've got yourself a winner right here!"

"Y'all fixin' to eat? We are starved," announced Doreen. I wasn't hungry at all but everyone in the room apparently was.

"I could eat," I lied.

All seven of us squished into the elevator, my arm being held firmly against Skyler's father's arm.

"You smell nice," he said to me.

"Thank you."

"Fuck, Skyler. God damn. No shit you can't last long in bed with her. Hell I wouldn't either. Look at the damn blue sundress she's wearin'! Mmmmmm."

I shot Skyler a look. The entire family was unbothered by his words which was even more disturbing.

"You know somethin' Taylor?" asked his father.

"What's that?" I was afraid of what his words might be.

"I made all *four* of my boys in under eight seconds and I'm damn proud of it. Skyler's momma here sure knows what she's doing!"

Everyone laughed. I tried to fake something that sounded like a laugh.

"*Four* boys?" I questioned. I only knew of Skyler and his two brothers.

"Yessum. These boys have an older brother. Different momma though. She's dead now anyway. Drugs or somethin' or other."

Everyone once again erupted with laughter. I guess I didn't understand ignorant humor. He was reckless with his words; nothing short of crude. I wanted to go home already.

Skyler's mother slapped me on the back. "Lighten up Taylor. He's only messin'." She must have noticed how uncomfortable I looked. I wanted Skyler to stand up for me. I was waiting for it.

"She's from up north, Doreen. I bet Boston folk don't giver' hell like we will! They are too busy drivin' round in their fancy cars throwin' their noses even higher. They all think they are better than us. She drives a BMW, Doreen," said his father.

More laughter. Skyler neglected to tell me his dad was such a comedian. He put his arm around me as we walked towards the car. Skyler's dad that is.

"So you think he's gon' make it Taylor?"

"Make it?"

"To the big league. You think Skyler can do it?"

"I believe he can do anything."

"Shit, he better! I got a mortgage that ain't gonna pay itself off. I'd like to retire early and get me a fishin' boat. Hey son, how bout' we hurry it the fuck up, yeah?"

"Trying," Skyler muttered.

I faked smiles and forced conversation with Skyler's family, who had no desire to get to know me over a spicy chicken sandwich meal at Chick Fil' A. They didn't wish health or happiness on him as most parents do for their children. They lived vicariously through Skyler, it was clear. It was almost as if he was an only child. One thing was for sure, they were banking on Skyler to give them the life they've always wanted. They were waiting to be paid back. I birthed you and now you're obligated to fulfill my wildest dreams. Overall first family impression: Yikes.

Skyler inserted the electronic key into our hotel room door.

"My dad's funny ain't he? Gosh we always have so much fun when the fam is together."

"He's certainly a character."

I responded the way pageantry had taught me to respond to opinion oriented questions without stating how I truly felt. How it forced me to color inside my lines and never stray too far from the neutral zone. How it made me a liar. I used these skills now. His dad was the ringleader of their family circus. Skyler's family was ruthless.

The first bus to the field was at 10:00 AM the next day and Skyler was on it. He never failed to be the first one to the clubhouse each morning. I wouldn't see him until ten o'clock that night. In a t-shirt and underwear, I ate leftover melted Reese's for breakfast in the hotel bed, while flipping through the limited TV channels. I spent some time looking out the window into the parking lot and neatly aligning my beauty products on the desk. I showered, dried my hair, found an outfit, and performed a makeup tutorial in the mirror. Best of all, and this is one of the greatest things about dating someone who was never around, I was able to keep my body's bathroom schedule regular if you know what I mean. There weren't any sneaky Walmart trips or excusing myself to the hotel lobby. Skyler left me religiously every morning and my bowels practically sensed his departure. It was beautiful.

Doreen texted me late morning, inquiring about a trip to the local mall to get us all out of the hotel. I agreed to tag along, inviting Sam to join in on the chaos as well. We piled into the Williams family caravan and headed straight for the interstate. We, minus Skyler's father. He chose to stay at the hotel to sleep.

Seven stores, all of which I'd never heard of before, lined the insides of the mall in Bowie, Maryland. Herds of old timers wearing white Reebok walking shoes with velcro straps brushed by us. We walked around to kill time. I'd never been more excited for a baseball game in my life. Skyler's massive thighs in baseball pants and his veiny forearms that bulged from his taped wrists, mainly due to poor blood circulation, would soon be on display. I just had to make it through this day with his family.

Seated on a bench inside the mall was a sleeping, elderly man. I assumed he might be waiting for his wife. Regardless, he was out cold. Sam, myself, Mamaw, and the Williams family shopped around a sporting goods store. I caught Doreen hiding behind a sale rack of clothing.

"Taylor watch this," she whispered to me. "I'm gonna holler at that man. Scare the living shits out of em!"

"*WAKE UUUP!*" she screamed. Her voice bounced throughout the silent mall. The man woke, jumping with confusion. He was clearly frightened. When he saw that he was in fact alone, his eyes closed once more.

"*BAHHHHH!*" Doreen screamed again. Her sons laughed. I was horrified. Embarrassed. I wished I'd stayed back at the hotel.

Skyler was thrilled I spent the day with his family. That, because of me, he was now complete. Come game time, the Williams family offered a different vibe. Skyler's parents sat in separate rows, moving from time to time during the game to get the best view of him during play. The stadium was empty, so, the seating options were endless. Mamaw sat above the dugout, alone, with her camera. She saw the game through a lens. Shia and Sheriden sat together in the very back of the stadium with heads buried in cell phones. Sam and I sat together in the designated family section behind home plate. Everyone was so unpredictable.

Following the game, we all went out for ice cream, Skyler included. Together we sat inside the ice cream parlor ingesting our frozen desserts. We sat in silence. The Sea Dogs lost and I learned one thing; the Williams family had no desire to converse with one another. Skyler isn't home eight months out of the year and nobody has anything to say? The highlight of the evening though, took place after dessert in the parking lot. We piled into the beige caravan one last time that night. Doreen was driving because Shane's back gets too sore when he drives. As we neared the exit of the parking lot, Skyler's mother accelerated towards a male figure crossing the driveway.

"Fifty points!" she hollered in her goofy accent.

"Yeeyeeyeeyeeyee!" her husband said before chuckling beside her.

It took a second for my brain to process what was happening. I heard their voices, looked straight into the distance, and felt the same fear the man in the headlights was feeling.

"*Doreen!*" I screamed.

The van came to a screeching halt.

"Are you out of your fucking mind!" The man approached the driver's side of the van; arms flailing and spit flying from his lips as he spoke. He was bullshit. As he should be. Doreen sped off once he was close enough and the Williams family commended her for being so spontaneous. They were proud of her. I was horrified and alone.

I spent the next two days in Richmond, Virginia— watching baseball games and battling through my time with the Williams clan. On our last night in Richmond, Skyler and I joined the family for one last dinner at Pizza Hut. Last one. Hallelujah. Doreen led us into the restaurant, blowing by the hostess stand, and seating herself. She barked orders, yelled for the waitress when she needed something, shook her empty cup of ice when she needed a refill, and called her name as she tended to other guests when she wanted the check. I was dining with *animals* and I was mortified.

"Look at that Benz," Skyler's father said as he pointed to a shiny, new Mercedes parked in the back of the lot as we left dinner.

"Bastard thinks he's better than everyone else parking in the back of the lot. Watch this. I'll show his ass."

Shane disappeared into the grocery store abutting Pizza Hut.

"Where's he going?" I asked Skyler.

"Who knows."

We waited outside the van for him to return. When he emerged from the automatic grocery store doors, he was carrying a sheet cake. *Happy Birthday Dylan!* read the cake.

"Was on sale! Guess Dylan forgot his own damn birthday cake!" his father yelled and snickered through his golden, yellow teeth. The Williams family didn't believe in going to the dentist. Shane had an evil sense of determination in his eyes as he made his way to the back of the parking lot. I had no idea what was about to transpire. I was scared.

"Watch this y'all!" his father said as he proudly hurled the giant cake onto the windshield of the Mercedes-Benz. I gasped. Skyler's mother laughed hysterically, practically cheering her husband on with pom poms from the sidelines. Mamaw directed Sheriden and Shia away from the scene. I grabbed Skyler's arm and did the exact same while evaluating our surroundings to see if we had witnesses.

"Someone's gonna call the police on him," I whispered to Skyler.

"He'll be fine."

His father proceeded to stuff cake underneath the windshield wipers, his mother now finger painting the hood with frosting. I stood in disbelief. I didn't know if I wanted to scream or break down into tears but they successfully destroyed the car without anyone noticing and it absolutely shook me to the core. I couldn't allow people like this into my life.

"Now that is how you show people with money they ain't shit!" Shane said diving into the passenger seat of the van. Skyler's parents were the people who chose to do the wrong thing while no one is watching. They were morally corrupt. Selfish, childish, entitled savages is what they were. Who raised my loving Skyler? I was degraded, mocked, made fun of, harassed, and embarrassed for a week straight and when asked by my boyfriend about my impression of his family, I had no idea what to say. I began to build a wall around Skyler and I; a wall that would keep his parents out.

Skyler was promoted to Triple A in Pawtucket, Rhode Island after returning to Portland. It was sudden and it interrupted our weekly dinner date at Chili's. I knew what was happening before Skyler got off the phone that night.

"This is him. Really? The Hilton in Providence you said? Yes. Thank you. Thanks so much. Yes. Bye."

We canceled our dinner orders, settled the bill, and raced back to the host family's house to throw Skyler's world into bins. I was excited for him. I mean, what a rush! Someone calls you and tells you to move to another state and without blinking, you just do. You have nowhere to live, just three days in a hotel covered by the organization, and then you're homeless. But that doesn't matter. We have three days to address the whole homeless thing. Skyler, on the other hand, wasn't as excited.

"It's late in the season. Guys are injured. They need help in the outfield. This "promotion" just means I'll go from playing seven days a week in centerfield to maybe two days a week in right or left. I don't even like left field!"

"You're still one step closer. If you're producing, I can't imagine they'd send you backwards."

"You don't get it. I'm not a prospect. I'm nobody. I wasn't an investment player. I won't embarrass anyone in the front office if I don't make it to the Bigs. I'm just here to fill temporary gaps for them. We gotta hit the road."

During a time that was suppose to verify all of your hard work and efforts, Skyler seemed *more* miserable than ever. It was the last and final step before reaching the majors, otherwise known as the "Show". All he had to do now was prove himself; time and injury already proved to be on his side. It was as if this promotion, and the bigger paycheck that came along with it, was an inconvenience. Maybe he didn't feel he was deserving enough. Maybe he was comfortable in his little bubble up in Portland. Maybe he just knew the business behind the game better than I did.

He followed me to Massachusetts where we dropped my car at my house so we could finish the drive together in his truck. And mostly because the Red Sox only paid to valet one car at the hotel. Pawtucket, Rhode Island was home to the Pawtucket Red Sox, but Skyler was given a three night stay at the Hilton in Providence as all promoted players are. Luckily for Skyler, my house was only forty-five minutes from the stadium in Pawtucket and my parents were willing to let him live there for some time, after his three day Hilton stay was over. Imagine not knowing the area or many of your new teammates and being responsible for housing when you have legitimately no clue as to how long you'll be on the team? Scary. Skyler said most guys are forced to pay to stay at the hotel. Even with the team discount, it was still one-hundred dollars per night.

Three hours later we arrived at a gorgeous hotel in the scummiest of cities. We were greeted by friendly concierge and the bellboy didn't allow us to lift a finger, even in the middle of the night. We were being treated as if Skyler were a major league player, and wow, we felt the difference. Our room, which was actually a suite, had two balconies and a selection of pillows to sleep on— depending on your personal preference of firmness and fluffiness.

"We can barely afford Dunkin Donuts for breakfast in Double A but we have a selection of pillows in Triple A. Something is wrong with this picture Skyler," I said as I fastened the belt on my plush, complimentary robe.

"That's why making it feels so good. Your whole world changes."

"How can they expect anyone to make it when they don't even pay enough for groceries?"

"You just gotta find a way to make it work."

The sweet sound of country music filled the bathroom as Skyler showered. He said he wanted to be the first to the field today, per usual, but I didn't think it meant getting up at the crack of dawn. He was nervous; I could tell. First day jitters. I drove him to the field as if I were driving my child to his first day of school. I tried to be his hype girl. I told him the PawSox were lucky to have him.

I told him he would be great. Then I returned to the hotel, showered, and watched TV before performing another one of my makeup tutorials to my audience, the mirror. *Next I'll be using Shape Tape Concealer by Tarte Cosmetics.* I found a Chipotle on the way to the field, ate dinner alone in the truck, and headed to the stadium to watch Skyler's Triple A debut. I too would have to make all new friends in Triple A. WAG friends. My mom drove down to watch the game with me so I wouldn't be alone in foreign territory— McCoy Stadium.

"A new face!" said a little, old woman at the Will Call window.

"Yes. Can I pick up player tickets here?"

"You most certainly can. And who do you belong to?"

My face fell blank. *Belong to?* Am I some kind of object? Does somebody own me?

"I need a name sweetheart."

"Uh, Williams. Should be two tickets under Skyler Williams."

"Wonderful. Best of luck to him and welcome to Pawtucket."

"I appreciate that. Thanks so much."

I opened the envelope of tickets to help me navigate. Well dressed women, some carrying children, passed by. They were much older than I, my nineteen year old self, and that made me feel out of place.

"Enter through the door behind me sweetheart. You'll see the doors to the boys locker room as soon as you get inside but take a quick left and you'll find the Wives Room and the entrance to the stadium," said the little, old lady.

"Thanks again," I smiled.

I politely pushed through a pit of fans waiting to catch a glimpse of what lay beyond the door I was about to walk through. They quieted down as I passed through, probably trying to piece together who I could *belong to.* I opened the door and was immediately hit with air conditioning, the last thing I expected to feel, and the scent of homemade food. Two even larger doors stood in front of me covered in the Boston Red Sox logo and surrounded by media folk and reporters waiting with microphones and cameras. I turned left as the lady instructed me to do so, following the trail of the fresh food. And there was the infamous Wives Room. I looked in from the hallway. The room was covered with children, pretty women, a plasma flat screen, and a spread of fresh food. I kept walking. I was too new and too alone to walk in there. I had a plastic chair out in the humidity calling my name. My mom needed to hurry up and get here.

Skyler started in right field as he predicted. The current center fielder in Triple A was healthy and had a major league debut under his belt so we knew Skyler wouldn't touch his position. He found me in the stands as soon as he took the field, as he always did, and gave me a head nod to acknowledge my existence. My mother joined me in the second inning and together we watched Skyler live out his promotion. He was exactly where he deserved to be.

"Sorry to bother you." I felt a tap on my shoulder. I turned around to a sweaty, overweight man with a hot dog in hand and a 2001 Nikon camera strapped around his neck.

"Dan Krader," he said as he offered me his hand.

"Have we met before?" I asked.

"Just a huge minor league ball fan. I noticed you cheering for Williams. You must be family; sister maybe? I just wanted to introduce myself and say hello. I know his girlfriend really well."

"*His girlfriend?* I am his *girlfriend*."

Dan Krader could barely make eye contact with me. He stumbled on his words, stuttering and excessively blotting his face with a mustard-covered napkin. I stared at the dirt embedded under his fingernails.

"His girlfriend's name is Kristina and she lives in New Jersey. She's one of my friends."

I could feel the eyes and ears of neighboring onlookers eavesdropping on our warped conversation.

"Look I'm just as surprised as you are right now," he said.

"Tell me Dan, how did this Kristina girl meet Skyler? How long have they been "together"? Enlighten me."

"Maybe a few months now. She lives in Trenton and they see each other whenever he has a series in town. Otherwise she'll make the drive to his Connecticut games."

"Have you ever met Skyler?"

"Yes. Twice. Both after games with Kristina. She misses him. She's so jealous I'm here right now and she's not."

"She couldn't make it to her boyfriend's debut? What a shame. What earth shattering obligation did she have tonight?"

"She's a waitress at Hooters and couldn't take time off."

"Of course she is. Have a good night Dan."

I pushed by him with a lump in my throat and tears forming at my eyelids. I was embarrassed because, for whatever reason, his words sounded innocent and pure. I fished for the car keys in my purse as his sentences replayed in my mind. My mother chased after me, begging me to slow down. It felt as if someone were holding a plastic bag over my head and watching me as I slowly suffocated to death. I needed Skyler; I needed to talk to him. I had no choice but to bask in this pain and wait. I always have to wait for him because he is never around. By choosing Skyler, by choosing this life, I was essentially choosing to put myself last. I'm choosing to wait. I pulled myself into the driver's seat of Big Red and hugged the tear-soaked steering wheel. Skyler's debut turned into the beginning of my end.

The driver side door swung open.

"Taylor! What happened? Why did you leave the game? What's wrong? I tried calling. I saw you leave. I've been so worried about you. What happened?!" Skyler was frantic. I lifted my head to look him in the eyes, feeling more defeated than ever before.

"Some man. Some random man!" I cried.

"A man?"

"Yes a man. He introduced himself to me at the game because he saw me clapping for you. He thought I was your sister! He said he's good friends with your *girlfriend* from New Jersey."

"He said that to you? Do you know his name?"

"Dan Krader. And your alleged girlfriend's name is Kristina from Trenton, New Jersey in case you forgot."

"Taylor. Baby," He pulled me into his chest for a hug. I pulled away from him. I wept. Hard. And I most certainly did not want to be hugged by him.

"Taylor I swear to you I don't know either of those people. I would tell you. They don't even sound remotely familiar. I swear I would tell you."

He rubbed my back delicately and wiped a few tears from my cheeks.

"You gotta understand something babe," he said. "People are crazy. Fans are crazy! You see how many nut-jobs wait outside to watch us board a bus right? They will literally do whatever it takes to get inside a player's world. Love and happiness is the last thing anyone wants to see nowadays anyway. Be strong for me babe and know that I love you. I'm not here to hurt you."

"He was just like so descriptive Skyler it was weird. He was so *sure*. You had to be there."

"I believe you babe. I don't doubt he was." His eyes filled with tears. His words grew shaky. My head was pounding at this point. I spent my day in the hotel bed but now I really felt exhausted; drained. Beat to a pulp.

"Wanna know something Tay?"

I looked at him.

"You are so beautiful when you cry. Your eyes get so green."

Really, dude?

"Where's your mom?" he asked.

"Home. I told her to leave."

"Is she mad?"

"She's just worried about me."

"Well let's get you home. There's something I'd like to ask you."

"Tell me. You can't make me wait after saying something like that."

"I'd rather not have this conversation in a sketchy parking lot."

"Skyler."

"Fine. I wanted to know if you'd move to Georgia with me for the off-season."

4

Governor's Cup Championship and champagne showers in a tarp-covered locker room later, Skyler's season concluded in Triple A during the month of September. Five months free of baseball was right around the corner, as was a move to Georgia. He told me it was imperative we spend the off-season in Georgia so he could teach lessons and make money. That he had a huge clientele lined up in the months to come. That his parents would be offended if he spent his free time up here with me because they never get to see him. So, with a very open mind, I agreed to make our latest temporary home Georgia.

I applied for jobs at outlet malls before we left. An online college student I was, but spring training would arrive sooner or later and we needed all the money we could get our hands on.

We would live in the basement of his parents' house. Skyler's bedroom was down there and it was where he stayed every off-season. He was twenty-seven and couldn't afford a place of his own. For me, this move meant depriving my duties as Miss Massachusetts Teen even more and putting my goal of auditioning for the Boston Bruins Ice Girls on hold. I was finally old enough to audition, but another year it would have to wait. He is away from his family for so long. I should be the one to sacrifice. Even if meant being stuck at his parents' house with no car.

We planned to spend one full week postseason in Massachusetts with my family. One week is all he gave me. He insisted we get to Georgia as soon as possible. We were driving; we had no reason to leave by any specific date. But Skyler was receiving immense pressure from his parents. I could see it in him. They had total control over his thoughts. He felt compelled to please them for reasons I do not understand. Skyler had to punch the time clock with them.

Like clockwork, we prepared ourselves to leave exactly one week after the season ended. Skyler had perfected goodbyes after all this time but I'd never left my family before. I was essentially moving out for the very first time and wow, it was painful. We laid our heads to rest in my bed one last time, and I cried and cried.

"I can hear your eyelashes against the pillow. What's wrong?" he said within the darkness of my childhood bedroom.

Skyler, the hunter, was creepily observant at times.

"I'm just sad to be leaving."

I thought about my cat. And my parents. My mother is my best friend in the world. And my brother; my shadow. I've never lived without them.

"Can we leave now?" I sat up in bed.

"Right now?"

"I won't sleep tonight. I'll just cry all night. Let's just get it over with right now."

"Are you sure Tay?"

"I have no other choice."

I cried in my parents arms in my kitchen that night. I hugged my brother. I buried my face in my cat's body. My heart was in pieces. I didn't want to go. I didn't want to leave my family. I didn't want to feel lonely. But I walked out my front door with Skyler Williams that night and I cried my way out of Massachusetts. I cried until my eyes were too tired to stay open any longer. It was Fall in New England, and just like the color of the leaves, the girl I once was changed; leaving in the wind for good.

"Where are we?!" I yelled to Skyler out the window as he pumped gas.

"Pennsylvania. Gettin' there." He climbed back into the truck holding a bag of donuts.

"Try one of these bad boys," he said while offering me a moist, gas station pastry.

"This gas station looks like it would violate health code laws."

"It's an apple fritter. Just try it. They are my favorite."

"Skyler it feels damp."

Virginia, North Carolina, South Carolina, and then Georgia. The longer we drove, the warmer it became outside. To think it was almost October and we could ride, without sweatshirts, with the windows down. The grass was thick and plush and every tree was green. You could say the foliage is delayed in the southern states. I rode with my bare feet on the dash, music blasting, leaving toe smudges on the windshield. It was a scenic drive and part of me could picture forever in such a breathtaking place. The roads were smooth; unlike anything I was used to. There were no cracks or potholes waiting to absolutely destroy the shocks on the car with an alignment that had already been tampered with. Cotton fields, farms, tractors, and peach trees. Them country songs weren't lying.

"We keep passing those Waffle House things. Are they any good?" I asked as I pointed to a high rise sign overlooking the freeway. Skyler laughed.

"You got a lot to learn," he said.

We crossed a two lane highway and entered a seemingly deserted part of town.

"That right there is Kenny." Skyler beeped his horn at a man riding his horse on the side of the road.

"Is he allowed to ride a horse in the road?"

"Babe you're in Georgia. You can ride a horse wherever you want.

He flipped his directional on to turn into a residential neighborhood.

"*Yeyeyeyeeee!* We home baby!"

Skyler's neighborhood consisted of small, identical splits with neat lawns and minimal use of plants. The landscape looked so bare. We were greeted by his mother who had been waiting for us in the driveway. His father was at work. Skyler and his mother shared an awkward embrace for some time as I stood by and watched. When they separated, his mother turned to me and said, "Taylor, you look like you've seen better days. How bout a shower?"

"Ah! I'm only kidding. C'mon Taylor. I'll give you the tour." She led me inside and up a set of stairs into the assumed living room.

"Oh.. My.. *Wow*," I said looking at the eleven deer heads mounted on the walls staring back at me.

"Yup! Skyler and his daddy caught every one of em'."

The living room resembled a taxidermy museum. Between the deer heads and the mounted fish, I felt like I had an audience. They had mixed-matched furniture with ripped cushions and torn armrests; the wood inside was exposed. I took in every detail.

"You'll never go hungry in my house, Taylor." His mother waved me into the kitchen and offered me a view of the pantry closet, her eyes gleaming with pride. I'm not exaggerating when I say it looked like the cereal aisle at your local grocery store. Cocoa Krispies, Apple Cinnamon Cheerios, Cap'n Crunch's Crunch Berries, Smorz flavored Apple Jacks, Froot Loops, Cinnamon Toast Crunch, Reese's Puffs, Lucky Charms, Trix, need I continue! There were assortments of Oreo's varying in all flavors as well as

Pop-Tarts, cookies, Honey Buns, Oatmeal Cream Pies, and every kind of syrup Hershey had ever concocted.

"That's not all!" She invited me into a room off the kitchen, presumably an office.

"We call this the tanning bed room."

There was in fact a tanning bed from the eighty's, a desk, and some office supplies. But the main purpose of the room was to store more snacks. Deluxe boxes of packaged snacks and drinks took up the space on the floor.

"Mamaw's got one of those membership cards to Costco. I go in there using her card all the time. Them idiots working there ain't caught on. I practically rob the place!"

I watched as his mother fell into tears laughing at her own words. I knew in that moment that our chapter in Georgia, though temporary, may be shorter than originally anticipated. I didn't belong here and I couldn't hide it.

I regained my conscious thoughts as I stood present in the tanning bed room.

"Wow, Doreen. You sure were right about having a house full of food."

She was glowing. Is this what created a professional athlete? Vanilla Wafers and Capri Suns? Where did my boyfriend learn to love fruit?

She showed me bedrooms, bathrooms, and the sanctuary of the Williams household — the gun cabinet. In her bedroom, directly next to the bed where a night stand would typically go, was an old China Cabinet filled with a variety of guns.

"Usually that cabinet is zip tied shut, you know, for safety. Shia and Skyler got into it one night and Shia threatened to blow Skyler's head off. I gotta get a zip tie back on there."

Suddenly Skyler's father's voice filled the entire house. "Who is ready for Mexican? I sure am!"

I found Skyler in the backyard playing with his dog, a German Shepherd named Sox, whom he purchased at a flea market with money from his signing bonus.

"Y'all ready to eat?" his mother yelled from the porch.

"Where we goin'?" Skyler asked.

"Eduardo's. Daddy wants Mexican tonight. Hurry up."

I turned to Skyler. "Mexican sounds dangerous after the car ride we just had."

"I know," he said. "I'm not even hungry."

"Tell them. We can grab something on our own if we get hungry."

"We have to go Taylor."

Before I could ask him *why*, the Williams family vehicle emerged from the garage. Skyler's youngest brother was in the back seat.

"*Let's go!* I ain't gettin' any younger!" screamed his father from the passenger side window.

"We have to go Taylor. Make them happy. They haven't seen me in a while."

Skyler began his way to the car.

"Um… shouldn't we put the dog in the house?" I asked.

"He lives outside." Skyler pointed to a small dog house in the yard. "That's why the yard is gated. Just make sure to lock it behind you."

I chased after him to catch up to him.

"So you never let the dog inside the house?" I questioned.

"At night we let him in to sleep. But he stays outside all day."

"What if it's cold? Or hot!"

"We put a fan in there when it's hot and a space heater when it's cold."

"Why wouldn't you just let him inside! His dog house is wooden. That could catch on fire with a space heater!"

"Taylor. Don't worry about it. This is how it has always been. He loves to be outside."

I turned back to lock the gate as instructed as a set of big, brown eyes stared back at me. I felt like I was doing something wrong. This sweet, fuzzy, angel of an animal deserved better. If I was stuck at home all day long, surely this animal would be spending more time inside.

I squeezed into the car and let the caravan door slide shut.

"Christ I thought we'd never get out of here. We are doing this quick I need to get to bed. Been bustin' my ass in the sun all day long."

Bed? It was six o'clock. I looked at Skyler. He opened his phone to type me a note, presumably so nobody would hear what he was about to say.

My parents go to bed at eight. If they are late, they get really mad.

I know. I'm thinking exactly what you're thinking. *Are you fucking serious?*

This is what our arrival got us from his father? Not a hug. Not a hello. *This?*

But I kept an open mind and a closed mouth. After all, this is family. And I just moved my entire life down here. By entire life I mean entire wardrobe, so I was willing to ride the waves for Skyler. At least for a little while. Our car ride was silent as was most of our dinner.

For parents that claimed to miss their son terribly, they sure didn't know how to show it. My blood boiled as I picked at the gray chicken inside my quesadilla. Nobody said much of anything and as strange as that sounds, it almost seemed normal to everyone else. We were together, physically, and that's what counted.

I woke the next day to a silent, empty house. Skyler was asleep beside me. The combination of Melatonin and Tylenol PM had him in a coma. The bitterness I carried from the impersonal interactions over soggy tacos seemed to fade as I stared at the peaceful expression on his face. I climbed over his still body to go make coffee. I was happy when Sox came to greet me in the kitchen. It was raining and if nobody else wanted to let him inside— I would have. I poured myself a bowl of sugary cereal and planted myself in front of the TV. I had nothing to do and nowhere to be and it was the oddest feeling I'd ever had. Until Skyler woke up, it would just be me and the deer heads.

Tomorrow my cousin Mark would marry his bride beside the ocean back home and though both Skyler and

I were invited to attend, he insisted we get home to his family. That enough time had been spent in Massachusetts [one week] and that his family deserved his time now. My only grandmother was sick, a rare blood cancer it was, and we knew her time on Earth was limited. Mark's wedding would most likely be her last wedding; the last time she'd share a room or a dance floor with her whole family. But Skyler told his parents we'd arrive on Friday and the changing of plans would upset them. I think I broke a lot of hearts the day we left for Georgia. I should have stayed home for the wedding. Instead, I clung onto the fact that my cousin Evelyn's wedding was one month after Mark's and because I was going to be a bridesmaid, Skyler and I would have to return to New England, even if it were against his parents' wishes.

Time passed as it tends to do. Skyler showed me Georgia the only way he knew how — from a four-wheeler in the red clay. I expanded my wardrobe in the camouflage department at Bass Pro Shops so I'd be eligible to hunt with him, or at least tag along for the ride. I would do anything for him and the friendship we shared together. I learned that blinds, in his vocabulary, are not privacy shades on windows, but rather a tent to hide in when hunting. And though I'd never pull the trigger on an animal, there is something to be said about watching the sun rise from the cold silence of the woods. I learned about tree stands, and how to climb a tree in order to get into the tree stand. I learned that climbing up is easy, and climbing down sucks ass. I learned to study the densely settled forest from a tree. I found so much peace up there. I learned about rutting season, trail cameras, and how we had to wash our clothes in scentless detergent so the animals wouldn't smell us. I learned how happy this sport made Skyler. I learned to find happiness within it too.

I shot my first pistol at a target in the woods. I shot my first crossbow into the ground because it was so powerful. Skyler never let me touch the crossbow again after that. I watched the gutting of a dead deer, I consumed my first venison burger, and I realized deer meat chili is better than chili with hamburger. I was out of my element, yes, but I was willing to find a way to fit into Skyler's little world.

We received free memberships to the local gym because Skyler had previously trained with the owner. We would start our days with a workout from the Red Sox training program booklet. Eventually, after giving his arm a brief break from throwing, we started playing catch together to keep his rage of motion. If we weren't at the gym or in the woods, we were expected to sit and watch all of Sheriden's baseball practices. Not games, practices. Everyday. Monday through Friday. Skyler had to make up for lost time and unlike what he had told me, he had zero baseball lessons of his own lined up. He just couldn't say no to his parents. Watching baseball practice every night was our only option.

People in town were always happy to see Skyler though. Seeing him was an open invitation to bombard him with the same, repetitive questions. *How was your season?*

What were you hitting? You ever talk to any of the Big League guys? Are they cool? Is David Ortiz a nice guy? You think you'll start in Triple A next season? Who do you think they will trade? The Red Sox need help in the outfield, do you think they will call you up? I stood by his side and smiled as he irritably answered the list of questions. It began to sound like a broken record. The only person who enjoyed these questions was Skyler's mother. She sat in her chair, nibbling on a bag of Twizzlers as the locals gawked over Skyler's season. He was her claim to a morsel of fame and she enjoyed every bit of the attention he put on her family.

Skyler struggled to find work for a while until an old coach, who owned an athletic training facility, invited him to take over some of his current baseball lessons. Skyler jumped at the opportunity knowing he had piss-poor insurance and a three-hundred-dollar Adderall prescription waiting at the pharmacy that he was unable to pick up.

We traded Sheriden's practices in for Skyler's very own baseball lessons. Watching him teach four-year-olds how to hit off a tee at the batting cages became the highlight of my day. I didn't have much to look forward to and being without a car made it even harder on me. I needed something that would get me out of my pajamas.

My resentment towards his parents turned to pure anger as the weeks passed. They were manipulative and controlling and had no desire to care for any of their children. They were obsessed with Skyler and Sheriden because of their natural ability to play baseball.

They were positive they would *both* be professional ball players. Shia, the middle child, and I'm reminding you because you probably forgot about him already just as his parents have, may as well not even exist. I never saw him, he never came home, nor did they speak of him. He didn't make his high school baseball team and I'm convinced they disowned him. They lack maternal and paternal instincts. They never cooked. They don't know how to. *Baseball keeps us so dang busy! We don't have time for any of that!* No. That's not how it works. Cooking a meal shouldn't interfere with a practice either. They live in drive-thrus. They allow Fudgsicles for breakfast. They don't tell Sheriden to change his clothes or brush his teeth in the morning before school. He was a child and his halitosis was already on another level. I missed home. Home cooked meals, tossed salads with wooden spoons, baking, and conversations with substance. I missed my family; my mom. Our shared talks in the living room over hot coffee. Our long car rides to nowhere just to chat. How could I tell Skyler I was unhappy in his world?

5

It was cold and rainy and the last thing I felt like doing this particular Monday night was putting on a bra to sit in a metal folding chair at a warehouse to watch Skyler teach lessons. It was Sheriden's birthday but they had a baseball practice to attend so I had the house to myself.

Skyler called me after his lessons.

"Hey babe. Should be leaving soon. These parents love to chat. I just want to get home to my girl!"

"No worries. Take your time. You know where to find me."

"Mom and Dad are taking Sheriden to Pizza Hut for his birthday dinner. I'll get dinner for us on the way home. Chipotle again?

"Now you're speaking my language."

Almost two hours later, Skyler's parents arrived home with Sheriden and Pizza Hut leftovers. They also had an ice cream cake. Skyler came walking in with them.

"You get lost?" I asked Skyler sarcastically.

"I swear those parents could talk all night! They all want their kid to be the best. I just want to tell them, *relax* your kid is only four."

I kissed him and took the bag of Mexican takeout from his hands.

"I'm gonna shower, Tay. I'm a sweaty mess. Go head' and eat."

I found a seat at the empty kitchen table and began devouring my burrito bowl.

"Haven't seen a soul use the kitchen table. Why don't you just eat on the couch like the rest of us do? Are you too good to eat on the couch?" Doreen laughed at me.

"I like eating at the table."

By the time Skyler reappeared to eat, I was completely finished and the only thing his family wanted was the cake.

"I'll light the candles!" I jumped out of my chair. "Where are the candles?"

"We don't own a single candle Taylor." Doreen said. "Never have, never will. Shane, get some paper plates."

"Well how about we sing! You guys sing Happy Birthday, right?" I asked.

Everyone looked around at each other before breaking into laughter.

"Just cut the damn cake Taylor and take you a piece. Enough of this nonsense. I just want to go to bed," Shane said.

My heart felt hot. Crushed. I wanted Skyler to interject. Why won't this man stand up to his parents! They are morons!

I played with the artificial frosting on my plate as Skyler's father gawked over the way his mother's ass looked in the spandex shorts she was wearing. We all sat in some sort of odd silence until his parents called it a night before the sun had its chance to set. They were always so quick to get to the bedroom. Skyler's father spoke too often about the 'adult novelty' store in town and how he loved to spoil his wife there. He also made it a point at family gatherings or in public situations to suggest that Skyler take *me* there. Their early bedtime was a blessing in disguise; it simply meant less time I had to deal with them and more time for Skyler and I to fool around by ourselves on his late grandfather's handicapped accessible bed that was passed down to Skyler. Lots of room for activities!

Our mornings were cyclical. Sugary cereal and "The Price Is Right" on the couch until we decided to move. But this morning was different. *Today* was different. My phone buzzed four times in a row on the ottoman holding both of our legs.

Jillian Peters sent you six photos on Facebook:
"Who is it?" Skyler asked as I reached for the device.

"*Jillian Peters*? Who the heck? I don't even know a Jillian Peters."

Skyler's spoon fell into his bowl with a clank and he hurried to dispose of his utensils in the dishwasher.

"Well I'm taking the four wheeler out back to check the trail camera. I'll be back in a bit."

"Hold on, Skyler. This has your name in it."

Jillian Peters sent me screenshots of text messages shared between her and my boyfriend. The messages had yesterday's date.

Skyler Williams:	Wow I just realized I give baseball lessons on Mondays 2 miles from your house.
Jillian Peters:	Who is this?
Skyler Williams:	Come on JP you know who it is.
Jillian Peters:	Oh, ha. Only one person in the world calls me JP.
Jillian Peters:	I thought about you the other day. I almost hit a deer. And I remembered how much you love to hunt.
Skyler Williams:	I want to see you.
Skyler Williams:	I know you want to see me too.
Jillian Peters:	What about your new girlfriend from Boston? Doesn't she live at your parents' house with you?
Skyler Williams:	Yes. She's at my house right now. Do you care? Because I don't care.
Skyler Williams:	Good talk. Hello?
Jillian Peters:	I'm not getting involved.
Skyler Williams:	I asked you a question.
Jillian Peters:	Please leave me alone.
Skyler Williams:	I need to see you. You and your daughter.

Jillian Peters:	Oh.
Skyler Williams:	Only problem is that it would be hard for this boy to just say hello. I mean. With a body like yours. You get what I'm sayin'?
Jillian Peters:	Gotcha.
Skyler Williams:	I'm one of the best secret keepers of all time. Nobody has to know.
Skyler Williams:	I just wanna have some fun with you.
Skyler Williams:	Put your daughter in her room, turn on the fan, and have some fun with me.
Jillian Peters:	"Fun"?
Skyler Williams:	I wanna be inside you again. I miss that feeling.
Skyler Williams:	If only every wish came true.
Jillian Peters:	I think we may have different ideas of what "fun" is.
Skyler Williams:	My last lesson ends at 8. I'll stop by after. I know you can't resist me.
Jillian Peters:	Skyler please do not come to my house.

The messages grew blurry as my eyes filled with salty droplets of anger. Who knew a stranger could suddenly shake my entire world? I tried to process. I tried to understand. I felt as if I'd been roundhouse kicked in the throat. Our sex life was incredibly active and he made sure he told me he craved me whenever he wasn't with me. Skyler was gone for three hours last night. He was twenty minutes from where I was. It was the first time I didn't go to his lessons. I had so many questions.

What if I had gone? I could have stopped this from happening. Is this my fault? Is this the *truth*? How did this happen?

"Skyler." I said. I was afraid. He looked up at me from the kitchen sink where he pretended to be busy.

"Come look at this."

I handed him my phone. He read the messages, then again, then again. Each time the look of confusion and disgust grew on his face.

"Did you go to that girl's house last night?" There was terror in my voice.

"Are you kidding me? I told you I was working and a group of parents held me up. Then I got dinner. FOR YOU! I was spending my money on *you*. Don't ask me stupid questions. This is insane. I don't even know what this is. Ex-girlfriends are the worst."

He threw my phone at me and darted for the stairs. He didn't want any part in this conversation.

"Skyler! Your phone number is on the screen because she didn't have your name saved. You did this! You begged your ex for sex as I sat in your bed and waited for you to come home. Stop lying to me!"

"*I'm not lying!* Christ. Get me out of this house. Crazy bitch." He spoke without a single care in the world.

"I need to leave. I have to go home. I can't believe I moved my life here for *this*."

I ran downstairs and pulled my suitcases from the closet.

"Go ahead. Get out of my house. I don't need this shit!" he yelled.

I began emptying drawers of my perfectly folded clothing into suitcases.

"Stop. Taylor. Wait a second. This is all a big misunderstanding, babe. I don't want her in any way. Please stop acting like this. You know I love you." He grabbed my arm in attempt to stop me from my packing rampage.

"Do not!" I pulled my arm from his grip and continued tossing clothes into suitcases in balls. I was angry. Then, out of nowhere, I was sad. On my knees I cried into my hands. Skyler met me on the floor to offer comfort, but he was quickly denied. Instead he watched me as I sobbed. That's all he could do.

"Do you know how scary it is to be betrayed by you? I left everything to be here with you! This is the only way you knew how to repay me? I need to call my mom. I need a flight home. I don't have the money for one. I'm fucking trapped here in your little world and this is how you show your appreciation. I'm done Skyler. I can't."

Skyler, now pacing in the hallway, began a meltdown of his own. It was the first time I'd heard his cries. He crashed onto the linoleum hardwood and punched the ground. He mumbled and groaned as his shaking body found its way to fetal position. I stepped over his quivering antics to continue my packing. I'd never seen such a dramatic performance before.

"You should consider a career in acting." I said. "You'd be fantastic."

He cried harder and louder.

"TAAAAYLOR! PLEASE! I don't know why I did what I did but I can fix this. I can make this right!" he screamed.

"So you did go to her house? I haven't even been here a month Skyler. I thought shit wasn't supposed to hit the fan until later. Not within the first month of living together."

I removed an entire drawer from the dresser and flipped it over into my suitcase.

"I know and Taylor I appreciate you being here more than you know."

"You don't act like it," I laughed.

"I don't even want her though! She has a *kid!* That's gross! Someone else's child came out of her."

"Last night's messages would tell me otherwise."

He found his way to his feet and stopped me dead in my tracks.

"I'll delete her. Block her. Delete all of the random numbers in my phone. Whatever you want, I'll do it. Just stay the night. You won't be able to get a flight that fast. Stay the night and just reassess this in the morning. If you still wanna leave me by tomorrow I won't argue. Just give me a chance to make this right. I would literally kill myself if I ever lost you."

"Don't you dare put that guilt on me."

Deep down I knew asking for a flight home with multiple pieces of luggage in the same day was unrealistic. I also knew that if I wanted to try and save my relationship with Skyler, my mom is the last person I'd want to know about this. Besides, since I'd been so public about my move to Georgia on social media, I was embarrassed to go home so soon. To see it fail. I felt like it was a lose-lose situation and I was trapped, there, in Skyler's little world.

"Block her fucking number Skyler. You haven't heard the end of this."

The saddest, most awful truth about the entire situation was that my heart knew the entire time it didn't want to leave Georgia. I packed those suitcases and made a disaster of our room knowing good and well that I wasn't ready to leave yet. Not him, not his family, not Georgia, not baseball. It was going to take more than a bad mistake to get rid of me. He was caught red handed and I, I accepted the situation. I stayed. I let him get away with it. I couldn't bring myself to say goodbye to the one thing that brought me to life.

> *"Weakness comes in a pretty, little package when the one you love betrays you. It's like someone plopped it on your front stairs and said, "You will have this now". Betrayal is unfair because it creeps up on faithful hearts and tells love to leave when it isn't ready to go quite yet."*
>
> — *Taylor Higgins*

This particular Wednesday morning I was awoken by the sound of a rifle being cocked nearly inches from my face.

Gasping for air, I sat up to locate Skyler. He was standing at the foot of our bed in jeans and a camouflage sweatshirt with a wooden rifle in hand.

"Are you fucking for real with that thing right now?" My heart was pounding in my chest. Normally I am a light sleeper but I'd taken Tylenol PM the past few nights to help me sleep with all that was on my mind. That, and I had a splitting headache.

"What's wrong? I'm just checking it out. It ain't gun season yet, I can only shoot with a bow."

"So why the fuck would you cock it right in front of me! I was sleeping!"

He smiled and slid it under the bed.

"Is that where you keep it?" I questioned.

"Never know when you'll need it. She's loaded too."

Part of me believed that in some sick, twisted way, he got a rise out of scaring me with that gun. To see my innocent face react at the sound of the cocking. To witness my eyes as they realized it was a rifle. I knew that he loved that. I knew he wouldn't actually kill me. I knew he just wanted to see me in fear. He wanted to kick me while I was down because he was down too.

"I'm going to check the trail camera since I didn't get to do it yesterday," he said.

"Sorry the blow out over Jillian Peters kept you from checking for deer pictures."

Taking advantage of my time alone and against Skyler's wishes, I finally replied to the messages Jillian Peters had sent me. I needed more. I needed *someone* to talk to about this. She immediately offered her number for a phone call. I took the keys to Skyler's truck and locked myself inside. I wanted to hear everything she had to say.

"Thank you for taking the time to talk to me. I know you don't owe me a thing," I said into the phone still feeling defeated from yesterday's events.

"Thank *you* for being mature and not attacking me. Most girls would claim I'm jealous or tell me I'm still in love with him. But that's just not the case. I would hope someone would tell me if I were ever in a bad situation like this. I can assure you if he's reached out to me then he's reached out to many others too."

"Can you tell me about your relationship with Skyler?"

"You'll learn a lot about him in a short period of time. I only dated him for two months, that's more than enough time for his true colors to show. He can only keep his mask on for so long, remember that," she said.

I knew her words were true because she spoke as if she'd been let down; hurt.

"Though our time together was brief, things escalated rather quickly," said Jillian. "We met at the gym last year— two weeks before he left for spring training. Within those two weeks, Skyler met my daughter Kensley, confessed his love for me, moved his belongings into my apartment, shopped for an engagement ring he planned to finance, begged to elope, and offered to legally adopt Kensley. It was a whirlwind. But he made me love him."

"Oh... my...," I said. "My relationship with him is oddly similar to everything you just said."

"I'm telling you. He knows what he's doing. A month into spring training, Kensley and I drove nine hours to Fort Myers, Florida, to visit him at camp. After two days, while Skyler was showering, I noticed a female's name pop up on his unattended phone. *Hot Blonde-Spring Training.* I opened the message, because why the hell not, and discovered his ongoing conversation with this girl, and lots of other girls too. Perverted comments, wants, desires, and 'I miss you's'. I was sick to my stomach. I picked my daughter up and was out the door before that monster even got out of the shower."

"Did you ever talk to him after that?"

"Of course. He called me crying. He called his mother crying. Who then called me and asked me to 'work it out with him'. As if my life was some sort of game. He begged me to marry him that whole week. And then he disappeared into thin air. This is the first I've heard from him since then."

"Wow," I said. "How terrible. And here I am, going through the same damn thing."

"Listen, take what you want from this. It's your life after all. But just know that he is a remarkable liar. He studied psychology in college and he can literally create the most methodical lies in seconds. He cries a lot because he is wrong a lot. His mother thinks he can do no wrong. His father is a pervert. Be careful. I have to get back to work. I'm a nurse. I wish you the very best. I'll pray that you find your way out of this mess."

When I exited the truck, Skyler was undressing from his hunting clothes in the garage.

"Anything good on the trail camera?" I asked. I wanted to distract his thoughts as to why I would be in the truck to begin with.

"I texted you. You didn't answer. I was wondering what you were doing in my truck."

"I made a phone call."

"Your mom? She get you a ticket home yet?"

"No. It was Jillian."

His eyes squinted as he looked directly at me. He was uncomfortable within his own mind.

"Well? She tell you how much of a piece of shit I am?"

"We just talked about the relationship she had with you. And that I should be careful."

"Careful?"

"She said you're a really good liar."

His fist bounced off the wall with a bang.

"Dammit!" he screamed. "I can't fucking talk about this anymore! I'm sick of people who want to ruin my happiness because they see something they can't have. I'm done. I don't want to hear about this again."

"Skyler that's not fair to me."

"Did you not hear me? I said I was done."

I don't know how to get mad. Well, I do. It just takes a whole lot to get me there. The nastier he became with me, the more I wanted to know *why*. I thought he could be better if he allowed himself to be better. I knew he had wonderful potential as a lover and that was my downfall. I'd fall in love with a million potentials if that meant prolonging a broken heart. I wanted to heal him. I didn't want him to carry so much anger. I wanted him to be the victim for once. I wanted him to recognize right from wrong and apologize. I wanted him to feel bad for me; to take the blame off my shoulders when I didn't deserve it in the first place. I wanted him to do better. To be better. He's given bits and pieces of a kind man to me before, I just wanted that kind man to stay.

That afternoon I received a letter in the mail from my parents' house. Inside was nothing but a piece of wrinkled stationary:

To My Granddaughter Taylor,

I'm writing to you because I finally have enough strength to do so. I am still surprised you decided to move so far away. I hope you made the right decision. I missed you at Mark's wedding. It really was a fun party and Nora really did look beautiful. Now I am looking forward to seeing you at Evelyn and John's wedding and meeting Skyler.

I spent the day with your family yesterday. Your dad took me to a doctor's appointment and then we went to one of his favorite places to eat in Southie. Veal cutlet sub from Joseph's Bakery. Bet they don't make them in Georgia. Then Sean (he had a half-day at school) and your mother, and the dog Bella (she likes me), came with all kinds of good things for me to eat. I was giving Sean

*a hard time because he's not doing well in school. I think
I need to work harder on him.*

*Looking forward to meeting Skyler. Hope he's as nice
as you say he is. He better be if he's going to be friends with
my granddaughter!! I'm getting very tired. I will try and
write more another time—*

That was it. I watched my dying grandmother fade in pen-
manship; a neat cursive to a messy scribbling of drawn
out letters. She didn't even have the strength to sign her
name. My mom called not long afterwards and insisted we
come home a few days earlier than we were anticipating
for Evelyn's wedding. She said Nana Higgins was fading
fast and that she probably wouldn't make it much longer.
My mother paid to have our flights switched and we flew
out the next morning. We no longer had time to focus
our energy on the infidelity. I was preparing for death and
quite honestly, I needed him by my side.

It was a gray and foggy November morning when we
landed in Boston. You could barely see five feet in the distance ahead. Skyler complained about the freezing temperature as it seeped into our aircraft. He expected cold
weather but even still, he complained about it as if it were
a surprise. I was just thankful I didn't have to listen to
his mother complain about driving us into Atlanta traffic to get to the airport anymore. *I just don't get why y'all
are leaving already. The wedding isn't until the end of the week.*
Hospice had moved my Nana into my Aunt Jane's house
and we planned to go straight there from the airport.

As we hovered over the treacherous, choppy Atlantic waves, I turned my phone on against the pilot's wishes, in order to text my mother.

Taylor: Landing now!! See you soon!!!

Mom: I just got off the phone with Dad. Nana just passed. I'm so sorry you didn't get to say your goodbyes.

The seatbelt sign went off and the crowd of people stood from their seats. Belts were clicking, babies were crying, and people with connecting flights were trying to escape, but my world was a frozen blur. I remained seated with my seatbelt still fastened and stared at the blank television screen in front of me. I didn't get to say goodbye. My Nana was surrounded by my family when she passed but I wasn't there to say goodbye. I was in Georgia with people that didn't love me. I never said my goodbye.

"You tell your mom we landed? I hate waiting at airports," Skyler said.

"My Nana just died." My words were stone cold and almost emotionless, for he knew exactly how to make every situation about him.

"Right now? Taylor. That's terrible."

"You never say you're sorry. Do you know how to apologize?! For cheating on me? For the death of my only grandmother? Anything?"

He grabbed my hand and held it carefully.

"Taylor you know that I'm sorry."

"It's felt more when it's actually said. Whate
have to go to Aunt Jane's house right now. My family is
there with her."

I found my mother parked outside the arrival doors of
the airport and ran into her arms as Skyler struggled to
maneuver two suitcases behind me. That task itself probably pissed him off but I didn't care. My mom was here and
the hug we shared told me I was safe.

The drive to Aunt Jane's was a quiet one. For the very
first time, Skyler would meet my family, who were in a
state of mourning over my newly deceased grandmother's body. He had never attended a viewing or a funeral
and I could tell he was nervous. For me, the denial of closure was the hardest part. I'll never have a final memory
with Nana. I remembered when her husband, my grandfather, died eight years prior after he lost his battle to
lung cancer. I used to call him "Pucka". I visited him on a
Tuesday and when I hugged him goodbye in his maroon
colored recliner, he squeezed my hand a little bit tighter
and said, "Yup, ok now, I'll see you soon," as he fought
back tears. A shy man of very few words, that was his way
of telling me not to let go. I remember that day as if it
was yesterday, but I'll never have a day like that with my
Nana.

The three of us entered a quiet Aunt Jane's house.
Tragedy practically socked you in the face when you
stepped inside. Sounds of sniffling and people blowing their noses into tissues filled the hallways. The floor
creaked underneath us all with our footsteps. I found

my dad in the sea of people and hugged him for a minute. He and his three older sisters were now parentless.

"She's in the back room if you'd like to see her before the funeral services come to pick her up," my father offered. It was my last and final chance to see her. I didn't know if I wanted my lasting memory of her to be nothing but a rigid corpse.

"Can you come with me?" I asked my dad. I didn't bother asking Skyler.

"Sure Taylor."

A nervous walk down a tiny hall led me directly to my grandmother's lifeless body in a bed. I'd say she was sleeping but her mouth was open unnaturally wide as if she died amidst her final breath. She wouldn't want me to remember her this way. I stared uncomfortably for a moment before backing out of the room.

I watched two men in black suits carry Nana out of my Aunt's house in a body bag, an advanced trash bag if you will, similar to the bag that holds our faux Christmas tree. It had to be one of the most inhumane things I'd ever seen, but I guess that's how it is done. They slid her into the back of a hearse at the same place we'd celebrated each and every Thanksgiving. Memories and voices filled the rooms and suddenly I was back over a warm Thanksgiving dinner in a previous year. Death is as cold as it sounds wherever you are.

6

We buried my grandmother on a Wednesday, and by Friday, we were preparing for Evelyn's wedding at her rehearsal dinner. It was a whirlwind of emotions to say the least, with very little time to grieve over the loss in our family. Evelyn extended the invitation of the rehearsal dinner to Skyler, but he declined. My dad had set him up with a job teaching baseball lessons while he was in town at an indoor training facility called the "DogPound". Skyler thought it would be more beneficial that he work his few evening hours instead of being my plus one to dinner. I think large groups of people he's not familiar with stress him out, but I could have really used the support. Skyler had never been to a funeral or a wedding before, and now he was attending both in the same week.

Skyler bragged about how he never owned a suit and that when he got married, he wanted everyone to wear blue jeans, including himself. At the beginning of the week, my mother took him shopping and had him fitted for two custom suits: a funeral suit and a wedding suit, and custom because, well, have you ever seen the body of a baseball player? I'm not even sure he was grateful for receiving the free suits. He only expressed his lack of desire to ever purchase something similar again on his own.

On Saturday morning, the day of Evelyn's wedding, I woke up with butterflies in my stomach. It felt as if I were the one getting married. I was elated to take part in her special day and the fact that Skyler was there made it that much more meaningful. I had an early morning appointment at the salon to have my hair done and Skyler would join me there so we could make the hour-long drive to Evelyn's mother's house right after. Her bridal party was asked to be there by noon and those with husbands or boyfriends were allowed to bring them to the house as well. As we prepared to get out the door as quickly as possible, it became obvious to me that Skyler was in a mood. He seemed agitated and tense. I assumed he was nervous and I decided not to feed into his unpredictable behavioral patterns.

"Skyler we gotta hurry or else I'll be late for my appointment."

He was purposely moving in slow motion, repeatedly telling me not to rush him while ignoring my every attempt to light a fire under his ass.

"I didn't even have time to eat breakfast because you've been rushing me all morning! All so you can get your stupid fucking hair done!" he yelled as we backed out of the driveway.

"Well you should have woken up earlier today. You've known about this appointment."

"See it's always about *you*. Who do you have to look good for anyway? I don't understand why you need to waste money and get your hair done. Who are you trying to impress? I'm right here. And I don't like you all fancy. So why are you trying so hard? Stupid bitch," he muttered under his breath.

Just another knife to my heart. I was rolling with the punches, I had been for a while, but everyone has a breaking point.

"There's a ton of places to get breakfast near the salon. Take my car and grab something while I'm getting my hair done."

"Why are you so selfish? I'd like to know."

"SKYLER. My cousin is getting married today. *Married!* Get your shit together. My family has been through enough this week. I do not need this from you right now."

I sent myself up in flames as I attempted to put out the fire he created. As I pulled into the salon's parking lot, Skyler opened the passenger side door and jumped out as the car was still in motion. I slammed on the brakes.

"Skyler!" I screamed.

"I'm fucking done Taylor. Go get your hair done so you can impress people! I'm going home. I don't need someone like you."

He ran for the main road. Hysterical me got out of the car to not only yell at him, but to close the passenger door so my car would fit in a parking spot and I wouldn't miss my appointment. People were staring. A random woman asked me if I needed help. I composed myself, temporarily erased the image of my boyfriend running down Main Street, smiled and opened the door to the salon. I made small talk with my stylist and searched for peace in the delicate scratches the comb made across my scalp. Surely he would get better after he's had something to eat. Breathe Taylor, just breathe. Blame it on low blood sugar. Find an excuse for him.

Then, like an angry storm, Skyler came barreling through the front door of the salon. I locked eyes with him in the reflection of the mirror sitting in front of me.

"Are you seriously going to lock me out of your car?" he said.

A humiliated me dove into my purse in a frantic hurry. He walked towards me to snatch them as if I'd inconvenienced him in some way. He grabbed them so hard one of the keys actually cut my finger.

"Is that your *boyfriend*?" my hairdresser asked.

"Yes. Uh, rough morning."

She shrugged her shoulders and proceeded with my up-do but disgust was painted across her face.

Leaving the salon I noticed my car parked out front, engine running, with the driver side door wide open. Skyler was nowhere in sight. I scanned the parking lot and quickly jumped inside my car expecting to find him on Main Street. I called him. Voicemail. I called him again as I burned rubber exiting the lot. Voicemail. I was one minute down the road when he finally called me.

"Where the fuck did you go? You just gonna leave me here in the parking lot? Wow. I see how it is."

"Skyler I didn't see you. Where are you? I'm turning around."

The line went dead. He hung up on me. When I returned to the parking lot, I still couldn't see him. I called him again. Voicemail. Suddenly he emerged from the back of the lot where I'd assumed he'd been the whole time; watching me as I lost my damn mind. He took his time getting into my car, making it completely evident that *he* was miserable.

"Do you realize this is someone's wedding day?" I asked.

He sat in silence.

"What is wrong with you!" I yelled.

Unamused by my words, Skyler continued to stare into the distance ahead with zero sign of sympathy.

"Did you at least get something to eat?" I asked.

"I don't like your hair," he said.

"Thanks."

We drove over an hour to Evelyn's mother's house in silence. I asked him questions only to receive blank stares. I'd turn the radio on to search for a song and he'd shut it off. I'd turn the heat on and he'd turn it off. He wasn't completely ignoring me. He still had intentions of breaking me. Even in silence.

We arrived to a house full of bridesmaids. Evelyn showed Skyler to the boyfriends' and husbands' room; a man cave in the cellar. I put my happy face on. There was a spread of food on the kitchen table; sandwiches, fruits, and cheeses. I indulged as the wedding party made small talk. I became calm after recognizing how incredibly calm Evelyn was.

I checked on Skyler nearly an hour later. The ladies were starting to put their dresses on but I wanted to make sure Skyler was done playing games. I wanted him so badly to enjoy this day with me.

"How you doing, boo?" I asked happily as I found a seat on the arm of the couch next to him. I hoped the tone in my voice would calm him.

"Good."

He wouldn't look at me.

"You alright?"

"I don't know. Would you be alright if you hadn't eaten a single thing all day? Would you be alright if I took you to a random house and went an hour without checking on you? You don't care about me. That's clear," he said.

The few spouses in the room pretended they didn't hear what he was saying.

"Skyler the kitchen is full of food. Go make yourself a sandwich."

"I don't want *that* food."

I took a deep breath and reminded myself not to cry.

"Then what do you want Skyler?"

"I want to go home. Georgia home. But that won't happen because I'm broke and you forced me here. Fuck!"

"Skyler. What do you want to eat? I will make you a plate."

"Ask your cousin where I can get a decent sub around here. That's all I'll eat."

"You want me to ask the bride, as she's stepping into her gown, where *you* can get a sub? Are you serious?"

He nodded his head. He still wouldn't look me in the eyes.

I stood from my seat on the armrest to make my way into the hall.

"There's an assortment of sandwiches in the kitchen. Figure it out," I said.

My anger quickly washed away at the sight of Evelyn's mother, my aunt, zipping her into her dress. She pinned her veil into her blonde curls; the sun from the window she was standing in front of made her skin look angelic. I was alone in the hallway and they didn't know I was watching but it made me wish for lifelong happiness. I wanted to be a beautiful bride in the sunlight someday. I wanted to find that kind of happiness.

The limousine arrived shortly thereafter and miraculously, Skyler, dressed in a suit and tie, made his way to the front yard where we had been taking pictures.

"Looking good," I said, as he approached me. He rolled his eyes.

"So we are about to get into the limo. Just follow behind in my car like the rest of the men. I'll see you at the church. Love you," I said.

"You mean to tell me I came all this way just to follow the limo?"

"Well yes. So we would have my car later on. I have to go. The church is right around the corner. I'll see you soon."

He turned toward the direction of my car while mumbling *what the fuck* and making it obvious that he was once again frustrated. The only thing he knew how to do correctly at this moment was break me over and over again.

The bridal party was assigned to two separate rooms at the church while the guests arrived. Evelyn and her mother passed corsages to those who were expected to wear one. Then there was Nana's corsage. She died a week before the wedding; of course there wasn't enough time to cancel her corsage. Instead they asked Aunt Jane, her eldest daughter, the oldest of my father and his three sisters, to wear it in Nana's honor. It was an emotional moment for everyone in the room. We were all so happy today, but so broken from Nana's unexpected departure, and it was confusing. I noticed Evelyn alone with her bouquet in the corner of the room. She tucked a small photograph of Nana into the flowers and carefully wiped her face clear of all tears.

Beautiful music filled the corridors and not even an hour later, Evelyn was a married woman. After the ceremony and a ton of pictures, I found Skyler in a crowd of my family members; joking with my brother and laughing with my cousins. I trod lightly into the situation knowing he was capable of changing moods in seconds.

Honestly, I thought he would be pissed about the fact that I had to walk down the aisle with one of the groomsmen.

"Hey babe. You looked so beautiful up there. I can't wait to see you walking down the aisle to me someday," he whispered in my ear.

I nearly fell over.

"Thank you."

I decided to refrain from asking any questions if it meant smooth sailing and a manageable attitude. Skyler and I drove to the reception in my car. He held my hand the entire way there. I didn't dare ask. I didn't want to know. Inside we found my parents and a drink at the bar and together we chatted as the bride and groom finished with pictures. Then, the bridal party was asked to meet in the back room for introductions.

"I gotta head back there. See you in a few!"

I leaned in to kiss him and he dodged my puckered lips; a strange look upon his face.

"No thanks. I'm all set. You'd better go. Isn't the bridal party waiting for you? The guy who walked you down the aisle is probably waiting for you." he said.

"Why are you doing this to me?"

He laughed in my face and then turned around to head straight for the open bar. I watched him order two beers as my eyes filled to the rim with tears. Compartmentalizing this day was exhausting, and so were Skyler's multiple characters. After being knocked down for what felt like the millionth time that day, I had to find another fake smile. This time for a room full of people.

Once the bride and groom shared their first dance, everyone was invited to join them on the dance floor. I expected to dance with the groomsmen who walked me down the aisle as he was standing right beside me, but Skyler swooped in out of nowhere and grabbed me. I didn't know if he was happy or angry. I'd been walking on eggshells all day, yet we still managed to have issues.

"You weren't seriously going to dance with that guy, were you?" He looked me dead in the eye for the first time all day. I think someone had found his confidence in the alcohol.

"I mean... we were just introduced together. It wouldn't have been a big deal."

Skyler laughed. "I can't believe you actually would have danced with him. How am I supposed to trust you? How slutty. I can't be with a slut like you."

We danced in circles with the rest of the guests; my arms draped around his neck and his, around my waist. People must have thought we were normal and happy. Around and around we went as romantic music filled the room. Skyler's breath reeked of beer and his eyes were red and glossy. His thoughts were careless and his voice cracked when he spoke.

"You're drunk," I said.

He smiled for the first time.

"So?"

"You're wasted!"

"I'm really not."

I worried about him and booze sometimes. He hardly drank in front of me but he admitted to me on several different occasions that baseball mixed with loneliness had caused him to drink himself to sleep during the season. I remember him telling me he kept a six pack of Bud Light on the floorboards in the back of the truck at all times. On his eight minute drive home from the field after games, he would drink the entire thing. Sometimes it was to put him to sleep, sometimes it was his pregame before he drove himself to the bars. He kept a bottle of Jägermeister in the center console for a quick pick-me-up when needed. Drinking wasn't his problem, it was knowing when to stop.

We danced until the song ended, whispering words fueled by anger into each other's ears, and then found our table along with the rest of the crowd. He seemed calm during this time. He was only semi-normal when I was by his side. If my attention was with other people, he lost control of himself.

As we made small talk with my family members while dinner was being served, he held me by my inner thigh.

"I love you," he spoke softly into my ear, then lifting my hand to his mouth for a smooch.

I scooped a spoonful of mashed potato on my plate (family style servings), and proceeded to help myself to a stuffed chicken breast as the dish passed by.

"Did you just put stuffed chicken on your plate?" Skyler asked me.

"Yes. Want some?"

"You never eat stuffed chicken when your mom makes it at home. You told me you didn't like stuffed chicken. Now you like it all of a sudden? Or did you lie to me? You're a fucking liar aren't you? I can't believe this. Fucking liar you are."

Our table fell silent. He had no regard for how uncomfortable he made people feel. The mood was tense and I'd never felt so awkward before in my life. My tears couldn't hide any longer.

"Babe can I have my car keys?" I asked pleasantly.

"I don't have them. I gave them to Sean."

I removed myself from the table and found Sean seated with my parents. I was the only person currently standing in the ballroom. Everyone was busy devouring their food. I tapped my brother on the shoulder.

"Can I have my car keys?"

"Er, I don't have them." He was confused.

One blink and I knew I'd lose every bit of water built up in my eyes and down my cheeks. I glanced over to where Skyler was still seated and noticed he was dangling the keys to my BMW in his hand. He was taunting me.

"Looking for these?" he sang as I grabbed them from his hand.

I started bawling as soon as I felt the cold, November night on my skin. My silver heels scuffed across the pavement as I rushed to be alone. To bask in my defeat in private. To hide my pain from those who didn't deserve to see it on such a day. But I wasn't alone. During my cries I heard footsteps that didn't belong to me. It was Skyler.

"Please let me be alone. I'm begging you! Let me be alone!" I cried out to him.

I could see my breath as I spoke.

"Nah. If you get to leave, I get to leave."

He jumped inside the passenger seat of my car before I could lock him out. A full day's worth of pent up emotions were allowed freedom as I hugged my steering wheel. My cries were loud and filled with pain and agony. I punched the steering wheel as hard as I could. The pain he inflicted on me made me believe I deserved to hurt on the outside as well. My fist rebounded off the frozen wheel and I cried harder when I noticed the busted skin on my knuckles.

I turned to him.

"How could you do this to me? You ruined my cousin's wedding! Our grandmother just died!" I was livid. Like, actually boiling.

He covered his face with his hands as if reality had struck him and he began to cry with me. Sobbing. Out loud. Like a little boy.

"I just want to go home! This isn't my home. I fucking hate it up here. I wanna be in Georgia. If I had the money to fly myself home right now I would. I'm calling Mamaw. I'll see if she can get me a flight home tonight. I can't do this anymore," he whined.

It was always about him. For the first time, ever, I numbly thought to myself: you need to let him go. I had no words for him. I knew he couldn't leave, nor did he actually want to deep down. Those were his fighting words.

Whenever he did wrong, he wanted the easy way out. He was cowardly. My body was quivering; my heart was racing. I was cold and I was tired. I begged my body to give in to cardiac arrest. That maybe the flashing lights from the emergency vehicles and paramedics strapping me into a bed in an ambulance would make him realize he'd done wrong. I wanted to be whisked away. In that moment, I thought if my body and mind decided they were too tired to go to work in the morning, I'd be at peace for the first time in a long time. I was ok with that.

I looked at myself in the rearview mirror. My once stunning makeup now dripped down my cheeks in black creeks of misery and onto my chest, intersecting with the pearl necklace that lay across my décolletage. I watched it ruin my dress. I watched it ruin my chances of walking back into the reception.

"*Taylor!* Are you drunk? What are you doing!"

It was my mother's voice and she was banging on my window. I rolled it down; inviting the frigid air inside.

"What is going on? Everyone is looking for you two! You missed dinner! Taylor, are you drunk?" She was screaming and I was panting and that was basically a formula for heated misconceptions. I'd hardly finished half of the solo glass of wine I had been milking since our arrival. I wasn't intoxicated in the least, especially now, but I knew she'd assume I was.

"It's *him*," I muttered. Sticky saliva clung to the top and bottom of my mouth, making my attempts to speak incredibly unattractive. I think I blew a few bubbles.

"*It's Skyler!* All. Day. He's. Been. So... Mean! He's been so mean all day. I. I. I can't. I can't do it anymore!"

At this point I was hyperventilating; forcing out as many words as I could. My dysfunctional breathing sounded pathetic. It was a cry for help honestly, but we were at a wedding, and nobody could save me right now.

"Oh get yourself together Taylor. *Look at you! We are at a wedding!* Clean it up. I expect to see you both inside in five minutes."

And then I was alone with him again. Alone in the dark parking lot. I wondered if his mind ever told him to hurt me. Sometimes I feel like he wanted to but didn't have the guts. I know he could kill me. I'm not talking about physical strangulation or a heavy blow to my head that with enough force, would kill me instantly. He's a strong guy and I'd already visualized what it would be like to beg for my life as his knuckles turned white around my neck. I'm talking about the mental state you travel to when you kill someone. He had it in him, mentally, to kill.

Skyler opened his door and exited the car without saying a word. I watched him circle around the back of the car only to lock my door as soon as I realized he was coming for me.

"Open the door Taylor," he demanded.

"No."

"Open the fucking door Taylor! Don't play games with me."

With what I assume was a shot of adrenaline and anger, I pushed the door open and stood up to face him. He grabbed my arm.

"We're going back inside. Come on. We can't sit out here alright. I'm cold." His voice was calm. Unlike anything I'd heard all day. It was like he was a totally different man. I was outraged.

"Take your hand off of my arm," I said sternly.

"I said *let's go*. Didn't you hear me the first time Taylor?"

His grip became tighter and he started to walk away, forcing me to move. He held my arm with a tight, pinched grip.

"Ouch! Stop! Wait! Ouch! Hold on! Stop! Help me!" I cried out.

In fear that someone would hear me if I continued to scream, he threw my arm as if he no longer wanted it. My elbow caught the side of my frozen car door and more cries echoed in the night. I discovered a deep gash on my forearm that was overflowing with blood onto my blue dress. It was a good wound, potentially good enough for stitches, and the sight of the blood drenching my dress made me even more hysterical than I was before. I struggled to find napkins in the glove box with my injured arm as Skyler stood there and watched.

"Are you bleeding?!" My mother suddenly reappeared at my car. I cried louder.

"You're covered in blood, Taylor! Your dress! Skyler, what happened?!"

He said nothing. He just stood there and stared at us.

"Skyler had my arm! He wouldn't let go! And it hit the door!"

My mental stability was decreasing between the freezing temperature and my exhausted body. I could barely form a proper sentence.

"Well you missed the family portraits Taylor. You should be ashamed of yourself."

My mother took a deep breath and pressed a handful of napkins onto the hole in my arm.

"I'm getting Sean and your father. We need to leave. This is a disaster. Neither of you are driving this car home. I will."

On November 14th, 2013, at twenty-seven years of age, Skyler Williams was able to cross *sabotage a wedding* off his list of unforgettable moments. My parents, naturally furious— my Dad, hurt as hell, made the energy at home that night unfathomable. Skyler's liquid courage had faded completely behind the four walls of my bedroom. He broke down in tears at the foot of my bed as I wiped makeup from my face. I'd been known to do one thing and one thing only for him and that was to comfort him. Tonight, I refused to do that. I was sick and tired of being *that* asshole that ran around with super glue for the fragile boyfriend that didn't know how to keep himself from shattering. I undressed before him as I had done many of times before, though tonight it felt different. I was timid. Shy, maybe. It didn't feel normal. I'd never been afraid to undress in front of this man (boy) that I loved so much, but tonight I held an oversized baseball t-shirt in front of my breasts as the blood-stained dress slid to the floor. I no longer knew the man (boy) that was crying at the foot of my bed nor did he deserve to see my body in such a vulnerable state.

I buried myself in the bedsheets farthest from where he was still sitting, waiting for me to ask him if *he* was alright.

He was waiting for my attention. He was waiting for me to assure him that it would be better in the morning. But not tonight. I listened to him undress in the darkness of the room. Belt buckle, zippers, shoe laces. He sniffled his way into bed with me, even whimpering at times. My body was firmly pressed against the wall parallel to the bed. I kept my distance but his body found mine. He pressed his wet face against mine, almost as if he was letting me know he was in fact crying, eventually dropping to my chest to soak my t-shirt with regret. I felt nothing for him. I had no response for him. It was my turn to be still; motionless. To just exist. I lay there beside him and did something I'd never done before— I let him believe he was alone.

I opened my eyes. Pure darkness. It had to have been the middle of the night. I was sober, completely, but I had been so physically and mentally drained by the abuse my boyfriend inflicted upon me that I could barely depict my whereabouts. There was a body hovering over mine. I could tell because of the little bit of moonlight that seeped through my shades. I stared at the wall, watching as this shadow danced over me.

"Skyler?"

"Sshhhhh," he whispered slowly.

He began kissing my neck. Each kiss delivered more and more aggression than the one before it. He thrust his body into mine. Though I was still clothed, I could feel that he was not.

"What are you doing! I have my period!" I cried as I made efforts to push him off.

"I couldn't sleep," he said.

My sleepy arms were no force for the two-hundred pound figure above me and now, he had me pinned.

"Taylor, relax. I love you. Don't you know that? Please love me back. Don't fight it. Just let it happen. I don't care if you get blood on me."

He groaned in my ear as if my efforts to remove him made this more of a pleasurable challenge. Was he actually getting off to this? When is this classified as rape? I was able to maneuver both feet onto his abdomen to shove him backwards. Nothing I did made a difference. He was so strong and overpowering. He grabbed my t-shirt and yanked it overhead, inviting himself to suck my nipples. I begged him to stop. He begged me to be quiet. He massaged, nibbled, and bit whatever he could to excite himself. I began to cry. My body fidgeted beneath his, begging to be freed. My pleas for mercy only seemed to fuel the fire in his mind. They made him work harder on me. I could call the police after his climax. His cum would remain on my body. Surely they would apprehend him, but such arrest could ruin his baseball career. I couldn't call the police.

"Just relax baby. I want to show you that I love you. You looked so pretty today. I can't wait to make you my wife."

He kissed my bones and my body tensed. The person who couldn't look me in the eye all day was now taking advantage of me.

"You know this boy loves you right?"

Tears continued to drop from my eyes. I wish he knew I was crying.

Taking control, he pulled down my pants and forced himself inside me. I lay still on my back as he fucked my limp body. This wasn't love. Tonight, I was a placeholder for his penis. His body slammed into mine over and over again, I laid there praying it would end. I didn't make a sound. Instead, I stared at the ceiling, patiently waiting to feel his ejaculation on my stomach. Normally it didn't take long. Tonight however, felt like eternity. Repulsed by my presence all day long, intercourse was not supposed to be on the agenda. He discharged the seepage from his penis. I listened as he found his way to the bathroom, assumingly to clean himself up and wipe away any excess semen. When he returned, he tossed a towel onto my body. I cleaned myself before rolling over; crying and disgusted with my own self. I was barely awake when he fucked me. Falling back to sleep was the easiest thing I'd done all day.

We didn't wake until noon the following day. Neither of us wanted to get out of bed and face the world; my parents. The inflammation surrounding my eye balls insisted I stay asleep. I was hungry, starving rather, from missing dinner the night prior and my bladder was ready to burst. My feet found the floor.

"Can we talk?" Skyler mumbled. He was face down in the pillow.

"I don't have anything to say to you."

"Did I ruin the wedding?"

"You ruined so much more than the wedding."

Though he was face down on the bed, I could tell he was crying. His body was shaking. I didn't know if his tears were sincere or if this was another academy award winning performance.

"Shut the door when you leave please."

I exited the room to use the bathroom.

"Taylor?" My mother's voice came from the kitchen. I froze.

"Come out here please."

I awkwardly made my way into the kitchen, where my mother and father sat in blistering silence. Humiliation and guilt consumed me, though I did not influence these emotions.

"Where's Skyler?" my father questioned.

"In my room."

"Well we should join him in there then," he said.

My father, a man of *less than* a few words, did not have a confrontational bone in his body. He wasn't one to unravel predicaments. In fact, he was the first to run from them. To see him commencing such dilemma made my eyes bulge from their sockets.

Skyler was still face down on the pillow when the three of us arrived at my bedroom door; a blanket draped over his head.

"How are you feeling today Skyler?" my father asked.

Skyler's shoulders shrugged, still not willing to move from his position on the bed. Not willing to actually *face* the mess he'd made.

"Were you drunk Skyler or were you upset about something?" These words came from my mother and they were gentle and understanding, as were my father's.

"I don't know. Both I guess," he said. "I ruined the wedding though, didn't I."

"Luckily Evelyn was busy enjoying herself. I don't think she noticed the chaos between you two, but you both certainly ruined the day for other people, especially us. I've never been so disappointed. That's all I have to say."

I felt the hurt in my dad's voice. He was disappointed and this killed me. My parents closed the door on us and Skyler dug his head deeper into the pillows and blankets to continue his crying. I felt no inclination to babysit his emotions all afternoon like I'd always found myself doing.

So, I left. I went driving. I drove to nowhere as Adele's voice cut into my heart like a newly sharpened sword. I belonged nowhere. I gagged on my tears. I was pathetic. If this was the prelude to our happily ever after, I think I'd better reconsider and get out— alive.

7

Forgiveness. Sweet, sweet forgiveness. Why must you come alive when I'm not strong? You tell me to turn a blind eye on others' mistakes; you tell me to *forget* when I know I shouldn't. Why is the trauma of his bad behavior forcing me to forget? I know by staying I'm becoming his enabler. He can have me; he can have whoever. He can *do* whatever. *Just leave him, Taylor!* I can't leave. It's that simple. I can't leave yet.

I found myself at Logan Airport boarding a flight to Atlanta one week after our arrival in Boston. After seven days of pure mayhem: death, marriage, rekindling relationships, and begging my family for forgiveness, it was imperative [to Skyler] we board this flight back to his one stoplight town. I didn't want to go back to his parents' house. I wanted to spend more time with my family. It was too soon! I was myself at home. I inherited depression in Georgia.

Our round trip flights were paid for courtesy of my freshly unemployed mother. Pharmaceutical sales, you are so inconsistent. Skyler told his parents we would be gone for one week. They had our flight itinerary and they knew exactly when to expect us back. They would be irate if plans were changed. If their expectations were inconvenienced. My mother offered to change our returning flights to give us more time in Boston and to spend Thanksgiving with my grieving family, but any delay in our arrival in Georgia had the ability to upset his parents and *that* was the last thing Skyler wanted. They operated like clockwork. They repeated each day of their lives with the same ugly patterns and anyone that interrupted this pattern of life was an asshole.

Thanksgiving morning in Skyler's hometown of Buford was a scorcher. The sun felt warmer and closer than ever before. I learned that *sweater weather,* something my New England blood looked forward to every August, would be postponed and that sixty degrees down South meant frostbite for the locals, and tank tops for this girl.

"Going to Kroger Taylor. Wanna take the ride? I needa pick up some ingredients for the dish I'm bringin' to dinner later," Skyler's mother asked me. *My mother not only would have already had the ingredients, but she'd be cooking and baking all morning. It's a holiday!* The voice in my head was the only rational voice I knew of these days. I talked to myself far too often.

"Sure," I accepted her invitation. What the hell, she was Skyler's mother after all and I'm all about finding the goodness in people. I took full advantage of my opportunities to leave the Williams household, even if it meant following Doreen around Kroger as she pushed a shopping cart around. Remember, I'm without a car. Doreen was an "extreme couponer" with a binder full of laminated coupons to prove it. She walked up and down the aisles in search of items she had coupons for. The items weren't needed, but she wouldn't dare waste a coupon.

"Think I'll get these frozen ice cream pies for Skyler. Buy two get one free!"

She tossed three frozen dessert pies into the carriage or "buggie" as they called it. I'd been corrected on the shopping cart terminology one too many times, though I still refused to refer to it as a buggie.

"He doesn't like pecan pie," I said as she organized her coupons.

"But I have coupons for them. I'm getting one free! Someone will eat the dang pies. Hell, I will myself. Why do you gotta act like you know everything?"

She continued to load the cart with items nobody needed or liked, just to use coupons. Why buy a dozen bags of potato chips when there's an entire section of the tanning bed room dedicated to potato chips? Not sure. Carry on.

"OK, now for the ingredients for my famous Thanksgiving dish. I'm making macaroni casserole," she said. We were staring at boxes of Kraft Mac and Cheese. She flung two boxes of spiral pasta into the cart.

"I have shredded cheese at home. All set. Let's get out of here."

I watched her argue about prices with the teenage cashier who gave zero shits about her saving forty-two cents on two jugs of powdered Kool-Aid.

"Taylor, go grab me another thing of cherry Kool-Aid. Says here I get one free with the points I just earned. Skyler loves the cherry flavor."

I raced to find Kool-Aid so that the people who were in line behind us wouldn't have to wait too much longer. I'll never go anywhere with her again.

Skyler's mother proceeded to lay on the car horn the entire way through the neighborhood on our way home.

"I do all the food shopping. I ain't bringing none of it in. When I honk, they best come runnin'."

My mortified self couldn't wait to get away from her as Skyler came running out to the driveway.

Skyler's mother grabbed her vinyl handbag and her "Big Gulp" of Mr. Pibb from the cup holder and waltzed inside without a single grocery bag.

"Help em, Taylor! Shit!" she yelled back at Skyler and I.

"Why are you so dressed up?" Skyler asked as we began stacking grocery bags on our arms.

"I'm wearing leggings and a t-shirt. I was worried about being too casual. It's Thanksgiving. Why, what are you wearing?"

"Um... jeans. My family doesn't dress up for anything. You'll see. You're overdressed."

Inside, I had the pleasure of watching Doreen create her specialty dish for the holiday. She boiled the pasta from the two boxes of mac and cheese, then spread the noodles in a small, pyrex dish before covering it with breadcrumbs and shredded cheddar. That, my friends, is the recipe to Doreen's secret mac and cheese casserole. Why wouldn't she just buy a regular box of pasta? Why Kraft Mac and Cheese? Does she know how blah this dish is going to taste? There goes the voice in my head again.

I learned Doreen was not a cook during my first week in Georgia. Not because of her obsession with fast food, but because of her *famous* chicken stew that she made for dinner one night. Her one and only recipe. She filled a stockpot with whole milk, butter, and a boiled chicken. She served it warm with crackers on top. I really struggled to get a few bites of that down while her entire family devoured it in front of me. That was a tough night.

I entered Skyler's grandparents' house to a room full of people I'd never met before. Everyone seemed to be dressed in sweatpants; everyone was seated and eating. I was struck by the powerful scent of cigarettes as I assessed my surroundings. Five or six of them shared the kitchen table and the rest were scattered around the house on couches and chairs. Not a single person looked up from their plate. Not even a *Hello*.

I followed the Williams family into the dining room where the food was spread to make our plates.

"That was awkward," I whispered to Skyler.

"They're eating. Why is that awkward?"

"Nobody greeted us. Isn't it rude they didn't wait for us to eat?"

"Why is that rude? Is that a law?"

I rolled my eyes at *his* rude tone. The holidays sure bring out the best in everyone.

"I've never even met your grandparents. You know what, never mind."

I didn't recognize any of the dinner options. Well, some. Gray turkey and sweet potato covered in marshmallows, syrup, and brown sugar. I genuinely did not know what I was putting on my plate. But what I did recognize was the arrangement of magnets on the refrigerator. Skyler. Skyler. And more Skyler. Skyler had a bunch of cousins on his dad's side of the family, not to mention his brothers, but this fridge acted as a shrine of Skyler's baseball career. Pictures, autograph cards, newspaper clippings, internet articles; everything. I thought, how odd? Skyler hasn't mentioned his grandparents once, nor does he ever talk to them. What kind of relationship could they have?

We found some couch space in the living room. The food was cold and made my paper plate sag in my hand. I scooped flavorless mush into my mouth and reminisced about Thanksgiving at home. At least I knew what was in the macaroni casserole.

"Momma this macaroni casserole is the best," Skyler said aloud.

Beaming, his mother responded, "Son, I know you love my cooking."

The macaroni itself was overcooked. The noodles were flat; practically wet. She also cooked enough to feed maybe four people. Small portions folks, small portions!

An hour after our arrival, people found their way into the living room to introduce themselves; including his grandparents. I braced myself for baseball questions that were coming Skyler's way. The less someone knew him, the more they asked.

"Skyler how was your season, boy? You gon' make it or what?" His grandfather's southern accent was the thickest I'd heard since I'd been here. I didn't know what he was saying at first. He pulled out a pack of Newports and lit one for himself and one for his wife. His wife, who was attached to an oxygen tank. They both suffered from lung cancer. Go figure. His grandfather jiggled the ice in his glass of sweet tea. Skyler shrugged his shoulders at his question. My blood boiled all over again as we got lost in a cloud of second hand smoke. He hated answering the same questions over and over. I hated listening to it.

"And you must be the famous Taylor. The "Miss Massachusetts" Taylor. Glad to meetcha."

I reached out to shake his hand. "So glad to finally meet you. Thank you for having me."

The room exploded with laughter.

"Look at this girl! She's looking for a hand shake!" yelled his grandfather.

"I'm sorry. Do you not shake hands?" I asked.

"She's bein' all proper and shit! What a lady you got here Skyler!"

I still didn't understand why I was being laughed at. For a handshake? I felt like I was six inches tall. It took everything I had to hold back tears. I didn't belong. I was hungry and alone every single day. I wanted so badly to go home. I also knew in my heart if I told Skyler I wanted to leave, he would tell me to go without him. So I stayed.

December came as did colder weather in Georgia. I'd spent the past few months tagging along to all things Skyler. I'd get up at three in the morning to dress myself in camouflage gear, drive an hour to the hunting club deep inside the woods, unload the four wheeler from the trailer, load the guns and backpacks onto the four wheeler, drive out to the hunting blind in the freezing cold of the early morning, and sit, like a dickhead, in a blind until ten that morning.

Sure it was calming, until the coffee you consumed on the ride there hits your stomach and you're forced to clench your fart hole for the remainder of the stakeout. I could detect antler rubs on bark and I knew a buck when I heard one, but man was I tired of watching my boyfriend spray leaves with bottles of urine or doe estrous. I didn't want to do another load of laundry with scentless detergent because "it's hunting season". I'd paid my Georgia dues and now, it was time to introduce Skyler to the word *compromise.* If we were going to do this baseball life thing, if we were going to be a team, I was going to need him to sacrifice for me as I had been doing for him.

Convincing Skyler to spend Christmas at my house was easier than expected and I think it was because he could sense my misery. I had no quality of life in Georgia and there was no denying it.

Against his parents' wishes, we left mid December. His parents think I'm unethical because I didn't abide by what *they* wanted, but the ugly truth was that Skyler was a grown man and didn't need mommy to clip his toenails in bed anymore. Yes, that was a thing.

We planned to call Massachusetts home until the start of spring training in February. It took six large boxes from the post office to get my belongings home. We flew to Boston, leaving the truck behind to save money. Skyler would continue teaching baseball lessons at the DogPound and I would finally start a job in retail at the mall.

New England saw one of its worst winters to date during Skyler's first encounter with snow. While he adapted to a new climate and learned how to use a snowblower, his parents slowly distanced themselves from both of us. They blamed me, completely, for taking him. I knew it was something they would never forgive. They never called or texted and when Skyler reached out, they were short and bothered. They filled his head with negative thoughts: Taylor tries to control your life. Taylor hates us. Taylor wants to take you away from us. In reality, I was done watching my identity fade in the basement of a house in Buford, Georgia. I was Miss Teen Massachusetts. I held a once-in-a-lifetime title. My life belonged in Massachusetts. I just wanted the people around me to understand that.

His parents only called to vent about the financial troubles they were facing. They asked him for money from time to time knowing he didn't have much to his name. They even asked him to purchase new baseball equipment for his youngest brother. They weren't positive people and based on Skyler's attitude, I always knew when they called. Skyler and I were fighting more than one battle and truthfully, we weren't strong enough for any of it.

On our first Christmas together, I asked for a ring. No, not that kind of ring, though I wasn't completely opposed to the thought of having a diamond on my left hand. I'd always wanted to be married at a young age. The ring I wanted for Christmas, however, was not a diamond. Instead, it was a thick band engraved with personal signs, sayings, words, and dates that I would bestow upon my finger for the whole world to see.

"Write down what you want this thing to say and I'll pay for it."

"I want you to surprise me. It's my gift. I don't want to know every detail Skyler."

"Make me a list of things you'd *like* it to say then. I'll choose from your list. I don't want you to be disappointed."

"Skyler. Write down the things you feel are most important to us and I won't be disappointed."

Skyler was easily frustrated. He was also easily overwhelmed. He hated confrontation, phone conversations, and parting with money. He especially hated parting with money because his mother had access to his bank account and she made comments about every transaction he made. Two months of spring training and about five months of minor league ball earned him around six-thousand dollars after taxes. Seven whole months of your physical being dedicated to one game that doesn't give a shit about your well being. *Oh, but it makes you work harder. It makes you want it more!* Bull. Minor league players are in debt up to their necks and are often times unsure of where they'll lay their heads at night, never mind being able to afford proper nutrition. And though most of them double their earnings in the off-season by teaching lessons, they all run back when it's time to report. *Why?* Because why quit now? This commitment has taken up so much of your life already. How can you quit now? What if this is your year?

The Red Sox have dangled *what if* in front of Skyler's heart for five uninterrupted years now. Skyler left college during his junior year to pursue a career with the Red Sox. I suppose it's better to suffer within the season than to live the rest of your life wondering *what if* I'd stayed for just one more.

I asked Skyler what he wanted for Christmas and in turn he said— a ring. A band that he could wear year round to let everyone know his heart was taken. Most of his teammates were married; engaged at least. The higher the level you played, the more married players you will find. Because, well, they can afford it. Kind of. I'm sure Skyler felt pressure. He wanted a certain type of commitment that neither of us could afford. We weren't ready, financially or emotionally, but we knew we wanted it to be us in the end. I found a charcoal gray, titanium ring with faint baseball stitching printed throughout.

Inside, I engraved these words: **I Love You Forever — Taylor**

My mother flooded our living room with gifts on Christmas morning as she had done my whole life. Perfectly wrapped packages consumed the floor space leaving no room for walking. I was thankful to be home; to celebrate in my mother's fashion. Skyler's parents mailed us a box of gifts to open on Christmas morning as well. The box, it was the heaviest thing I'd ever felt.

Sean, Skyler, and I waited patiently for my parents to join us in the living room before opening anything. My mother prepped Christmas breakfast so we'd have a hot meal when we finished opening. Sunglasses, clothes, shoes, workout attire, watches, makeup, and stockings full of gift cards later, Skyler and I moved onto the gift from his family. The weight of the box derived from over fifty bags of hard candies. Dollar Store candies. Gum, mints, bags of chips, and socks. A cat necklace. They mailed us the entire Dollar Store. I'm all for *it's the thought that counts*, but I knew they didn't have a lot of money and it pained me to see them spend it on everything we'll never need. A twenty-five dollar gift card to Chili's would have been more meaningful [helpful] to us, but that's what happens when you try to gift people you barely know, even if that person is your son. Skyler needed new gear to start his season, gear that is terribly expensive, but they didn't even know that.

Last but not least, we shared our personal gifts to each other in the privacy of my room. He handed me a big box and a little box.

"Which should I open first?" I asked.

"The big one."

I ripped through candy cane covered paper to find a teddy bear in a box. His fur was camouflage and he was dressed in a Red Sox uniform.

"Press his foot," he said as he gestured towards the bear's limb.

"I love you sooo much!" It was a recording of Skyler's voice.

"Now press the other foot."

A recording from the chorus of 'our song' began playing.

Hey Pretty Girl, it feels so right
Just like it's meant to be
All wrapped up in my arms so tight
Hey Pretty Girl, it feels so right

Kip Moore, you are a genius with this one. We decided a long while ago that this would be our first dance song at our wedding someday.

"This is so sweet babe. I love everything about this bear," I said.

"It's to remind you of me when I'm on the road. I even sprayed his jersey with my cologne."

"This was so thoughtful. I love him. I will cuddle him when baseball takes you away from me."

He handed me the little box. I knew exactly what was inside. In a vintage box sat my ring atop a cushioned palette. It was heavy; one pound to be exact. I flipped it around to read all the words: Taylor & Skyler, Massachusetts, Georgia, Our First Christmas, Leo & Cancer, July 20 & July 26, Hey Pretty Girl Let's Build Some Dreams, My Beautiful Future, I Love You, Princess, My Baby, Mine Would Be You.

"Look inside the band. It's the exact coordinates of where we first met."

"Skyler. I'm speechless. This is incredible. Thank you."

"I hope you think it's perfect."

"This surpassed any expectation I ever had. I am in awe."

The vibration of his phone shook on my nightstand.

"Hey Momma. Yeah I was just about to call you. Merry Christmas to you too. No, no it's fine we ain't doing nothing right now. We already opened gifts with Taylor's family. Yeah I can talk, of course. Did y'all have a good morning?"

I could hear her voice.

"Was alright. Your brother had us up real early. You know how it is."

"We just finished opening the box of gifts you sent us. Y'all are amazing. You're too good to us. Thank you so much."

It's Christmas Taylor. Be nice. Stay calm. She called smack dab in the middle of our sentimental gift giving session and Skyler didn't even have the nutsack to tell her because she might get offended.

"So son, I noticed five-hundred dollars come out of your bank account. What was that for?"

Fumes I tell you. Fumes pouring out of my ears. My eyeballs! Skyler's face turned white as I dared him to tell her the truth with my stare.

"It was for…ah… Taylor's Christmas present. I got her this special ring she'd been wanting. It has our names on it and stuff like that."

"You spent five-hundred dollars on a dang ring for her?"

"Yes Momma."

"Well if that ain't the biggest waste of money I don't know what is. A dang ring. Wait till your daddy hears about this one. I gotta go son."

The line went dead.

"Merry Christmas to you too, Momma," Skyler said to the dial tone.

"I'll wear this ring until the day I die Skyler. It means a lot to me."

"I know. Momma's just weird about me spending money. It's cause they don't have any. Anyway, where were we?"

I handed him a small box. Delicately, he peeled open the wrapping paper.

"What, are you planning to reuse the paper next year? Rip it!" I yelled with excitement.

When his eyes met his ring for the very first time, they filled with tears.

"I love it Taylor. I feel so loved. Thank you. Thank you."

"There's a message inside the band."

He began to cry. "I'll never take this off Taylor. Only for games. You know, because I don't want to lose it. I love you so much."

"I love you too."

8

Three weeks after celebrating our first Christmas together, we flew back to Georgia to get Skyler's truck and continue our journey south to Fort Myers, Florida. This would be our first spring training camp as a couple. We would spend a single, dreadful night at Skyler's parents' house to break up our traveling.

Every millimeter of space in the truck was packed to capacity, but Skyler's mother insisted we take the twelve cases of bottled water she bought for us.

"There's plenty of room in the truck bed," she said.

"They are really heavy, Momma. Why add extra weight if we don't need to? I'm already spending a fortune on gas as it is." Skyler expressed his concerns.

"We will get water at the grocery store as soon as we get there," I chimed in. We were giving her the politest no thank you possible.

"So you mean to tell me I bought all these waters for no reason?"

She was insulted. As if she'd never made an unnecessary purchase before. As if *water* was something that would go to waste.

"No Momma. We will take them. I was just worried about the weight."

"Well quit talkin' and load em onto the truck, boy. It's cold out here and I wanna get back to bed."

Skyler still refused to share the driver's seat with me on road trips. Something about my lead foot and my ability to rack up speeding tickets made him believe he was the better candidate for the job. He swallowed an Adderall dry as we pulled into the Chick Fil' A parking lot. Spicy chicken biscuits with cheese were a traditional start to our long car rides. With my bare feet pressed against the windshield, my food baby put me to sleep.

I woke up in a pool of my own sweat and glanced out the window. My pale reflection in the mirror outside reminded me how badly I needed a tan. The scenery no longer consisted of winter beiges and browns, but of palm trees and blue skies.

"*IT'S ALIVE!*" Skyler said as I arose from my groggy stupor.

"How long was I out this time?"

"Almost three hours."

"I'm sorry. I should be helping you stay awake."

"This is my sixth time making this drive Taylor. I've done it alone five times. I can handle it."

"I guess. Where are we?"

"Tampa. We'll be there in an hour. Close your eyes."

A lawn mower was the final thing that woke me on our drive. We were in an empty parking lot with an empty baseball stadium sitting in front of us.

"Welcome to JetBlue Park! It's right off the interstate. Figured I'd show you around the office before we check into the hotel."

"It's so beautiful here," I replied. "Can we walk around?"

"We can do whatever we want. I work here."

As I overlooked six practice fields and an exact replica of Fenway Park, I suddenly became excited to call this place my temporary home. Lee County, a particular piece of Florida's Gulf Coast, was now *our* home. And though I'd never seen a Publix or heard of places like "Steak n' Shake" and "Zaxby's" before, my old soul was willing to build a life I'd grow to know so far from home.

In sweatpants and slippers, I followed Skyler around the complex. We walked across practice fields, passed through batting cages, and stood on mounds where pitchers practiced with catchers. I saw the weight room and the dining hall and, as I inhaled the sweet scent of freshly cut grass, I thought about Boston's most legendary players walking these same steps as I. Not everyone will get this chance.

A gate in the outfield of Fenway South was left wide open, practically waving me inside. The grass exemplified perfection and I felt sorry for walking on such beauty, but the impeccable silence of the stadium made it the most glorious sight I'd ever seen. I crept into centerfield to admire the view Skyler knew all too well. With each exhale, I was thankful. Something as beautiful as this ball park in southwestern Florida would surely be the reset button Skyler and I needed. Something *this* beautiful could only attract more beauty.

Lodging in Fort Myers during spring training gave me headaches throughout the off-season. I'd spent much of my time researching hotels and rental properties in the area that were affordable. *We don't accept month-to-month guests. You must pay for at least six months. We are not in your budget. We do not offer furnished properties.* I could continue. Skyler had a host family in Florida, but with four children under the age of seven and three dogs, I insisted we get our own place. And by our own place, I meant a run-down extended stay hotel. For the next two months, Room 244 at the Crestwood Suites was it.

"OH. MY. GOD. What is that *smell?*"

I was horrified when I opened the door to our room. It was bad enough I had to relish in cigarette smoke as the woman at the front desk found our missing reservation, but to be hit in the face with the smell of death as I entered the room I'd be living in was another thing. Musty, stale cigarettes, dirty bedding, and poor air ventilation made for a bitter combination. I struggled to get my suitcase through the heavy door that continued to close on my body. Two decrepit, full-sized mattresses dressed in raunchy, brown comforters stared at me from across the room. My slippers stuck to the knockoff hardwoods in our kitchenette as I made my way around for a closer examination. An old fridge with warm insulation and moldy food, a dirty kitchen table, a stained sofa, and a tiny TV from 1996. The curtains were dusty, the lampshades were yellowed, the wallpaper was peeling, and the air conditioning unit made strange noises. I was very afraid.

"There is *no way*. I can't stay here. This is not right. I requested a non-smoking room with a queen mattress. I just can't."

"Taylor we don't have another option. We'll go to the store right now and buy cleaning supplies. All this place needs is a good clean and some fresh air. I've seen worse. Trust me."

Before unloading our lives from the truck, we found a Walmart. We bought cleaning supplies, cleaning gloves, and other necessities that homes need. Bleach, candles, detergent, dryer sheets, shower curtains, and new bedding. We pried the windows open and stuffed dryer sheets into the air conditioner to mask the odors for the time being. On my hands and knees, I scrubbed the black grime and the different stenches right out of the room.

Once disinfected, I assisted Skyler in carrying the bins and suitcases up two flights of stairs. Our building did not have an elevator which made the thought of carrying cases of water bottles to our room a thrilling task. I made my first trip to Publix and, while I was gone, Skyler took it upon himself to push the two full beds in our room together to create more living space. Of course I'd rather be staying in a furnished townhouse in a gated community with an attached lanai overlooking a golf course with dancing fountains in the nearby pond like other players were, but we didn't have that luxury quite yet. Skyler didn't get a million dollar signing bonus nor was he rostered on the forty-man. For those who might not be familiar with the term "forty-man", it is essentially a list of players that are available for major league use. Skyler didn't wake up with job security and comfortable paychecks, but if living in a grungy hotel room with no stove and a handful of channels to watch on TV means I won't have to go a day without Skyler, then sign me up. It's only temporary. Besides, the toothbrush holder he made by sticking our toothbrushes into an upside down styrofoam cup really made the old room feel like a home.

I nuzzled my way into his arms on our new, giant bed and rested my head on his chest as day turned to night. We drifted off to Forensic Files, one of our five channels, until Skyler got up to use the bathroom. I heard him digging through the cosmetic bags.

"What are you looking for?" I asked.

"My Melatonin. And the Nyquil. What did you do with them?" His voice was frantic.

"They should be with the toothpaste."

"Found them." He was calm again. He reappeared at my bedside, downing a full gulp of Nyquil and then swallowing a few Melatonin pills.

"Skyler you've been driving all day. How are you not tired on your own?"

"Oh I'm exhausted."

"Then why take all that medicine?"

"I'll get a *better* sleep."

"It's not necessary to take all of that. Let your body fall asleep naturally."

"I forgot you were a doctor."

We slept in late the next day. Real late. Skyler didn't have to report to training camp until the following day, which basically gave us a free day in paradise to do whatever we wanted. I requested Waffle House and a trip to Fort Myers Beach. Skyler hated the beach, I knew this. He hated sitting in beach traffic and feeling drained from the sun. I guilt tripped him into going though because of how lonely baseball made me feel during season. Sad face. Tomorrow, a new journey down an old path would begin again for Skyler, but there I was, seemingly a minuscule detail on the infinite road of chasing the dream. Would my role in the baseball world remain as small as I felt?

I drove Skyler to JetBlue Park in my pajamas on the morning of his scheduled report date so I wouldn't be trapped in the room all day. I'd order a black coffee from Dunks on my way home, and after creating much confusion in the drive-thru with my thick, Boston accent, I was back in Room 244 before sunrise. I sipped hot coffee in bed while watching the country music video channel and pondering about what to do with my day. I fell back to sleep before finishing my morning brew.

Three hours later, I woke up for the second time that day. The room was warm and the sun was finally awake. I microwaved the remainder of my coffee, poured myself a bowl of cereal, and went back to bed to dine. Our kitchen table didn't come with any chairs. I showered, made the bed, and began unpacking our belongings. My clothes filled a small closet. Skyler's were crammed into the solo bureau that held the TV. Skyler was neat so I made sure everything was exceptionally neat when he came home.

I would have liked to explore the area; to see what was around us, but wasting gas was a real concern of ours. Skyler reset the mileage on his truck every time I used it by myself. He knew where I went and how much gas I used. I couldn't afford to fill the truck.

I kept my phone nearby at all times in case Skyler called to tell me he was done for the day. He hated when I was late. Eventually, he did call. His physical exams were complete and he was cleared to start the season. I picked him up exactly where I had dropped him off.

"Hey babe!" I said as he lifted himself into the passenger seat of the truck. His head fell back into the headrest and he reclined the chair completely with his eyes already closed.

"How was testing today?" I asked.

"I'm dead. That sun is fucking hot. We were running sprints all day. They told me I'm the strongest guy they own right now, physically. They were happy with my off-season workouts."

His skin was red and his eyes were tired. He slowly pressed a bottle of water to his lips.

"Well that is amazing! I'm so happy for you."

"Taylor look, these days are tough on me and it's only going to get worse. I warned you about coming to spring training. I'm gonna be tired and irritated all day every day.

I don't want to explore. I don't want to go to the beach. I don't want to go for a walk. I just want to eat and go home and sleep."

"I get it. I know how hard this is. I'm here for you."

"As long as you know. Can you drive? I'm starving. I wanna get food. Let's go. Gas is on the right."

My hand jumped to the shifter. A long drive down Daniel's Parkway, the most traffic infested road in all of Fort Myers, would bring us to Skyler's favorite place to eat. I bought lunch for the two of us as Skyler found a table on the outdoor patio. We ate in silence. Skyler inhaled his food as I attempted to learn about his day. I wanted to understand his routine. He barely wanted to discuss it.

"Well if you don't want to talk to me that's fine but I have some things I'd like to say to you. I'd appreciate it if you could meet me halfway with groceries. The rent plus food is just too much for me to handle on my own. I need help Skyler."

"I told you I wasn't interested in paying a single dollar for you to stay here with me. I don't have the money. I'm not even paid to be here right now. I could have stayed with the host family for free. I could have stayed at the team hotel. I told you to stay home if money was going to be a problem."

I dropped my fork. His words made for storms beneath my skin. A million emotions danced throughout my veins. I wasn't hungry anymore.

"I am just asking for help every so often. You are eating the food I buy."

"Fine. I won't eat anything you bring home anymore. I'll eat at the field."

"Skyler."

"I'm getting twenty dollars a day in meal money. My salary pay hasn't even started yet. I can barely support myself, let alone the two of us. I can't help you. Get a new job."

Skyler got into bed as soon as we arrived back at the hotel. Eat and sleep; he wasn't kidding. He was out cold. I laid beside him, wide awake and staring at the ceiling. I listened to his breathing and gently stroked the hairs on his head. I watched a muted episode of Forensic Files in a dark room as he slept away a sunny day.

I reminded myself I had come to spring training to support Skyler's goals. To support our relationship. That's what I told everyone. I quickly learned this was all a lie. The feeling of being completely alone delivered me truths I didn't want to face. I felt compelled to be there. Like, I didn't have a choice. I suffered so much pain in his lies about his ex and I didn't dare give him the chance to make the same mistake twice. I was here to prevent mistakes— cheating. To prevent pain that would come if I was in Massachusetts. I was here so I'd know exactly what was going on at all times. I was here because I wouldn't be able to survive the distance of a love that's already been unfaithful. I thought about Jillian Peters more than I'd like to admit. You know, his ex from Georgia that he visited while I was at his house. She was a part of my days. I brought her everywhere with me. I thought about her when I woke up in the morning, and at night before I fell asleep. I thought about her in the car and in the shower. I thought about her while I had sex with Skyler. When he was on top of me, it was her face that I saw. I thought about their time together. She intruded my daily thoughts without the slightest clue of the damage and disruption her name brought me.

My days in Fort Myers became something of a bad dream. They were a broken record; a pre-recorded song stuck on repeat. Skyler was confident he'd be assigned to yet another year in Double A. He said he was lost in a sea of prospects in a business that was already overcrowded. I told him to think his greatest desires into existence.

We started fishing together. It was inexpensive and therapeutic and it got us outdoors together. I had faith out there. The sun on my skin and the sound of the smallest current crashing along the shore rejuvenated my belief that Skyler and I were deserving of the most admirable of loves. This hobby helped our bond in brand new ways.

I struggled daily with the thought of going home to complete my year as Miss Teen Massachusetts and to crown my successor in March. I wasn't strong enough to go home. Skyler struggled to find his place in the system at work. He knew he was good, but he also knew he wasn't good enough. Together we struggled to maintain a peaceful relationship. If his parents weren't causing a riff, his job, money, or social media was. He asked I delete all forms of my social media, which I agreed to do, but by him cutting me off from the world, I felt lonelier than ever. He feared I would meet new love online eventually and this frightened him. This forced me to re-download the apps onto my phone every morning once I dropped him at the field. I did this to post about the magical times we were having in Florida, even though the two of us were clearly unhappy behind closed doors. I had to post. I had to share our love with the internet. Peoples' comments on our photos brought me to life: *What a gorgeous couple you two make! I'm so happy you're happy! I hope to find someone who looks at me the way he looks at you!* These comments fulfilled something inside me. Something I was missing. They made me whole for a second, knowing I was able to fool the outside world. People told me I was fortunate. I wish they knew me on the other side of the four walls. Would they recognize me at my worst?

On Valentine's Day, my mother sent us clothes, cards, and candy. She had the ability to make any holiday special from another part of the country. Skyler bought me roses and I surprised him with a parasailing excursion after practice. It was a cold and cloudy day, but I wanted our first Valentine's Day to be something to remember. Ironically, Skyler's mother called us on our way to the beach.

"Son, I've been looking at the transactions in your bank account and I'm noticing you're spending more money than usual. You're at Dairy Queen every night. One ice cream doesn't cost ten bucks. Why can't Taylor pay for her own ice cream. I don't get it!"

"Momma it's just ice cream. We like to go there. I can manage."

"It's ridiculous. Waste of money."

Tell her what my family has sacrificed for us. Tell her what they do for us. Tell her what they pay for. Tell her it's because of my family that we have a roof over our head and food in our stomachs all the time. Fucking tell her! The little voice inside my head was going ballistic.

"Hey Momma I don't mean to cut you short but Taylor is taking me parasailing for Valentine's Day. We are almost at the beach. We are excited. Neither of us have done this before."

"Hope nothing goes wrong and you go crashing down into the water. You could die."

"Alright, Momma. Thanks for that. I'll talk to you later."

"Yeah I hope so. I hope you don't die. Taylor and her dumb ideas."

My eyes filled with tears beneath my salt water stained Ray Bans. Skyler didn't even notice. Why can't he be my teammate? Why is she allowed to talk to him like that?

Post parasailing, we capped off our day at a popular Japanese steakhouse and to my surprise, Skyler picked up the tab. I had one final gift for him. It was hidden in my closet beneath a pile of clothes at the hotel. I debated giving it to him the whole way home. We'd had a good day. Skyler was happy and his temper had been even. I didn't want to offset him. He held my hand as we drove and told me he couldn't imagine doing another year of this lifestyle without the love I'd given him. He was so thankful. And in that moment, my mind decided, NOPE, not giving him the gift tonight. It was a book. I did a professional boudoir photoshoot before coming to spring training. I anticipated giving it to him on Valentine's Day. A book full of my body clad in tasteful lingerie, expressing the sexiest forms of vulnerability. I intended to show him what was his and only his. He didn't like me to be in front of the camera, though. He didn't want my picture to be taken. I thought these photos might ruin his mood and I didn't want to ruin our night. I didn't want to upset him. The book would have to wait.

The energy was playful as Skyler unlocked our front door. My eyes were begging for more than I could offer in words. He sent the keys to his Chevy spiraling down the molecular bit of counter space we had. He charged at me, lifting me onto the chair-less kitchen table. I wrapped my legs around his body as we struggled to find our way to the bed through the intense kissing we shared. I was thrown backwards onto the bed where we would continue devouring each other's mouths. He sucked my bottom lip until I tasted blood. He found the foundation of my neck with his tongue. I could feel the muscles contracting from his lips around my bones. I thought he might remove flesh from my body. Our breathing turned into groaning. Dense, substantial cries filled the room. The walls at the Crestwood Suites were paper thin. We knew this because we'd spent many of nights with our ears pressed against them listening to our next door neighbors' arguments turn into fuck sessions. Tonight the neighbors would listen to Room 244. Skyler tugged on my dress.

"Take this thing off," he begged.

He helped guide the clothing up and over my head. My bra disappeared shortly thereafter, allowing him to bury his profile between my boobs. Licking, spitting, sucking, and biting. Oh, the gnawing. My chest was shiny; a coating of saliva soaked my skin. It matched the ring of wetness around his mouth. My spinal cord had a conniption. I arched my back and released the most agonizing renditions of each vowel. He stood to undress himself. I love watching him undress. He left me alone for a moment. There. On the bed. Naked. But I wasn't completely alone. My demented thoughts were back to haunt me. *Jillian Peters. Will he do this with others when it's not physically possible for me to be with him? I know he's lied to me.* He grabbed my calves and maneuvered my body to the edge of the bed. His fingers crawled underneath the worn, elastic lace band of my panties that rested neatly across my hip bones. He softly drew my kneecaps apart. His tongue moved to my clitoris. I fidgeted as the blood circulated inside me. He hardly ever licked me down there, but when he did I'd go to heaven. I grabbed handfuls of the sheets. He submerged his penis into me. Slowly at first, but gaining great momentum with each stride. I'm not sure if there's anything more satisfying than recognizing the initial moment when your lover is completely and perfectly inside of you. We were sweating together. I was covered in his perspiration and he was covered in mine. Together our salty bodies made the most rhythmic love. Our homemade lubricant made for easy gliding. As he continuously thrusted into me, my pelvis begging for kindness, he interlaced his fingers with mine. His palms were soaked.

"I love you Taylor. Do you love me?"

He told me he loved me and asked for reassurance every time our bodies combined.

"I do love you. So much."

My response never changed. Skyler was the first man to deliver me a real orgasm. Before him and vibrators, I was unaware my body could reach such nirvana. And then, I felt it coming. *Cumming.* My insides were overwhelmed with a complicated warmth. A head to toe, full body experience if you will. For a few moments, I went to paradise. He owned me and I had not a care in the world. I wasn't even present on this planet. *Cum inside me. Create a baby with me. Let's start our family now.* I'd never felt closer to him in those moments of craziness. With clenched fists, I released the bed sheets from my hands and exhaled the most gratifying of noises. Rise and shine residents of Crestwood Suites.

"I can feel that," Skyler whispered as I spasmed beneath him. I pulsed hot bursts of liquid onto his penis. My body was his to keep forever. He pulled out and finished around my belly button. He fell beside me on the bed to catch his breath.

"I love you so much," he said.

"I love you darling."

He got up to fetch a towel from the bathroom and wiped the semen from my stomach as I lay there, examining his every move. I prayed every night that it would be us in the end. My best friend. Oh, my heart beats for this man. I can feel myself inside of his soul when I look into his eyes. His eyes; a familiar home that I've known all my life. I was made to take great care of his mind. My laughter. My happiness. I reside within him. I promise we are more than arguments and random sex. It has to be us in the end.

9

To maintain some sort of sanity, I'd sneak out to Fort Myers beach with my morning coffee to watch the sunrise on occasion. I'd beat traffic which saved big time on gas. Just me, hot coffee, an occasional read, the white sand, and my thoughts.

I continued my domestic hotel room chores so Skyler could focus on nothing but his game. Every afternoon when he came home, the bed was made, the fridge was full, and the laundry was clean and folded. I carried baskets of dirty clothes down flights of stairs to the laundry room with detergent, dryer sheets, and coins only to carry those same things back up flights of stairs when they were done drying. I carried bags of groceries, gallons of milk, cases of water, and energy drinks from the parking lot up to our room in the sweltering heat without a single complaint. I didn't want to make waves. Skyler needed to focus. I applied for a job at a local boutique and the manager seemed excited to have me join the team.

I didn't know how we would make it work having only one car, but I was willing to try. After seeing my driver's license during the application process and realizing my residency here in Florida was only temporary, I never heard from the manager again.

Finally, Sam arrived in spring training. She planned to stay for the remainder of camp with Kyle. I so looked forward to female interaction. Skyler hadn't been much of a presence, and the only face-to-face conversations I'd been having were with the lady that worked the front desk at our hotel who was in a different mood each time I went to pay rent.

"I love it here," I said as Sam and I caught up over spicy tuna maki. We sat outside, surrounded by vivacious plants and palm trees at one of Fort Myers most popular sushi joints.

"It will get old. This freedom, I mean. The sunshine. The pool days. The lack of responsibilities. I've been doing this for too long. Trust me. I just want to settle in one place. So honestly, how have you been doing?" she asked.

"Great! We've been fishing and…"

"I said *honestly*." She cut my sentence in half.

My face fell blank.

"It has been decent. We've had our share of ups and downs. I guess we are still learning about each other. Skyler's tired all the time and I'm lonely. He refuses to support us financially. I feel like I'm starting to struggle with this life. I feel lost." My voice began to crack as I confided in the only friend I had in this new world. The beating in

my chest began at an uncontrollable pace. Sam was signifi-
cantly older than me; six years to be exact. She'd followed
Kyle around the country for years, making her a veteran
WAG. She's supported her husband through countless
trades, injuries, surgeries, recoveries, and releases. She
has worked as a bartender, waitress, and chain retail store
employee to keep her life with Kyle manageable. She mas-
tered the lifestyle and she was someone I could always
learn from. Sam flipped her sunglasses on top of her head.

"Taylor do you know what happened between Kyle
and I?" she asked.

I shook my head no. I truly did not know.

"Skyler didn't mention anything to you about us?" she
asked again.

"No. I swear. I know nothing. What are you talking
about?"

"Kyle and I have been married for two years. I met him
when I was bartending at a local tavern. His baseball team
was in town for a few nights. We fell in love almost immediately. A month after we met, I moved in with him. I've
been traveling the country since."

"No way!" I said. "That's pretty amazing."

"Yeah. I met him in July and we married that December.
It was a whirlwind but we were inseparable and when you
know, you just know. Our wedding day was the best day of
my life and our honeymoon was something out of a fairytale. One month into our marriage, Kyle left for spring
training. I decided to stay behind, finish my degree,
and tend to the home we had just purchased together.

Our relationship was rock solid. I was sure we could handle the distance."

"You two didn't waste any time," I laughed.

"As soon as he walked out the front door for spring training, Taylor, he stopped talking to me. I thought he was dead, honestly. We shared a cell phone bill so I was able to look up his activity. That's the only indication that would tell me if he was alive or not. He was calling and texting random numbers at all hours of each day and night. But not me; his wife. I lost my damn mind Taylor. I was alone in our home in Texas. My family lived in Tennessee. I was alone and I had no idea why."

"Holy fucking shit, Sam."

"I lost forty pounds when my body didn't have forty pounds to lose. My hair fell out. I'm talking, literally balding. I slept for days on end. I didn't eat. My skin broke out in hive-like pimples. I still have scars all over my body from them. I was so sick. Eventually I just got up in the middle of the night and drove to Fort Myers by myself. I hadn't showered or changed my clothes in lord knows how long. I didn't pack a bag. I just drove through the night. When I got to Kyle's apartment in Florida, his roommate answered the door. He looked at me like *oh shit*. I walked straight passed him in search of my husband. He was in bed. On his phone. I stood at the foot of his bed and begged him for answers. You know what he said to me Taylor? Absolutely nothing. He said nothing. Hours of begging. Nothing. I drove another fifteen hours back to Texas, to our house, and promised him a divorce. I was so distraught I don't even remember driving home. It's a miracle I'm alive. The worst part? My family doesn't even know. They would be broken. I've never had anyone to talk to about this."

My hands covered my mouth in shock. My heart hurt for her. I almost couldn't find words.

"Sam. I am so terribly sorry. I had no idea. How did you ever resolve that?"

"He didn't talk to me until the end of spring training. Two months of silence as newlyweds. Betcha' don't hear that one every day. When his little vacation in Florida ended and he was sent back to Double A for the fifth year in a row, reality sank in. He doubted his career. He could sense the end. This doubt made him afraid and he didn't want to live with that fear alone. So, he called me. He knew I'd be there to love him when baseball didn't."

I believe Kyle killed something inside of Sam the month after he vowed to love her for the rest of their lives. She was the file to his jagged edges and he needed her only at specific times. She was on call for his emotions. I knew she wasn't happy.

"I don't believe in divorce Taylor. That's why I chose to work on things. But I'm embarrassed and I live my life waiting for it to happen again. Kyle doesn't think twice about the fact that he took years off my life as I monitored the numbers he was texting with Fort Myers area codes. Every night I'd fall into a medicated sleep thinking about how many of those women my husband had sex with. I hacked his social media accounts and his email address only to find millions of ongoing attempts to meet new women. He drank. A lot. He even admitted he was always drunk. He told me he's had sex with fans, team photographers, and his teammates' sisters while we were married. My life hasn't been the same since. It never will be."

I shook my head.

"Sam," I said.

"No, it's alright. He blamed it on baseball. He says it fucks with your mind and makes you do things you wouldn't normally do. He says baseball makes you a bad person, whether you want to be or not. I mean, I get it. One minute you're good enough and they want you, then suddenly you're being replaced. Is he making excuses for his actions? Yes. But I do believe that baseball is a business, *only* a business, and the organization treats its players like chess pieces. And then on top of all that, Kyle tore a ligament in his arm. As a pitcher, those were some heavy words. We were able to reconcile our relationship over his injury. He needed a nurse and I just flat out needed him. I often wonder what would have happened to us if he didn't get hurt."

My perspective on the most beloved ball game in America was quickly changing. It wasn't a past time nor a hobby, but a production company that slammed doors on dreams.

"The point of my story Taylor, is this. It takes a remarkable partnership to withstand a relationship with a professional athlete. This game changes people. You've both got to want it. We are in love with someone who is never around. We trust that they keep our love sacred when we're forced to be apart. I lost myself to this game. My world is dull and my spirit is anxious. You're so young. Please don't lose yourself to baseball. And remember, your gut is always right."

Her speech was heart wrenching. I was petrified to love Skyler the way I did. I knew to proceed with caution, but I could relate to Sam's experiences to an extent and that scared the shit out of me.

We spent the afternoon soaking our sweaty bodies in a pool at a local YMCA. It cost us each one dollar per day to use the pool. If it meant paying in quarters, so be it. It was our only joy anyway. We did this until the boys called us for rides after practice.

As I roasted away under the Florida sunshine, I thought about home and other things. I would have been a freshman in college; living in a concrete closet of a room and incorporating booze into my daily regimen. But instead I was here, adapting to a new way of life. After all, some of the best lessons come from experience, right?

"Ugh. Skyler's done at the field. Same time tomorrow?"

I wrapped a towel around my waist.

"I'll be here."

"Hey thanks for confiding in me today, Sam. I needed to hear that."

"I will always have your back."

I drove to JetBlue Park with a wet towel still wrapped around my waist. The same giddy, excitement hit me the second I saw Skyler exit the player complex.

"Hello babydoll!" I sang as my weary boyfriend plopped his body into the passenger seat of the truck like he'd done many times before.

"Did you drive all the way over here like that?" he asked.

"Like what? In my bathing suit? Skyler there's a towel covering half my body."

"You look like a whore. I'm out in the heat all day trying to make a living and you're driving around in *my* truck like a fucking whore. God damn, Taylor."

"Your windows are tinted Skyler. Nobody can see me."

"I'm embarrassed for you."

"Seriously?"

"Just get me home. I don't wanna be in the car with you."

He grabbed a bottle of prescription pills from underneath his seat.

"Have those been in here all day?" I asked.

He popped an Adderall into his mouth.

"It's not good to leave medication in the car you know. Especially in this heat."

"Again, are you a doctor?"

"No."

"Didn't think so."

I slammed on the brakes.

"Why are you so fucking irritable Skyler! I can't catch a break."

"Just *drive!*"

My boyfriend was addicted to ADHD medication. I now blamed his unpredictable behavioral patterns on tiny capsules of amphetamine salts. *I've been taking them since college and I'll never stop.* That was his excuse. I was failing to support an emotionally unstable human. I was supposed to be the one that kept him from cracking. This bomb that he was; exploding when you least expected it and without reasoning. I did what I could to keep him from erupting but nothing seemed to work. My energy was spent pasting his rips and tears back together. No adhesive I'd offer was strong enough; I was not enough. He made me nervous. I was a punching bag for his emotional outbursts. He carried a heart of confusion, concern, and frustration, and I carried our sanity. He told me Florida would be hard, but I was struggling to find my purpose in his life, period.

Back at the hotel, the landline on our nightstand rang. It was the front desk. Skyler and I had received mail.

Miss Taylor Higgins & Mr. Skyler Williams

The site of another wedding invitation made me cringe. My cousin, Candace, Evelyn's sister, was ballsy for extending the invite to Skyler after he nearly destroyed her sister's big day.

"Well I won't be going to that wedding. Opening series is that week. I'm sure you'll find someone else to bring."

"Skyler you haven't even been assigned to a team yet. You don't know what your schedule will be."

"Ah, no. I do. I'll be in Portland. Again. And we are on the road that week. Find another guy."

Skyler knew how to beat the hell out of me with his words. Simple conversations with him were exhausting because he made them that way. The kinder I was and the more I reassured him, the meaner he became.

"I've been wanting to tell you something," I said softly.

He fluffed his hands enforcing me to speak.

"The Miss Massachusetts organization offered me a spot in the annual St. Patrick's Day parade in South Boston this year. It's a family tradition to attend this parade, and I think it would be a nice tribute to my Nana if I went home for it."

"And?"

"So I would have to go home a week before spring training ends."

He sighed. "You know I hate this pageant bullshit."

"I'm aware. But I think it would be special for my family."

"It's all fake. I can't have you parading around town while I'm trying to play ball. That's not the type of person I want to be with and you know that."

"I'm literally doing this to honor my dead grandmother."

He stood up abruptly, grabbed the car keys, and slammed the door shut behind him.

"Do whatever you want. I can't date a pageant girl."

10

One week and several arguments later, my solo self landed in Boston. I had to come home for the parade. I just had to. I brought back with me as many of my belongings as I could so there would be plenty of room in the truck for Skyler's baseball bags on his trek north. I was leery of leaving him alone in the place we'd called home for the past few months. Unpleasant scenarios unfolded in my mind as I waited to deboard the aircraft. I chewed on what was left of my acrylic fingernails. My heart throbbed so loud I assumed everyone around me could hear it too. I pictured him drunkenly escorting another woman into our bed after hiding my leftover belongings in the closet. I wondered if my absence would make his ring find a temporary hiding place. In his jeans; a jacket pocket, a drawer, perhaps? He had been unfaithful in Georgia, I knew that in my soul. The truth Jillian Peters delivered me still lived inside my bones. The messages she had exchanged with my boyfriend were clear as day in my memory. Was I insecure for allowing my imagination to travel to such dark places? *But I do love him.*

It's only one week, Taylor. I talked to myself because I didn't feel comfortable confiding in anyone. He has games every day. He will be so busy. The March sun in Florida will put him to sleep after his games. But the scenarios in my head refused to rest. Was the negative reel of film in my head replaying itself because I'd been beat so badly by his words?

Boston's frosty air touched my golden, olive complexion all too soon. I wondered briefly why people chose to endure our cold winters when given the choice to live anywhere in the world. Anyhow, the site of my mother's face flushed the unpleasant climate from my mind. Being home and without Skyler reminded me of what life was like before I had met him.

"How was Fort Myers? How is Skyler doing? Does he know where he will be playing yet? How are you? I'm so glad you're home."

My mother came full of questions per usual. I did my best to fill her in while refreshing Skyler's Twitter page.

"Ugh Taylor! You're no fun to talk to. Your heads always buried in your phone!"

If only she knew. I tell my mom everything. Point blank. But not this. I couldn't. Not yet. Handling my own emotions had been a challenge of its own. I wasn't ready to juggle a worried mother's emotions at the same. No thank you.

The St. Patrick's Day parade was the next morning. I drove to East Fifth Street in South Boston with my family to meet the man from Mercedes-Benz of Boston who'd be driving us in the parade. We met in front of what was still Nana's house. My dad and his sisters had yet to sell it. A banner hung on each side of the beautiful Benz convertible with my name and the name of my sister queen, Miss Massachusetts. More importantly, it held words to honor Nana throughout every street in her beloved Southie.

In Loving Memory of Sis Higgins

The scripture was green and surrounded by shamrocks. Just the way she'd want it. My immediate family came to watch the parade: Mom, Dad, and Sean. A few friends came, and a few neighbors did too. My extended family, aunts and cousins and such, decided it would be "too upsetting" to attend the parade this year. I don't think they'll ever realize how disappointing this was to me.

As my mother draped an Irish Knit afghan that Nana made over our laps in the backseat of the convertible, I received a text.

Skyler Williams: Have fun in the parade babe! You look beautiful. Wish I could be there with the family to see you. I love you so much!!

His kindness made me assume the absolute worst. Instead of being struck with happiness, my heart sank to my stomach. Something was wrong, *very* wrong! Regret sank in, forcing me to soak in my terrible decision to come home. My fingers froze in the cold as I refreshed his social media while waiting for the parade to begin. Every two seconds, no exaggeration, I refreshed my boyfriend's accounts. He knew my time was occupied. What lines would he cross during this time?

As our vehicle slowly began to join the parade, a woman named Leslie Finn followed Skyler on Twitter. I held my phone low in the car. *Refresh the page, refresh the page, refresh the page.* I couldn't stop. I had to remind myself to look ahead, smile, make eye contact with onlookers, and wave back to them. Moments later, he followed her back. Smile and wave, smile and wave, look happy, smile and wave, take a picture, smile and wave.

I took screenshots. I had to build a case for myself so I could confront his lies. I was prepared for denial. I needed all the physical evidence I could get to avoid being manipulated. His lies became so perfect that I'd even began questioning whether I discovered anything at all. Did this even happen? I don't remember. Why don't I remember? Am I seeing this correctly? I'm sure there is a valid explanation. Tomorrow will be a better day. Am I losing my shit? I need to get back to Florida. Why did I come home? I'm definitely losing my shit.

Based on her profile, Leslie Finn was a blonde haired, blue eyed orthopedic surgeon. She was also a single mother of two teenage girls and a self-proclaimed baseball fanatic. She proved to be twice the age of my boyfriend with her wrinkled, leather handbag skin and her saggy example of a boob job. The incredible gap between the cannonballs on Leslie's chest obviously didn't faze her based on the number of provocative photos she chose to share on her page. Random fans followed Skyler on social media all the time, but my gut told me there was reasoning behind this particular follower named Leslie Finn.

Sam's words replayed in my mind: *Your gut is always right. Always.* As I waved to friendly pedestrians along the sides of the road I thought to myself, why in the fucking world would he follow this hag? I was angry. Smile and wave T, just keep smiling and waving. And I did. For three hours I smiled, waved, and took pictures with the prided [drunken] citizens of South Boston. I brought joy to others when internally, I was dead. I needed out of this parade. I needed answers.

When we passed my family, they jumped the ropes to take pictures with me. I knew my dad was especially proud in that moment. I wish more people would have been there to support us all. As we neared the end of the route, we passed an obnoxious crowd of intoxicated people.

"Taylor Higgins! Taylor Higgins! It's me! We went to high school together! Guys, I went to high school with her!" I glanced over at the crowd, trying to locate the female voice. I made eye contact with a peach haired girl with three inches of black rooting on top of her head. She wore a drawstring backpack and had a cigarette in one hand and a red solo cup in the other. Immediately, I knew who she was. She had never been nice to me. In fact, she was friends with the girl who pushed me into a locker in middle school. I wanted to ask her what jail was like or if the joint she

smoked in the school cafeteria was worth her expulsion, but instead I stared blankly. I scanned over her crew of friends who were basking in a smoky cloud of weed and then turned my head forward to look into the distance ahead of me. I wanted to laugh, yell maybe, or flip her the bird. Inside I was doing all three, trust me. Instead I kept my composure and handled it the way society insists title-holders should— I did absolutely nothing in fear of who I would offend.

As grateful as I was to ride in such a legendary parade, the number one thing on my mind was cantaloupe tits. By the time the parade ended, he had unfollowed her. Like I said: screenshots. He can't tell me I'm crazy if I have screenshots! Does that sound crazy?

I didn't confront him right away. Skyler, a delicate grenade, is unpredictable when he explodes. Suffering quietly to myself was easier than causing him to lose his temper.

Skyler was abnormally descriptive while I was home. I'm not sure if I'd been submerged in paranoia for too long or if he was, by rare chance, telling the truth. On the phone he told me every little detail about his day. What he was doing, who he went fishing with, and as soon as he tucked himself into bed at night with a bowl of mint chocolate chip ice cream in his lap. His descriptiveness made me unsure. In the meantime, I set out on my own investigation of Leslie Finn. She followed minor league ball players all across the country. *Only* minor league ball players. She responded to player's tweets and proudly donated money to player's charitable organizations they advertised online. Hmm.

Skyler Williams: I can't wait to have my beautiful wife
                     back in my arms! I miss you so much
                     baby! Only one week until we are back
                     together!! I just want to kiss you!!!! I am
                     not the same when you are gone! You
                     are my WORLD!

The seventeenth of March fell on a Monday this particular
year and I was thankful for that. I assumed partying on a
Monday was unappealing and would attract little to none
because, you know, work. Rookie assumption. Skyler spent
his St. Patrick's Day afternoon fishing and getting dinner
with some teammates afterwards. Allegedly. He sent me
a picture of our prehistoric TV captioned *In for the night!*
around six that evening. Six! I could see his hairy ankles
hanging off the foot of the bed in the picture. My reaction?

I was on the first direct flight to Fort Myers Tuesday
morning. That is what I have to say about "being in bed"
while the sun is still shining on the evening of St. Patrick's
Day. I told Skyler I'd be returning first thing in the morning.
He told me I was wasting money, which I was, but I'd rather
waste money than spend my nights worrying myself to death.

*You must think, you stupid girl. So young, so dumb. He keeps
giving you reason to leave and you choose to stay.* I'm still not
ready to leave yet. I'm not ready to quit. You see, when
it is good, it's truly good. When it is bad, which typically
outweighs the good, it destroys me but I can't see my life
without him. It is he who I picture walking down the aisle
to. He who will be the father of my children. He who will

be my life partner. It has to be him. We must find the balance of long distance relationships and communication. We will grow together through all of this. Watch us.

My trip back to Fort Myers would be my first opportunity to ask him about Leslie Finn. I can't confront him over the phone because he will erupt and abandon me. It *has* to be in person. I wish he didn't have total control of my emotional being.

Sam picked me up from the airport because I arrived in the middle of a minor league matinee. From the airport, we went straight to our sushi spot with another WAG who recently arrived to spring training from the Dominican Republic. We knew her from the Double A days in Portland. Anything was better than frying our butt cheeks on metal bleachers and getting an awkward tan for three hours. Alandra, girlfriend to one of the Red Sox's most valuable catching prospects, happened to also be one of the first WAG friends I made on this journey. I made splashes in my soy sauce with my chopsticks.

"You good, mama?" Alandra asked me.

I was nervous; scared. Happy to see Skyler, but dreading what would follow.

"It has been hard. Learning to adapt to this lifestyle all by myself."

"Girl, what did he do?" Alandra spoke sternly through her Spanish accent.

"I just have a feeling something is wrong. I don't trust him."

Sam and Alandra exchanged looks and then nodded.

"We have something to tell you," said Sam.

I knew they were about to ruin my day, my appetite, and potentially my relationship with some truth. I anticipated what the reality could be and what my short trip home could have caused. My heart was still. My body; stiff as a board. My mind sensed disappointment all too well.

"We saw Skyler at Boardwalk Bar last night. We were walking the pier and we bumped into him. He was with a group of guys from what we could see, but he was trashed. He saw us." said Sam.

"Did he say anything to either of you?" I asked through the lump in my throat.

"He asked us to keep this from you. That he just wanted to have a good time with the guys without you freaking out. I'm sorry you're finding out this way but we couldn't hide it from you," Alandra said.

Panic and betrayal yanked on my heart strings. I knew what suffocation felt like because of him. Imagine being suffocated to death time and time again but for some reason, your heart lives on. You continue to exist in a nightmare. You're afraid of your own life. That was *my* life.

"The sad part is he sent me a picture of himself in bed last night. I flew back today because I sensed he'd been lying to me. I don't know what to do anymore."

I had to sit through the end of Skyler's game in order to talk to him. With his eagle eyes, he found me the second I found a seat on the bleachers. He winked at me and flashed a big, cheesy grin. The anger in my veins intensified. The voices in my head get louder every minute.

I was on edge. I waved to him. My ass burned against the aluminum; my flesh dissolving into the metal. My sadness was used to waiting its turn. I was surrounded by beautiful women varying in age. Some pushed babies in prams, some held expensive dogs on leashes, and others came alone with curled hair and big sunglasses. We all came from different parts of the country; world rather. Yet we were all here for the same reason. We all loved someone with a dream. I embraced the small talk and wondered one thing: how many other women sitting with me were putting on a front right now, pretending to be happy, and hiding their pain behind a wide smile. Pretending is easier than explaining; forgiving is easier than divorce. Remember that.

When the game ended, Skyler rushed off the field for a kiss. He picked me up, spun me around, and told me how happy he was that I came back. He pulled the truck keys out of his bag and handed them to me.

"Be out in ten baby. Gotta take a quick shower," he said.

I carried my duffle bag through the player complex and towards the player parking lot. Other minor league games were still being played which meant I was stared down, whistled at, and had vulgar things yelled at me as I passed by each team. The away players were known to give the opposing team's WAG's a hard time. I finally found Big Red and climbed into the passenger seat to blast the air conditioning, hoping to salvage the remainder of foundation on my face.

Skyler, who compulsively organized his truck, kept his vehicle immaculate at all times. Today, however, it was in disarray. There were men's t-shirts crumpled into balls on the floor boards. Shirts that didn't belong to or smell like Skyler. Yes, I smelled them. It wasn't Skyler's detergent or deodorant. Green party beads were shoved into almost every cup holder and shamrock sunglasses were randomly displayed throughout. The passenger seat was pushed so far forward, almost into the glove box, leaving little leg room. I also noticed a pack of cigarettes on the floor next to the gas pedal. But *my picture.* Skyler kept a picture of me on his dashboard near the radio ever since we started dating. Today, though, my picture was nowhere to be found. I opened the center console in a hurry. There, lying neatly across some junk and some nips, was my picture. He hid me from someone.

"Hey, hey!" Skyler jumped in the driver's seat.

He kicked the pack of cigarettes underneath the chair.

"What's wrong?" he asked as soon as he saw my face.

"Can we talk when we get home? I don't want you to drive when you're angry."

"God damn, Taylor! Back for two minutes and you're already picking fights with me. Why didn't you just stay your ass home? I don't need this shit. I don't need you here!"

"Please drive home."

"I ain't moving from this spot until you tell me what the fuck is wrong with your miserable ass."

"Please Skyler."

He flung the truck into reverse and backed out at an aggressively fast speed. He peeled out of the lot only to stomp on the brakes when he felt like it to jerk me around and cuss me out for causing more drama. My body went crashing into the dashboard because I hadn't been wearing my seat belt and he knew that. Tears began to fall as soon as my forehead hit the windshield. I checked for blood. Nothing. He yelled some more and pretended to drive off the road.

"You make me want to just drive us both into that ditch! I could fucking kill both of us right now! Maybe then I wouldn't have to listen to you bitch!" he screamed.

"*Skyler!*" I yelled as I pushed the wheel; forcing the truck away from the ditch. He swerved at the last second and I tumbled into the door on my side of the car. I thought he might kill us both. I think he really wanted to this time. I cried softly to myself as I visualized the car wreck Skyler so badly wanted to create. Police officers, firefighters, EMS. Who would arrive on scene first? Who would be the first to witness an upside down Big Red? The engine is smoking; Skyler is bloody and unconscious against a shattered windshield. A Jason Aldean song is still playing on the radio as a local patrolman locates my filthy corpse several yards from the truck. Jason Aldean is my favorite. Medical services would wipe me from the pavement to the sound of country music. If only Skyler would have driven off the road.

Inside our hotel room, our home, everything appeared to be the way I left it. Skyler planted his body on the edge of the bed and, with arms folded across his chest, he demanded I speak.

"Go ahead, Taylor! Tell me what you're bitching about now!"

"What did you do on St. Patrick's Day Skyler?"

"Oh Christ! Is that what this is about? Your little friends snitched on me? Trying to catch me in a lie? Ain't gonna work cause I ain't a liar."

"You were out drinking when you told me you were in bed. You told them not to tell me."

"You're such a dumbass. One of the guys called me looking for a ride home. He was hammered and a few of them needed a ride so I went to pick them up. When I got there, none of them were answering their phones. I got out of my car and went into the bar they told me they were at. That's when I saw Sam and Alandra. If you weren't such a psychopath I would have been honest with you. But to avoid a fight, I decided to keep that from you. I was only trying to help them out."

More tears fell from my eyes. How dare he insult me right now?

"My... my um."

"Um fucking what, Taylor?! Spit it out. Dang. Everything is always about you."

"My picture. It was hidden in the center console. Who were you hiding it from?"

"It wasn't hidden. The guys were drunk and they kept messing with it. I put it in there so nobody would ruin it. Are we done or do you have any other pointless fights you'd like to start?"

His carelessness made me cry harder. I struggled to find courage. I struggled to project my voice.

"Who is Leslie Finn?" I asked.

"*Who?*"

He spoke as if it were his first time hearing that name.

"Leslie Finn. Who is she? You followed each other on Twitter a few days ago."

"The old lady?"

Skyler chuckled at the sound of her name.

"Who the fuck is she Skyler?"

"She followed a bunch of us guys on Twitter and nobody knew who she was so I followed her back to find out. She's like a mom or something. She's old."

"So it was your responsibility to take one for the team and find out who she is? Ever think she could be a fan?"

"You just love to fight, huh?"

"Why isn't our relationship enough of a boundary for things like that? You would lose your damn mind if I did something like that!"

"Talk... talk... talk. All you ever do is talk. Do you like hearing the sound of your voice or something?!"

His southern accent made the word *talk* sound repulsive. A sound I will never forget. *Taaaulk!*

"You should have stayed home. A week apart would have done us good. I can't deal with this bullshit Taylor, I really can't. My love for you will never be good enough. I will never be good enough."

"I just need the truth. So I can move on from this with peace."

"I gave you the truth. Now end it. I don't want to hear another word come out of your mouth."

I gently lowered my weakened body down onto the bed to weep silently into the pillow. For a split second, I stopped crying to inhale any scents that could have been left behind on our cotton pillow cases. I searched for an unfamiliar scent. A female's perfume, dry shampoo, hairspray maybe. Anything. They smelled like our detergent.

"Here we go again. Cry, Taylor. Cry it out. This shit is so old. I'm over it."

He started the shower, leaving his phone to charge on the kitchen counter outside the bathroom door. I waited until I heard the jingle of the shower curtain being pulled along the rod before jumping out of bed to investigate his device. His phone was locked with a passcode. Thankfully I knew the passcode, not because he told me, but because I'd studied him doing it time and time again for instances like this. He didn't know that I knew. His inbox on Twitter was empty. Naturally. His email, a different story. His Twitter notifications were sent directly to his email. After days in agony, I finally read what was said between Skyler and Leslie, and who initiated this exchange.

Skyler Williams:	Do I know you?
Leslie Finn:	No. But I'd like to know you. I've been following your career for a while now.

| Skyler Williams: | Thank you I appreciate the support! You should text me. |
| Leslie Finn: | I think I'll need your number in order to do that. |

Cue my boyfriend sending his number to wrinkly jugs. My eyes focused solely on the numbers that made up his phone number. The shower shut off. I made sure his phone was positioned exactly where he'd left it, including the way he wrapped the charging cord around its body. I got back in bed and acted as if I had been deeply enthralled with an episode of Forensic Files. I dried my sniffling eyes and listened to the towel wipe the moisture from his skin.

"You *bitch!*" he shouted. You touched my phone didn't you? You touched my fucking phone!"

His accusations grew louder each time.

"Skyler. Please."

I was afraid. Flat out petrified.

"I can see your fingerprints on my screen. I know you touched my phone. I cleaned the glass before I went into the shower to see if you'd touch my phone and you fucking did! You don't trust me!"

His temper was rising; I could see it in his eyes. He would make me pay for this.

"You want to keep fighting? Well let's fight. Let's do what *Taylor* wants because the world revolves around *Taylor!* Let's fight! Come on!"

He began throwing things from the kitchen counter-top. Food, water bottles, and eventually the glass vase from my Valentine's Day roses. His eyes were bulging from his skull; I could see the veins in his face. He made his way towards me where I now lay in a ball; knees tucked into my stomach and covering my head. My body expected his hands. I knew they were coming for me. He slammed the mattress beside my face. I flinched. He laughed. He was in control. He knew I was scared and he loved it. My big, desperate, saucer eyes pleaded for compassion. I knew he could kill me with his bare hands. Suffocation is the quietest way to take a life; we learned that from Forensic Files. Maybe he would like to test that theory. He always said he wondered about it.

"I saw your conversation with Leslie," I said.

I had to fight back with my words. They were all I had left.

"What the fuck did you just say to me?"

Drops of his saliva landed on my skin.

"You gave her your phone number."

I lifted myself into a seated position on the bed. He stood before me.

"You're a coward Skyler. And a shitty liar. I caught you."

The word *coward* struck him like lightning. His daddy probably used it on him once or twice before. He stared at me. The look in his eyes was unlike anything I'd seen before. There was a demonic presence living inside his pupils.

Skyler turned around and opened the door to the closet that held the remainder of my clothes. He grabbed the suitcase I'd left behind and flung it across the room. I watched it ricochet off of the wall and onto the floor.

Because it was made of plastic, it cracked in a million places.

"Go home you piece of shit! Here you go, I'm helping you pack! I'll even drive you to the airport! Call mommy, tell her to put you on the next plane. I'm done! So fucking done with this!"

He ripped my shirts and dresses from the hangers as they joined my dilapidated luggage on the carpet. As he worked his way into the shelving of the closet, intentionally whipping pairs of shorts at me, I realized something. *The book.* His freaking Valentine's Day gift that I'd ever so unfortunately forgotten about was sitting on the top shelf in between the clothes. I prayed it would slip past him. Then, I heard an object spiraling through the air. It crumbled against the wall. I jumped up to retrieve it.

"What is that?" he questioned.

I held the book against my body to protect it with all I had.

"It's nothing Skyler."

"Let me see what you have in your hands."

I closed my eyes as he reached for the book. He shoved me onto the floor in order to peal the book from my hands. He struggled to break my grip and, for a while, he couldn't. This only pissed him off more. One by one, he removed each of my fingertips from the frame of the book, completely destroying it in the process. A book that was meant for him to begin with— I begged him not to look. I cried and I begged. He pushed me backwards every time I attempted to keep him from looking.

I watched him flip through the smushed, broken pages with horror in my heart. His expressions were repugnant. Tasteful images of myself that I once found to be beautiful were shredded in front of my face. I now felt like the ripped art in those photographs; shredded and torn to pretty, little pieces of nothingness.

"What is this trash? *You slut!*"

"That was supposed to be your Valentine's Day gift except I was too nervous to give it to you on Valentine's Day because I was afraid of your reaction. We were having such a good day. I was afraid of *this*. I had it custom made for you."

"Custom? A photographer took these pictures which means you were half naked in front of another person. How does that make you feel? Stop lying to me. This wasn't custom. You know I hate this shit!"

"Skyler I thought it would be sentimental. Women do boudoir shoots for their significant others all the time. It's very normal."

"I'm embarrassed to say I ever dated you. To think I could have impregnated you! You can't even take care of yourself, never mind a child."

He threw the remainder of the book at my chest.

"I'm done arguing about this. I gotta eat. This Adderall has me shaking. I wish you would just understand that I love you and quit your bitching. Please stop fighting with me. I have nothing to hide from you. I have never lied to you and I never will."

I had no words.

"Are you coming? I'm going to get food."

I looked at him. Confused, trembling, unable to regulate my breathing and gargling the thick mucus in my throat.

"I'm not hungry right now Skyler. Thank you."

I was frozen inside a cloud of emotional trauma. My tremors were violent; my pulse rapidly beating out of control. Such dismay brought heart palpitations to my chest. My pallid skin mirrored the sufferings I felt inside of me.

"Fine. Starve for all I care."

By now I had our arguments figured out like they were some sort of equation. Complication plus confrontation equals abandonment. My body wouldn't move; my mind, still trying to process what had just happened. When the adrenaline disappeared and my awareness reminded me I was in fact present in this disaster, the heartache of unanswered questions returned. I was left to bargain with him once more. We'd spent so much time screaming about fingerprints on cell phones that I wasn't even allowed to address the fact that he had contacted another woman.

In a painful silence, I cleaned the tornado of a mess Skyler had created in our bedroom. I hung my dresses, folded my shirts, and tried to recover what was left of the book as if I planned to stay in Florida. I had zero sadness left inside me. My emotions were disappearing. I'd become immune to being helpless. I wanted to know how a human being could love someone in such a distorted way. My mission now was to locate the root of his problems; his anger. His heart was trapped behind bars beneath the bones of his chest and I dreamed I'd be the one to release it from its shackles. If I couldn't, with my patience and purity, nobody could. But seriously, why Leslie Finn?

11

We managed our last week of spring training together, somehow, without slitting each other's throats. Skyler had a magical way of pretending our arguments never happened and I just didn't have the energy to continue fighting an uphill battle. He always returned a calm, kind, and compassionate man willing to use the argument as a lesson on the road to building a stronger relationship. I believed him every time. I would do anything to keep him in my life. He made me so sick.

Our final day in Fort Myers was a rainy one. It was gloomy and miserable and it suited the recurring theme of our story just right. Our home was once again an empty hotel room and our belongings were bagged and boxed. I picked Skyler up at JetBlue Park one final time. He walked out of the complex with two, massive baseball bags with Red Sox logos hanging over his shoulders.

"Going back to Portland. Third season in Double A. Told you," he said as he flung the bags into the backseat.

"Seriously?" I didn't want to believe him.

"Yup. Another year of being broke and living in some- one's basement."

"I really thought you'd—"

"You thought wrong," he cut me short."Nothing I can do about it. Too many of our top prospects are coming up. They'll work their way up through this organization faster than I ever will because I don't have millions of dollars attached to my name. That's the difference between being a first round draft pick and an eighth rounder like myself. Prospects have to produce and climb the ladder quickly or else it will make the important people in the front office look stupid."

"You'll get there Skyler. It doesn't matter how long it takes."

"Whatever."

In a monsoon of wind and rain, we squished our lives into Big Red back at the hotel. Florida, your rain is unfor- gettable. It reminds me of the fake rain they use in movies; those downpours are completely unrealistic. Closing the door to our room was like closing a chapter of our lives. That tiny space held memories Skyler and I would carry forever, and then some we didn't want to carry but were forced to anyway. This tiny room was significant to me. I'd learned several lessons, both good and bad, and I'd discovered a lot about my young self.

I stared at the green Crestwood Suites sign in the side view mirror through the fog and the rain as we drove away. It would be the last time I'd see that sign for a while.

Forever maybe. I was sad in that moment. Spring training was a giant experiment for our relationship. As trying as it was for me emotionally, I believed in my heart Skyler and I were still meant to love each other, if only he would accept that he must love himself too. The love we shared was a love I was willing to eternally fight for. I was willing to fight even on days Skyler chose not to. I stared at him as he drove. The only thing I could hear was the windshield wipers going a mile a minute. Placing a hand on the base of his neck, I gently stroked his spine. My fingers moved easily from the oils on his skin. He loved to be rubbed.

"Forgot to tell you. They released Kyle Creedon this morning," Skyler casually blurted out.

"Today?! How did you forget to tell me that!"

"Yes today. He practiced with us and everything. We were all cleaning out our lockers and packing when they called him into the office. He started crying because everyone knows what *"Coach needs you in the office,"* means at this point."

"I feel so bad. I have to text Sam. Did he say anything to you?"

"He came out of the office, said they released him, and shook my hand. That was it."

My heart broke for them both. Imagine that your career, your dream, was in the hands of fate. That, no matter how hard you worked, you just might not be the right fit. Or, in mine and Sam's case, to be placed into friendships with someone you would have never known if it weren't for this game, a friend that is now considered family, only to have them taken from you in the blink of an eye by some geezer in the front office that doesn't even know your first name. Poof. Our lives were tiny, insignificant pieces to the big game of baseball. Sam was gone from my life and there was nothing we could do about that. Maybe being released would give them time to make their marriage stronger. I worried for Sam. I worried for their happiness.

The hurricane followed us from Fort Myers, Florida straight into Buford, Georgia. Our plan was to spend the night at Skyler's parents house and then continue the drive north in the morning so he could see his family one last time before the start of the season. Blessed. Skyler was the only person they cared about in this equation, in any equation really, and that was evident. There'd been an unidentified anger, an elephant in the room, since that day in December when we decided to spend the remainder of the off-season in Massachusetts with my family. His mother hated any instance where she didn't have complete control over him, his money, or his time. As if spending his entire signing bonus on his family wasn't enough, they continued to act as a constant reminder that they were depending on his success in baseball. The latest, easiest way to describe the Williams family— greedy individuals that wanted no part in things or people that didn't profit them.

We arrived in Skyler's hometown after ten hours of driving. His ability to drive ten consecutive hours was sponsored by none other than his usual: Adderall, donuts, and energy drinks. Skyler called his mother.

"Momma, we will be at Kroger in five minutes. Yup. See you soon."

Confused, I asked, "Why are we stopping at Kroger? It's so late."

"Momma fills my tank every year to start the season. It's a ritual we have."

We parked at a pump outside of the grocery store. His mother's caravan came rumbling in behind us, turning heads at the gas station with each screech and pop the vehicle made. Skyler jumped out to hug her and together, they shared a moment and forgot all about me.

"I missed you son. Now I'm gonna pull my car up real close behind yours. Fill it up then hand me the pump real quick. Im'a fill mine too while we're on Mamaw's tab," she giggled.

What? Did I hear that correctly?

"Hi Doreen!" I yelled through the window.

"Hiya, Taylor."

His mother didn't come to chit chat, she came to scalp a free tank of gas off her elderly mother. She was strictly business at the pump.

"You good?" Skyler questioned on the way to the house.

My mind had been blown for the trillionth time.

"Your mother never ceases to amaze me, Skyler."

"What do you mean?"

"She just stole from your grandmother. She's literally taking advantage of an old person."

"She ain't stealing, Tay. Mamaw wouldn't mind."

"Well I'd bet my life that Mamaw doesn't even know! I thought she wanted to buy you a tank of gas! Not Mamaw!"

He shook his head as if I were being irrational.

After too many hours in a moving car, all Skyler and I wanted to do was swan dive into a mattress. As we made our way into the Williams neighborhood, we noticed the street was aligned with cars on both sides near the house.

"Looks like someone is having a party," he said. "Probably the new neighbors."

"Is that your cousin's car?" I asked.

"Oh, shit. It is. My whole family is here."

Fuck. We dug through boxes in the truck in search of some attire for the following morning and then walked into a house full of guests ready to talk and ask questions. We survived the drive on fast food meals and various gas station snacks. Our limbs were stiff and our greasy skin needed a hot, soapy shower. *Skyler how was spring training? Where will you be playing this year? Did you get promoted? I heard an outfielder is hurt, does this mean you have a chance? The Red Sox need help in centerfield, this will be your year. The Pawtucket Red Sox play the Gwinnett Braves, we'll finally get to see you play this year if you get to Triple A!* It was all noise.

"I'll actually be starting in Portland again this year. I'll be lucky to get to Triple A this season," he said.

And, *crickets.*

"Everyone! Find a seat. I have something to show Skyler!" his mother announced.

"Momma we don't have to do this right now. I'm tired."

"Well it ain't my fault y'all took forever to get home. We do this every year. Don't be selfish, boy."

A recorded Red Sox spring training game appeared on the TV. During spring training, certain minor league players are asked to sit in on big league games that happen to be nationally televised. The actual rostered players elect not to play a full game to prevent a preseason injury, allowing minor league players to get some time on the big field. It's your time to shine, really.

"I recorded every game Skyler appeared in during training camp," she boasted.

I sat on the living room floor to leave couch space for the old folk to watch reruns of games I'd seen in person. Granted his mother fast forwarded to all things Skyler, but it was brutal. I stroked the neglected, obese family house cat, Frosty, whom Sheriden would so often throw into the air, forcing it into a backflip— forcing me to go ballistic. But what's worse than watching a live baseball game on television? Watching a pre-recorded version of a spring training game while my boyfriend struggled to stay awake across the room as questions were fired his way.

Hot beads of water splashed my face as I stood under the shower head. My sore eyes remained closed and I held onto the wall for support. Skyler was in bed waiting for me. The shower, my one place of peace, made me anxious now. I felt Skyler near me even behind a locked door and a shower curtain. He was famous for dumping cups of iced water on me in the shower, or just peeking in to sneakily watch. He loved to hear me scream either way, but when my eyes met his in such privacy, he was amazed with my level of fear each and every time. It never got old to him. I established a fear of closing my eyes to wash my hair. I tried to do it as quickly as possible so I could watch for him again. He has seen me naked and unaware when I trusted the walls to hide my body for a moment. My poor mind was restless.

The voice inside my head began a pep talk as I finished my shower thoughts: *The sooner you fall asleep, the sooner you'll wake up and say goodbye to these people. Who knows when you'll see them next!*

I went into the bedroom, locking the door behind me, and allowing my wet towel to fall to the floor. There was a knock at the door.

"Y'all decent? Can I come in?"

"Just a sec, Momma. Taylor just got out of the shower."

She sighed outside the door.

"My underwear is in my bag in the bathroom. Guess I don't need those tonight," I said.

I threw one of Skyler's college tees over my head and hid under the covers to hide myself from his mother.

"I'm waiting," his mother whined in the hallway

"You can come in now Momma."

The door flung open.

"Dang. About time!"

She planted her bum on the foot of the bed to rub Skyler's legs. I was expecting her to ask about spring training or the upcoming season but she said nothing. She rubbed him without saying a word. The three of us sat in a weird silence; me half-naked and she, going to town on his feet with coconut scented lotion. I looked Skyler dead in the eyes and, without saying a word, told him to get her out of the room.

"Alright, Ma. We are pretty tired. We should get some rest before our drive tomorrow."

"It's you that needs the rest. Taylor doesn't have to do a damn thing."

"She keeps me awake. She's my co-pilot."

I bit my tongue. Completely offended, she left without saying goodnight to either of us.

I'd never been more excited to begin an eighteen hour road trip in my life. Saying goodbye to his family was indescribably satisfying and because they didn't believe in traveling, I was sure I wouldn't see them for a very, very long time. The rain let up for our drive to Massachusetts but the wind currents were stronger than ever. We stopped for gas in Virginia and I thought I might be sucked into the sky on my way to the restroom. I knew we'd hit New England when the truck went to war with the roads. Skyler was convinced Big Red would fall apart in New York. It sounded that way at least. Cracks, potholes, roads with faded lines, and weather eroded tar stood as one, big welcome home sign for me.

The first thing I noticed when we entered my hometown was how narrow the main roads were compared to the ones in Florida. My house was without a doubt the best thing I'd seen in a long time. I knew I was here to stay this time around. Home fulfills you in a way that nothing else can, and I was ready to be whole again. Skyler's season would start in two days. We planned to spend the night with my family and make the drive to Maine tomorrow morning. My phone vibrated as we pulled into the driveway.

"Who texted you?" he asked with crooked eyes searching for the name on the screen. Skyler practically jumped down my throat whenever I got a text message. *Who is it?*

"It's Sam, relax. I texted her about Kyle's release."

Sam Creedon: Hey there! We are just getting home. Thank you for checking on us. Kyle and I will be alright. We are hoping another team will pick him up, though that's almost impossible at the beginning of the season. I can't say I'd be completely upset if his baseball career was over. It would probably be the best thing for us actually. Maybe our marriage will have a chance at normalcy. Wish Skyler the best of luck this season from both of us. Promise to stay in touch! And if you're ever in Texas, know that you have a place to stay! Taylor, you are so kind and so beautiful. Never let anyone take that from you. Chase those dreams of yours!!! You promised me you'd audition for the Boston Bruins Ice Girls team this year and I'm holding you to that! You are made for big things! Love you sister!

I fought back tears from her words. My chest had a certain sting inside of it. What if I never see Sam again? My mom met us at the front door. I'm sure she heard the exhaust from the truck before we came up the street. Unlike Doreen's van, Skyler paid to have a rowdy vehicle. Mom hugged me for a really, really long time and proceeded to do the same with Skyler.

"I'm so glad you guys are home! Spending an hour a day on the phone with Taylor just wasn't cutting it anymore!"

We walked into a fully prepared, home cooked meal. For the first time in months, Skyler and I devoured real food. *How was the drive? Did you hit any traffic? Do you want salad? You guys must be exhausted! Did you enjoy your time in Florida? You missed a helluva winter here! Are you ready to start the season?* My parents asked all of the right questions. I came to life almost immediately.

The following morning came too soon but I knew Portland was a manageable distance from home. The season opener was in Binghamton, New York which meant I'd spend just one night in Portland to help Skyler get situated at the host family's house before driving his truck back home to Massachusetts. This also meant I'd spend a week without Skyler while he was away for the series. Our constant countdown of a life could be compared to a cracked hourglass that ran out of sand too quickly. I depended on a body that was hardly present; a mind that was barely available. His words would hold me when nothing else could. I craved the one thing I would never have on a daily basis: his touch.

Time would never heal such aching in my heart. Distance would always be a strain and I had to accept that.

We spent our first night in Portland unpacking Skyler's necessities by a single, shadeless bulb to light the room. The host family moved Skyler's bed into one of their kids rooms, so he was without a bed. We bought an air mattress and a memory foam pad at Target that would suffice. Leslie Finn's existence still cooked slowly in the back of my mind and I refused to start another season with this uneasiness simmering in my chest. I would die just to find the truth. I suppose there's never really a good time to ask someone about their infidelity, but my feelings refused to linger longer than they had. Road trips were set to begin again and I needed honest answers before he headed off to another state alone.

"Skyler I'd like to talk to you about something without you getting angry. Please can we have a normal, adult conversation?"

"Uhhhhhhh! What now Taylor! Can we go one night without an argument?"

"I don't want to argue Skyler. I just walk to talk."

"You just wanna *fight, fight, fight!* It's OLD! What? What do you want now? *Talk!*"

His eyes were squinting. The wrinkled lines across his forehead were perfectly defined horizontal lines. I hoped his temper wouldn't wake the family upstairs.

"I saw your conversation with Leslie Finn on Twitter. You gave her your phone number." I said.

"This again? You are legit insane, you know that? There is something wrong with your head. You're so fucked up! Just go home. You're mental."

"Why did you give her your phone number?"

"I already told you *why!* I wanted to know who she was and why she was following my teammates. We were curious. Now leave it alone. I'm done talking about this."

"That's absolute bullshit and you know it. I need the truth. I can't live like this."

"Then don't. Nobody's forcing you to be here. Go! I gave you the truth. She's old as shit. Do you think I wanna fuck her? Here's an idea, trust your boyfriend for once."

I knew the truth, part of it anyway, but Skyler had a way of telling me his version of the truth. He spoke clearly and confidently about his actions. He made me feel like a fool for not believing him. I was willing to forgive his mistakes, no matter how many he made, because of the severity of love I had for him. I just wanted to know *why* he acted the way he did.

"I'm done talking about this. You can either believe me or cry for the rest of the night. Your choice. Either way I'm gonna sleep like a baby. Tomorrow is my first day of the season and that's all that matters. Nice way to start it off though, Tay. Good job. I don't need this."

"*Skyler please!*" I cried.

"I sleep well at night knowing I'm a loyal man. Now lay down and go to sleep. This boy loves you. I mean it."

His head fell to the pillow. He pulled at my arm in hopes I'd lay down beside him but I resisted, staying seated on my side of the bed.

"Alright then sit your ass up all night. I'm shutting the light."

What I knew about Leslie Finn that day might be all I'll ever know about her.

12

Portland's home opener brought me a brand new batch of WAG's. I met women from Australia, Ohio, Virginia, Texas, Baltimore, Puerto Rico, Kansas, California, New Mexico, Arizona, and Louisiana. The wives and girlfriends of the game consisted of college students, working professionals, and those who chose to leave it all behind to become an attachment to the lifestyle as a baseball gypsy. Temporarily residing in a random city isn't always rainbows and butterflies for a WAG. At first, it's fun. Road trips, late nights, pizza in bed, hotel hopping, new people, dinner at midnight, iHop dates, being homeless, chasing the god damn dream by your man's side! Well, for starters, whomever created minor league baseball said, "AND LET EACH STADIUM EXIST IN THE MOST DESOLATE OF PLACES ACROSS THE COUNTRY!" Binghamton, Trenton, *Pawtucket!* Lock your car doors.

"What's it like to be a WAG?" said everyone ever. WAG's have a lot of time to do virtually whatever they would like

to do until first pitch. When the old timer who rides the golf cart around the stadium becomes your pal, you know you've truly paid your game day dues. GPS becomes your bestie because you never know where the fuck you are and your excitement will stem from things like strawberry farms and panini cafes. *Off-day plans anyone?!* And it's all done in the name of love. Because being completely invested in a relationship can make you do just about anything. But every day is the same. *Baby, you are my rock. You make this journey so much easier on me.* Fucking duh! At the expense of [my sanity] boring, empty days. But what human being needs purpose, right? Some WAG's work in their home state and visit periodically. Many become teachers to allow themselves a summer with the hubs. Some pick up jobs near the stadium to ensure decent conversations and help with the mountain of bills. Us WAG's are the stabilizer in this broken world of baseball. We are all one, big family.

Watching baseball games in the freezing rain at an empty stadium will be the norm, you'll make a home out of an unfurnished structure, you'll adapt without a car of your own, you'll be comfortable living in several different places throughout the year, you'll learn to prepare a meal with minimal ingredients, and the groceries will always find their way into the fridge because the man you chose as your life partner spends over twelve hours per day at the stadium. The travel is lonely, you'll stay up late then sleep in the next morning, your body will consist of snacks and takeout food, and living without a stove or an oven will become easy. The one day off he'll be able to spend with you every few months will excite you like noth-ing else, friendships will keep you afloat, you'll create a blog to provide a purpose for yourself— a vlog if you're really feeling adventurous, team photographers will go to great lengths to have sex with the man who sleeps beside you each night, fans will be mean to you, the media will be even meaner, everyone will assume you are rich when you are poor, and you'll handle life and all that it throws at you alone because, well, he has a game and it has to be you. You'll never complain, you'll see the best in every situation, and you'll remain serving as the strength your relationship needs. He will survive because of you. You will survive because you have to.

Sure, WAG's have green juice dates and wine nights with charcuterie plates. We need each other's company. We need to socialize and we crave a reason to get out of our yoga pants. To feel normal. Then, when it's game time, we'll make sure to drive ourselves to the stadium in a beautiful car that we did not purchase. The car belongs to him the same way we belong to him. We are posses-sions to our baseball playing owner. That car will be your identity. To fans; to everyone. Strangers will know who owns you by the model car you arrive in. We will park it in a lot with the other beautiful cars only to rejoin our fellow WAG's in the stands. We'll pray our man has a good game to avoid a silent car ride home and unpredict-able mood swings. Our kindness and uplifting words will never change his attitude if he didn't produce during the game.

Post game, you and the other WAG's will hang near the locker room and chat as the guys shower. One by one a player will come out, and one by one a WAG will leave. *"See you tomorrow."* By now it is late. You finally get to see him. You're excited! He is exhausted. Your only quality time together has no quality at all. He wants to go to bed. You want to go to dinner. He eats the clubhouse food, eyes closing, leaving you to fend for yourself. The best part is? Tomorrow will be identical. And the day after. And the day after that. Because, *love*.

I started cosmetology school in April in Massachusetts thinking it was a career I could pursue in any state. I thought I'd be golden no matter where Skyler ended up on the map. *I'm going to have a career and make this work!* I was completely wrong, I left hair school shortly after I began, and it was in *that* failure that taught me that I should probably start making decisions to benefit me, myself, and I. I needed to locate my true passions for myself, not because it would help me to spend more time with Skyler.

My cousin, Candace, married her now husband, Jake, in April as well, and after an eleven inning matinee in Portland, Skyler surprised me at their reception. To this day, I'm still shocked he was allowed to attend her wedding after his performance at Evelyn's wedding. To my surprise, our relationship was growing stronger than it had ever been before. With time, I stopped asking about people like Jillian Peters and Leslie Finn. It was easier to live happily within those dark secrets, than to live without him at all. I didn't have the whole truth, and because of that,

I couldn't walk away. Our love, like the antidepressant it was, was erasing all insecurities and damaged thoughts I once had. We'd never been better and I had never been more sure that I'd eventually get to call this man my husband, regardless of how much I still stalked his social media.

Then came July. Our second consecutive July in Portland, Maine. My birthday month, Skyler's birthday month, and my brother Sean's birthday month. Skyler and the rest of the Portland Sea Dogs had a home stand through the Fourth of July weekend. I'd known this for a while because I'd carefully checked the team schedule at the beginning of the season to mentally prepare myself for Skyler's whereabouts on holidays, birthdays, and the ever so dreaded "off-day" while on a road trip. I hated off-days, but I prayed for off-days in Portland as opposed to another city. Game free, practice free, workout free off-days. Sure the guys deserved the break, but I couldn't bear the thought of free time, far, far away from me. It simply meant one thing: bars, girls, and intentional mistakes. Yes, I said intentional.

"There is cheating to cheat, and there is cheating because your current status does not make you feel fulfilled anymore, though you are not entirely ready to begin the coping process of the person's physical disappearance."

— Taylor Higgins

I thanked the universe for allowing the Sea Dogs to play at home on the Fourth of July. As stable as our relationship had been, my heart lived in fear of putting it to the test. I still carried Skyler's lies within, all of the unanswered questions lived beneath my skin, but we were doing well. I couldn't bring myself to make waves about the past anymore.

I wore an oversized baseball jacket to the July Fourth game to smuggle a spicy tuna roll into the stadium. I tucked what would be my dinner into the waistband of my jean shorts and proudly joined my baseball sisters in the stands, knowing I'd found a way to eat decent meals at a normal time. After eleven godforsaken innings, the Sea Dogs took home a win and us WAG's were invited onto the field for a firework celebration. We paired off with our men in the grassy outfield to watch the show. With my back against Skyler's chest, I leaned on him as he held me in his arms. I was fully present with him in that moment; cherishing each second and knowing sooner than later, a charter bus would take him away from me again. My mind struggled to remain positive at such a beautiful time. *Silence your mind, T. You will never heal unless you shut off these thoughts.* As fireworks danced in the sky above us, an extreme feeling of paranoia entered my body. Well I suppose it lived there, but I usually kept it secluded. The stadium was full of fans tonight, thousands of them, and I felt each and every pair of eyes from behind. The fingers on my left hand were interlaced with those on Skyler's right hand. He gently massaged my palm with his thumb and whispered sweet words into my ear. My mind battled remorseless thoughts. *How many women in this crowd know Skyler? How many women in this crowd know who I am and pursue Skyler anyway? How many women in this crowd have Skyler's phone number? How many women in this crowd are laughing at me right now? How many women in this crowd think I'm stupid?* I was eaten alive by the negativity that now possessed my inner being all while in my lover's arms. He couldn't protect me from the damage he'd done. Will I ever escape this mess? I kissed him on the cheek for anyone that had been watching. I did it over and over again because I felt I had to. I'll show those women! He is mine.

I spent my days uploading pictures and documenting how unbelievably amazing our relationship was on social media. The more I struggled to control my thoughts, the more obsessed I became with sharing our relationship with the public. Deep down I was bothered and frightened, but I had to prove to everyone that we were beating the odds. I was a liar, the worst kind, because I knew how to lie to myself. I lied to myself until I eventually believed my own web of lies that my broken brain conducted out of a sad unsureness. The fireworks ended but the inconceivable theories repeated themselves. Betraying trust is simply an introduction to mental suicide in slow motion. Don't know what it feels like to lose your damn mind in slow motion? Ask someone you love to lie—. Who am I kidding? We've all been fucked over. We exhaust ourselves in search of truths we hardly ever find. We beg for pain and devastation because it's expected; it's accepted. We hunt for placeholders and temporary distractions in dusty bar rooms when life challenges us. Does love carry any quality anymore? I'm beginning to think not.

On July fifth, Skyler played an afternoon game before boarding a bus back to Binghamton, New York. He delivered me a pre-game cola with the word *soulmate* written on it. Giddy ole me did what anyone else would do in this situation. I uploaded a picture of it to Instagram.

As my buttocks clung to the plastic seat with summer perspiration, I dreaded the "see you later" I'd soon be faced with. Days like today made me pray for extra innings. *If the game ends at five, he'll be on the bus for at least six hours, plus the bus stops for food a few times, he probably wouldn't get to the hotel until midnight so bars will be closing, yup he will go right to bed. Perfect!* Those were the conversations I'd have with the voice in my head. I didn't get the extra innings I had hoped for though and our goodbyes were only getting harder.

"I wish I could bring you with me," he said as he wiped tears from my sun kissed cheeks. He says that every time he leaves and I, well I always cry. I blasted music and sung my lungs out the entire drive home to Wilmington. *This is what happiness feels like!* Sunshine, a happy heart, beautiful memories, and a good man. His love made me invincible. I thought.

When I returned home, I was starving. I scooped a hunk of peanut butter onto a plate of sliced apples and planted myself on the couch. Instinctually, I refreshed Skyler's social media accounts. He naps on the bus so I wasn't expecting to find anything new. His Twitter was clean, naturally. I felt almost no desire to look, but out of habit I logged into his email account. You know, just for the hell of it. He didn't know I had access to his email still but I guess that's why they compare upset females to veteran detectives.

Welcome to the demise of Taylor Higgins. My life hasn't been the same since. A conversation via email was unfolding in front of my eyes. Word for word:

Skyler: Hey it's Steven! My texting is fucked up idk why haha.
Brianna: Hey stranger! How have you been?!
Skyler: I'm a lot better now that I'm talking to you! We are coming to town tonight. Our bus gets in at midnight. Hope you don't have any plans. You wanna pick me up again?
Brianna: Haha idk Steve! That's really late and I have work in the morning.
Skyler: Come on! You know it will be worth it. :)
Brianna: You really think so?
Skyler: YES!!! I'll see you at midnight babe.

I watched as this unforgiving conversation transpired on my device. *Steve? Really?* My vision was hazy. I couldn't hear anything; I couldn't speak or swallow. I thought about crying but no tears were forming. I thought about sending him a vicious text message in lieu of a phone call in fear he'd ignore my call or hang up on me after hearing something he didn't want to discuss. I thought about driving six hours to Binghamton to have this conversation in person knowing I wouldn't be able to fall asleep with these messages harboring in my head. *If I leave now, I'll get there by midnight.* Then I thought about driving to Portland to destroy his pride and joy, Big Red, that sat alone and unattended in the player parking lot. I fantasized about engraving his Chevy: *Brianna, Leslie, Jillian, AssFace!* I wanted him to come home to a masterpiece. Welcome back, you dick. I erased the destructive thoughts shortly after realizing I would be chewed to pieces as an inmate. I ain't no prison wife. But I did muster up the courage to call him. I calmly, considering the circumstances, dialed my [sleeping] boyfriend. Nervous was an understatement. And worst of all, based on their conversation, this wouldn't be their first encounter. I found my way to the Portland Sea Dogs schedule as I anticipated the sound of his voice. The last time the Sea Dogs played in Binghamton was the week of my cousin Candace's wedding in April. He surprised me at her wedding reception, and the day prior he'd been in Binghamton. I had goosebumps. Who was this cheater?

"Hello?" Skyler muttered into the phone as if I'd woken him.

"Skyler I need to talk to you."

"Alright. Well spit it out, dang! I'm trying to sleep."

"I'm. So. Afraid."

"TAYLOR! WHAT DO YOU WANT? YOU JUST WOKE ME UP!"

"I just saw the messages between you and Brianna on your email."

"What messages? What are you talking about? I've been sleeping the whole time. Somebody must have hacked my email account because I haven't been talking to anyone. I've been asleep, just like I told you. Because I'm a man of my word. I can't deal with this right now. You're literally insane, wow! Get off my email and leave me alone. The whole bus is listening to our conversation and everyone is laughing at you. How does it feel to be known as the mentally unstable girlfriend? I'm sure as hell not proud. Everyone feels bad for me."

Then he was gone. Just like I knew he would be. I called him back like I'd done many times before. Reminding myself to breathe was imperative at this point.

"WHAT DO YOU WANT TAYLOR?" he screamed into the phone.

"To talk! Please just talk to me!" The line went dead.

Hysterical me fell to my knees on my bedroom floor. Slouching, I held my head in my hands and sobbed. Nobody was home at my house which invited my wails to become comfortably louder than normal. I continued to call him, for it was in those few seconds of ringing that put my cries to rest in case he decided to answer. I found peace in the ringing; it was my only hope. *Your call has been forwarded to an automated voice messaging system.* The sadness and discomfort returned immediately. Rage, too. I kept calling.

"Listen you psycho cunt, everyone on this bus already thinks you're a lunatic. Do yourself a favor and stop fucking calling me."

"SKYLER! Just wait a sec—. He hung up again. I knew his words were lies.

My panic-stricken self went back into his email to find that the messages had been deleted. I had screenshots, but what if I'd never seen these messages to begin with? I needed the answers I deserved. If Skyler wasn't willing to give them to me, I would find someone that would. I searched Brianna's full name on Twitter and easily found a blue-eyed brunette from Binghamton. I opened her profile picture to stare at the face that interfered with my relationship. She was Hispanic and pretty and her smile was captivating. Skyler always begged me to dye my hair brown, could this be why? I stared and stared before concluding: screw it, I have to message her. If she had a heart in the slightest, she would give me the truth.

Taylor: Hey, apologies for this random message but I am desperate. I found a rather explicit conversation between you and my boyfriend in his email and I'm just looking for answers. He's claiming he never sent the messages. His name is Skyler. We have been together for over a year and any info would mean the world to me at this point.

She responded within a minute:

Brianna: Hey. First of all, I am so sorry. Are you referring to Steve? He told me his name was Steve Smith. At least that was the name he used on Tinder. He told me he did not have a girlfriend. That he'd been single for "too long" to be exact.

Taylor: His name is 100% Skyler Williams. Have you met him in person before?

Brianna: Yes, once, this past April. We had sex multiple times if that's what you're wondering. I'm so confused by all of this. He made me feel so wanted.

Taylor: He has a way of doing that.

Brianna: I wouldn't have gone near him if I knew he had a girlfriend. Again I'm sorry. Feel free to message me if you have any other questions.

That day I learned many new things about the man who owned my heart. Out of everything I learned, the thing that bothered me the most was the discovery of his fake, online identity fueled by the desire to fuck strangers as I slept. On road trips, Skyler would bombard me with sweet words, but he was never alone. He couldn't stand to be alone. He attempted to have sexual relations with a girl after he'd spent the weekend making love to me. I felt dirty. My body had been violated. No amount of excessive showering could wash away this kind of filth.

I called him again. Now, my number was blocked. I curled into a ball on the floor and cried more. I was suffering in enormous amounts of pain. No broken bones, but perhaps a broken organ. The vessel of life thumped slowly in my chest. I thought I might die today. I shook, teeth chattering, and melting in long, uncomfortable cries. My hands, unsteady against my kneecaps, quivered in distress. I felt bad for myself. I felt shame. I'd enabled Skyler. I had accepted his mistakes in the past because

I was not ready to accept his physical absence in my life, and by doing so, I'd authorized the most inconstant of disloyalties. I was struggling too often and living too little. How will I recover from this?

I heard the front door. My mother was home from work. I listened as her high heels came clicking up the stairs.

"T, are you home?" she yelled.

I didn't say a word. I wept silently on the floor while trying to control my breath. I didn't want her to hear me panting like an animal. I didn't want her to see my purple face. As I listened to her movements carefully, I found my reflection in the mirror across the room. My face was brick red, eyes irritated and beginning to swell. I wanted to abandon the girl in the mirror. I was embarrassed to look at her. And even still I looked for answers instead of jumping to goodbye. *Where did we go wrong? What can I do to fix him? What caused him to act this way?* This isn't normal behavior, something made him do this. I hammered my mind with questions. Why, *why, WHY!* My heart went to war with my brain as I yearned for the strength to say: SCREW YOU. I AM GONE.

My mother made her way down the hall to my bedroom. I knew I would have to be truthful; there was no way of hiding this one.

"Taylor?"

My door was ajar. She pushed it open and gasped at the sight of my body on the floor.

"Taylor!" she screamed. "Are you alright?"

I didn't know where to begin. Quite frankly I didn't feel like reliving each stage of events so she could hate Skyler's guts as I tried to wrap my head around things myself.

"Are you sick? What happened to you?!" She was frightened.

"Mom. I am clearly upset. Your energy is not helping me right now."

"Talk to me then Taylor. Is it Skyler?"

"Yes. He... he uh, he lied to me. He told me he was napping on the bus but when I checked his email he was actually just conversing with a girl in Binghamton so they could meet up for sex *again*."

Her face went white as a ghost.

"I don't understand," she said. "I thought you had an incredible weekend together. That's what you told me."

"I'm not sure about much of anything right now, Mom. But I do know that I need some time alone."

She looked down, nodded, and left without saying a word. If you know my mother, you know that her silence is unusual. A woman who always had something to say, had absolutely nothing. Skyler broke both of us that day.

An hour turned into several hours. The sun sank and the darkness of the night reminded me all over again of my abandonment. I did manage to get off the floor and into my bed. I called Skyler's phone over and over again even though he had blocked my number. I was hoping he would want to talk after he calmed down. Midnight came and went and I never got a call. I wondered if he stranded me for Brianna. I spent all hours of the night searching for Steve Smith on dating apps and on Facebook. I found nothing. I just cried. I cried and I cried and I cried until my eyes no longer opened.

It was early morning when I passed out from exhaustion. The melatonin helped, too. It was easier to go to sleep than to be awake. I don't know the exact time, but the sun was rising and the birds were chirping. Isn't it funny how the world goes on even when you feel like yours has stopped? *One foot in front of the other, T. This pain is temporary.*

My phone vibrated under my pillow.

Skyler: I'm not arguing about this anymore. I slept the entire bus ride to Binghamton. I never messaged ANYONE from my email. I've never heard of a "Brianna". We got to the hotel around midnight as planned and I went straight to bed. That's it. If you can't believe me then we can't be together, it's as simple as that. My own girlfriend doesn't even trust me! But I'm done talking about this. I don't want to hear another word about it.

He sounded so strict and so evil. It was all about him. Always. He didn't have the right to decide whether or not we were done talking about this. We hadn't discussed anything at all! He had mistaken my love for weakness. In fact, he abused my love for him. Alone I was strong. Together, he made me weak. This was déjà vu. *Who is Leslie Finn? He must have gone to Jillian's house that night in*

Georgia. Tell me I'm not crazy. Somebody save me from my mind.

By now I had literally no energy left to defend the evidence in black in white. If I showed him screenshots he'd call me a liar. I sent him a picture of my eyes captioned: This is what you do to me. Nothing more, nothing less. My sockets looked like two, angry welts. My evergreen eyes told stories sad enough to erase daylight from existence. My eye bags had bags and my skin, a shade of gray. I was willing to accept the truth. I expected a remorseful response to the photo I'd sent him.

Skyler: I don't do shit to you. You do it to yourself. You overthink everything and it's pushing me away. Keep crying, Taylor. I'm ready to leave you. Crying doesn't make me feel bad for you.

Skyler spent the week in Binghamton without communicating with me at all. Come midweek, I accepted the fact that he did not care to resolve anything because, in his mind, it didn't happen. I stayed in bed, avoided the world, stalked Brianna's Twitter page, and refused meals from my mother. Days were tolerable, but I feared the nights. Alone in the silence with nothing but my demented thoughts to carry me into a depleted coma. I cried so hard. I ached for him. He was the only one who could save me but he chose not to. He was taking years off of my life. I had to write to him. My words were my final fight.

Brianna proudly shared her attendance at each Sea Dogs game on social media. She caused havoc in every square inch of my body. With the shades drawn in my bedroom, I overanalyzed my life. I poured my heart and soul out to Skyler via email. It was the only form of communication I still had access to. I knew he wouldn't read it, or respond, but I sent it anyway. My mother begged me to eat; she begged me to take rides in the car with her. She knew my love for mesmerizing drives, the movement of the car is so satisfying, especially when partnered with music. A drive with my mother was a temporary cure; a band-aid for a wound that needed stitching. Ninety-three south and twenty-minutes later I could see the Boston skyline greeting the stars. I'd quietly cry to song lyrics and my mother would cry because I was crying. She was the only thing saving me.

A week without Skyler's voice meant I was agitated, nervous, and apprehensive. I inherited bad anxiety, something I was not familiar with, and it strangled me to death. This feeling of anxiety figuratively handed me a noose as I stood atop a chair and it kindly asked me to step off. Going beyond the four walls of my bedroom was a task I was no longer able to complete. I thought about him; Brianna. I pictured them at their most intimate hour. I wondered about the lies he told me back in April in order to buy himself enough time to have sex with Brianna. It drove me mad. He sent me flowers that week in April; a massive arrangement of roses with a beautiful letter. He made flowers look so hideous now. *His ring.* What did he do with his ring as he penetrated her insides? Of course he didn't wear it. Was it tucked into the pocket of his jeans, the jeans that I bought, that were thrown on the floor beside the bed? A symbol of our love bestowed upon his ring finger was hidden. *Our love* was hidden in exchange for a few, meaningless minutes inside another woman's vagina.

I didn't know it at the time, but Skyler's lack of communication with me during the week was a blessing in disguise. It was healing. I didn't have to answer to anyone and I found comfort in the ability to make my own decisions without reporting back to somebody that wanted to shelter me from society. I'd spent many of those lonely nights soaking in a blistering, hot bath. I'd sink down until the water touched my chin and the wet strands of my hair covered my bare shoulders like individual streams of gold. The dripping of the faucet at my feet chained each beast in my imagination. I debated running away with my newfound freedom. I could ditch Skyler at any moment. It was *my* turn to abandon a love that didn't deserve me. I was undisturbed in that tub; under the water. I could have escaped to heaven right then and there but I chose not to. It wasn't my time to go. Tears slid down my cheeks and into the large container of water that held my body. I bathed in my own sorrow, literally. His neglect only gave me more time to fantasize about the way he'd murder me. I believed he was capable of premeditated murder. Maybe he would butcher me as he did with his deer. Maybe he would strangle me. Alone in my bath I could feel his hands around my neck, holding me beneath the water. He was in

Binghamton, so far from where I was in my bath, yet the terrors he'd left me with were enough to disturb a psychiatrist. Nothing would ever be the same between Skyler and I. I'd have to move on.

The team bus departed Binghamton on a Friday morning. He unblocked my number to inform me of his ETA. The Sea Dogs had a seven o'clock game that night and Skyler invited me to Portland so we could talk after the game. Because I'm a female and I crave closure, I accepted. Truthfully I missed the shit out of him, but he wasn't allowed to know that. I told my parents I'd left some of my belongings up in Maine and that I was going to tell him goodbye in person. They were rooting for me. I began my drive after the game had started so I wouldn't have to see a single inning. I drove there feeling empowered. Today would mark the start of a new beginning.

Arriving at Hadlock Field for one final time was bittersweet. I was forced to keep all of my adventures there as distant memories. The game was crawling by upon my arrival, with four innings to go. I entered the stadium to say goodbye to my second family, my baseball sisters. I owed them proper farewells and they deserved to know about my sufferings. I told them everything from the Jillian Peters issues in Georgia, the hauntings of Leslie Finn, to the discoveries of Brianna from Binghamton. I told them about his split personalities and his bipolar-like behavior; how he controlled and how he manipulated. He was an abusive liar; a narcissist. He targeted me with manipulation and his destabilizing ability to control me. He sabotaged my memory and humiliated me as often as humanly possible. The only consistency he offered was persistent, uninterrupted denial.

The girls genuinely felt sorry for me. They told me they'd me miss but they made me promise I would leave him. I promised. I welcomed one final panoramic view of the stadium knowing I would never live in this moment again. Three of my closest girlfriends knew I'd be confronting Skyler post-game and they insisted on staying to ensure my safety. *Bradley and I will stay in the parking lot until we see you leave. He will jump out of the car and wrestle him to the ground if he touches you! We won't let him get out of line at all!*

Skyler was one of the last guys to appear from the clubhouse doors. He took his sweet time for obvious reasons. My car was parked next to his truck, and three other cars were positioned behind our vehicles in the deserted player lot.

"Hi," Skyler said as he approached me.

"Hi."

It had been so long since I last touched him. I wanted to.

"So what's up? What did you wanna talk about? Better not be the whole Binghamton thing. I've had enough of that."

"Would you mind if we had this conversation inside my car?" I asked.

The headlights from the three cars behind us practically had us in a blinding spotlight. We got into my car.

"Do you have any idea about what you've put me through this past week?"

He wouldn't look at me. He couldn't. I'd known this situation all too well.

"Skyler. Look at me."

"Fuck, Taylor. I can't live like this anymore. You stress me the fuck out."

I fell silent.

"You're right. We can't live like this anymore. I love you but I cannot be with you anymore. I have to put my health first."

The waterworks were forming; I could feel them coming like a flood from a broken dam. I was surprised I allowed those words to leave my mouth. *Who am I?*

"I never told you this but right before we met I was introduced to a girl named Lacey. She was part of the field crew for the Red Sox and she knew a lot of players. One night, I was invited to a concert with some of my buddies and she was there. I saw her a handful of times after that but we had exchanged numbers that night and she instantly clung onto me. She started talking about a relationship so I started pulling back. The more I pulled back, the crazier she got. She threatened my life; my career. She told me she'd make sure I'd remain single for life. I brushed it off thinking this short, hefty chick hadn't seen attention from anyone with a penis in years. Then, I met you. I fell in love with you the second I met you and I wanted to tell the world about you. When she found out, she went on a social media rampage. Her bitter, petty accusations made me think you'd leave me if you ever found out. I told her I would file a restraining order on her if she ever bothered you. But ever since I met her, I've been having problems with my passwords: social media, Skype, everything. I know it's her. Look, I saved some of her messages," he said as he flashed his phone at me.

Lacey: Looks like you're dating a teenage Barbie doll now. I didn't know you were into underaged children. You're a pervert. I'm reporting you.

Lacey: I can't wait to have you arrested for child molestation. You will lose your job.

Skyler: Please leave me alone or I will have to go to the police.

Lacey: Can we talk?

Lacey: I was kidding about your girlfriend. She's just young for you.

Lacey: What happened to us?

Lacey: Does she know about me?

Suddenly I was losing sight of the break up I'd rehearsed over and over again in the shower.

Lacey: You're an asshole Skyler.

Lacey: Coming to Portland for the game tonight. See me after? I wanna fuck you. You don't have to talk to me ever again. I want it to be our little secret.

Lacey: You suck. I just want sex. Nothing else.

Confusion set in as I read the messages.

Lacey: I'm at the pub next to the field. Come see meee!
Lacey: Hello???
Lacey: Ok.

"So this Lacey character seems like a total whack job but I had a legitimate conversation with Brianna and you felt the need to avoid me all week SO some things are not adding up," I said.

Skyler broke down in tears.

"I can't lose you Taylor. It killed me not to talk to you all week but there was no easy way of telling you this over the phone. I wanted you to believe me."

"What is there to believe Skyler? You fucked her. Simple as that."

I texted the girls to let them know that I was fine and our conversation was nowhere near heated.

"Who are you texting?" he asked.

"The girls. They waited to make sure I would be alright."

He cried harder.

"MY TEAMMATES KNOW ABOUT THIS? Why the fuck do you tell people our personal business. This doesn't involve them. WHAT THE FUCK!" he screamed.

"I came up here to dump you Skyler. I came up here knowing my boyfriend screws randoms on the road every other week. It's time I got on with my life— without you. How do you make me better? You don't. You restrict me from doing things I want to do. I've given up so much to make this as easy as possible for the both of us. I walk on eggshells to ensure that it is impossible that I am the cause of a bad game. And this is how you repay me."

"Taylor I want you to be Mrs. Williams. I've never done anything to hurt our relationship. This boy loves you! You have got to believe me."

Numb, I inhaled and exhaled over the feeling of a fluttering heart beat.

"From now on I will tell you the good, bad, and the ugly. I should have told you about Lacey sooner. I promise to be wide open from here on out. I will tell you every step of my day and I'll send pictures to prove my words. Come home with me. We can talk more in the morning. It's too late to drive back to Wilmington. I don't know anyone from Binghamton. That wasn't me."

To be blunt, I didn't leave him. Call me a fool, an imbecile, call me whatever, but *I wasn't ready*. I can't explain to you why I continued to stay other than the fact that I was not fucking ready. Week after week I watched my spirit vanish into dust. I knew it wasn't healthy to stay but I wasn't willing to cope with a life without him; the loneliness. I wasn't ready to watch him love somebody else. I couldn't let other women defeat us, even though it was him who gave into them every time. I had too much pride for public defeat. I would fight until I had nothing left and trust me, I was almost at that point.

Skyler's birthday, July 20, came as fast as it went and though I was technically considered a living being, my spark died Fourth of July weekend. The sparkle that once lived inside my eyes was now dull. I forgot how to laugh, and the simple sound of laughter from others brought me to hatred. I no longer appreciated the simple things: a sweet, garden tomato, a good song, the scent of brownies baking in the oven. I barely communicated with others. I avoided it at all costs actually. I heard voices and I saw moving lips, but I was not present. I stared at the tips of noses because my mom once told me if you couldn't look someone in the eye, look at the tip of their nose and they'll never notice the difference. So I did just that. I was no longer existing, I was way beyond my rock bottom.

I forced myself to attend every home and away game. It was time consuming; a full-time job rather. Skyler had become my full time job. He was all I had. I'd rather exhaust myself with travel than be ripped to shreds by my thoughts. Even when my eyes begged for rest, I got into my car and drove. I was lost in his world. Nobody knew how much pain I was in. *Why was I doing this to myself?* When my mind allowed it, I slept, only to wake feeling more exhausted than before. My mom insisted I talk to a therapist, but I didn't need therapy, I needed change. Therapy attempted to heal a past and I needed something that would catapult me forward. I needed to find my own way to personal victory. Besides, he or she who is paid to understand my troubles will not authentically improve my state of mind unless they too have suffered through identical heartbreak. Experience trumps all.

Six days later I turned twenty. Skyler had a series in New Britain, Connecticut, so obviously I spent my birthday in New Britain, Connecticut. My mother cried knowing I'd drive three hours only to sit alone at a minor league baseball game in the middle of nowhere. Happy Birthday, T. Skyler had committed to a genuine attempt at crystal clear communication and me, helpless as ever, survived off of his average efforts.

I sat alone in an empty stadium as my mother predicted. Skyler found me in the stands and winked at me each time before entering the dugout during the game. I didn't mind the loneliness, I was comfortable with it now. The goofiest creature of a woman decked out in Red Sox gear found a seat next to me within the hundreds of empty seats. She had brown, frizzy curls, glasses, clothes that were far too small, and a disposable camera in hand.

"You must be Taylor!" she said while offering her hand out for a shake. Each of her fingers held a mood ring.

I shook her hand.

"That I am. And you are?"

"My names Patty! I am a *huge* Red Sox fan, well, *minor league* Red Sox fan. Well, I am a huge major league fan too, but I follow a lot of the minor league players. It's fun! I take pictures of all the guys! They call me the "crazy camera lady". Have you seen some of my photos online?"

"Oh! Yes, I've seen your pictures. It's very nice to meet you in person."

"Same here! It's an honor to meet you, actually. I am a big Skyler Williams fan but I've enjoyed following your journey as Miss Teen Massachusetts just as much. Mind if we get a selfie together?"

She leaned into me and began snapping away on her camera.

"Thanks Taylor! Anyways, I love when the Sea Dogs come to town. They are my favorite team. So many hotties on that team too. Sky's a sweetheart. You're very lucky! And he's *hot*. I met him after a game one night. I waited at their bus to get autographs and he was one of the only guys who stopped for me. He's awesome! Love that guy! Do you think you could set me up with one of his teammates? I've been crushing on Boyle for a while now. I would make such a great baseball wife. I only work twice a week so I'm pretty much free to travel whenever. How cool would that be? Traveling with your hot husband and taking care of your babies? I love babies. I'm so ready to have babies. I work at a daycare."

Holllllyyyyyy talks a lot. And *Sky*? Nobody calls him Sky. She continued snapping pictures of me during our conversation.

Faking a stupid chuckle, "Yeah, Skyler's a good one."

The game was almost over but I needed to abort mission ASAP from Patty.

"I'm gonna use the restroom before the game ends. It was so nice meeting you!" I said.

"Where are you going, little lady? We got a whole inning left!"

"Just really need to use the bathroom."

"Well you better hurry back. Wait, do you really need to go to the bathroom or are you trying to ditch me?"

I was dumbfounded. My face went blank.

"I'm just messing with ya! I'll huntcha down after the game if I have to."

I didn't have to pee at all. I rushed to my car, locked the doors, and refreshed the minor league baseball app so I could pretend like I saw his last at bat. Thankfully, the Sea Dogs won.

Skyler called me in dismay from the locker room.

"Where did you go? I saw you leave before the game was over!" he cried.

"Relax. I was escaping a crazed fan."

"Crazy camera lady?"

"Nailed it."

I waited in the parking lot as my boyfriend showered. My phone buzzed again:

Skyler: Pizza Hut for dinner? Not much of a birthday cel-
         ebration but it's about all that's open right now.
Taylor: You know the way to my heart.

As I listened to the dial tone awaiting a response from a Pizza Hut employee, I noticed a piece-of-shit car circling the lot near the team buses. The muffler was dragging on the ground, sparks practically flying, and it was making all sorts of disturbing noises. It was covered in rust, dents, and dings. The bumper was covered with stickers and fuzzy dice dangled from the rearview mirror. I'm no mechanic but I was pretty positive this heap of junk wouldn't pass an inspection. My eyes tried to focus on the driver of the shitbox. It was Patty. She hung her head out her window as she scanned the parking lot. She was clearly looking for something; *someone*. I slid down in the seat of my car, scolding myself for not having tinted my windows enough, and ordered our pizza. *Please don't see me, please don't see me.* I texted Skyler.

Taylor: OMG! Patty is legit circling the parking lot. I think she is looking for me. HURRY UP!

Moments later, Skyler entered the parking lot after avoiding a crowd of anxious fans surrounding the door to the team bus.

"You OK?" he said as he greeted me with a kiss.

"Yeah," I said. "I think she's gone. I bet she's pissed."

"Who cares. She's a stalker."

We returned to the team hotel just as our pizza box was being delivered. I showered to rinse my "daily oils" as I like to call them and then climbed in bed to devour a boatload of carbs.

Skyler picked up a slice of pizza.

"I'd like to make a toast," he said.

I too held up a slice of pizza.

"To the most amazing girl in the world. Happy Birthday, babe. Cheers to you."

We clanked slices.

"Cheers, lover."

13

By August, I felt our relationship was back to normalcy (considering), though I still found myself waking in the midst of the night with panic attacks. Sweaty and winded, I'd wake from a creepily realistic nightmare, only to jump for my phone to check Skyler's social media followers. I'd lay there in tears stroking my rib cage to feel the bones I'd exposed by starving myself. I never have an appetite when I'm upset. I was fragile and underweight and the hands that touched my bones told my conscious that I was pathetic. Reassurance was a survival tactic but I searched for ways to break my own heart constantly. Like I said, normalcy.

It was a Monday. I spent the morning sipping iced lemon water on a float in my pool. The Vitamin D from the sky said hello to the melanin in my skin and awakened my freckles. I squeezed the lemons from my drink into my already white hair. There's no such thing as *too blonde*. Skyler had a game that evening but Portland was expecting major thunder showers so I decided I wouldn't make the drive. Besides, the Sea Dogs had a makeup game early the next morning so I wasn't worried about any potential extracurricular activities. I was calm with my decision; I was relieved I wouldn't have to make the drive. I was tired. And while Skyler's communication skills had improved dramatically, I still continued to refresh his social media accounts by the minute, even in my pool.

Following: 281, Following: 281, Following: 281. I kept refreshing his page. *Following: 282.* WHAT! He's not even texting me! I raced to find his newest victim, praying it was a he, but anticipating a she. My heart was thumping, my appetite escaped, my world was stopping all over again. *Emilee Wood.* I clicked on her profile hoping to learn more from her bio.

*Emilee * Sophomore - Portland High School * 15 years young *
Follow for Follow*

Seconds later, Skyler gained a follower. Emilee Wood. Every bone in my body was tense as I debated on how to properly handle this situation. *I have to be gentle with him. If he feels attacked he will accuse me and shut me out.* Fuck it! I called him.

"Really Skyler? The one night I tell you I'm not coming to Portland you're following new victims online? She's fifteen fucking years old!"

"*What are you talking about?*" he asked in pure confusion. "Yes I'm on Twitter. Yes I've been scrolling around but if I've followed anyone it was a complete accident. Chill out."

"I changed my mind. I'm coming to Portland tonight."

I hung up on him. When I returned to his Twitter, he was no longer following Emilee. I ran into my house to rinse the chlorine from my skin and to make myself look presentable for his game. Presentable ended up being wet hair and pajama shorts because I just *had* to get there.

Normally I never go to Will Call to pick up my ticket in Portland. What's the sense in waiting in line when I could just enter the stadium through a gate in the back parking lot? Skyler always put my name on the ticket list because it was mandatory, but I never actually picked them up. But *tonight*. Tonight was different. I went to the box office with ulterior motives. A young guy, probably in high school, was working the window.

"Hi!" I said. "Skyler Williams was supposed to leave tickets tonight for my entire family but I'm not sure which name he left them under. Can you read me the names he listed?" I asked innocently.

The boy fumbled through some paperwork to find the player's ticket and parking list. I wanted to hear him say Emilee's name; I was ready for it.

"Looks like the only name on his list is *Taylor*. Taylor Higgins. That you?" he asked.

I was relieved but at the same time I wanted to jump the counter and take a look at the list myself. I knew Emilee's name would be on there. One of his teammates probably did him a solid and left her tickets under their name as an alibi.

"That would be me," I said.

I was almost disappointed. I sat alone per usual during the game, scanning the crowd for the face of Emilee Wood and avoiding my WAG sisters at all costs. I knew they wouldn't agree with my decision to keep Skyler in my life and I wasn't ready to defend him either. I was tired and unhappy. I was the living definition of *beat to a pulp*. But not witnessing Skyler's exact whereabouts had become unfathomable. So much for staying home.

After the game I asked Skyler to show me his phone. I put him on the spot and, naturally, he hated it. What liar likes to have their back against the wall? I chased after the truth knowing how angry that made him. I slowly lost interest in his anger. It was easy to get a rise out of him, though, and I was addicted to it. His bad behavior was my drug. I didn't need answers because my gut already knew the truth. I also knew he'd never admit to anything because he is incapable of being wrong. I shared a bed with this person. I chose to over and over again.

Negative energy devoured me. I lived in fear and I was too weak to make any changes. Too weak to escape. I knew I had to hack my way back into Skyler's email account to find answers. His social media was linked to his email and he was confident I'd never find my way back in. While doing eighty in the fast lane, I entered his email address into the login information and thought long and hard about what his new password could be. I tried his old password, only changing the few numbers at the end to the current number on his baseball jersey. *I was in.* It was too easy. Idiot. Instantly, I recognized Emilee Wood's name from a Twitter notification.

Skyler: Hey, text me again. I lost your number and I have a question.

Emilee: Okay!!

My world ended all over again. There was no one to blame but myself. I'd kept him after all he'd put me through. He thinks he can get away with anything. He knows I love him too much to leave him. He knows he is indestructible. This was all my fault. Again, I found myself reaching out to another stranger online who very well may already know of my existence. Who may be waiting for my message to come. I had to pour my heart out to someone who might not even give a damn about my pain. I put my life, my happiness, in the hands of a stranger. He left me no choice.

Taylor: I just found a conversation between you and my boyfriend on his Twitter and I just wanted to ask you about it. His name is Skyler Williams. He told me he didn't know who you were but we've hit a bit of a rocky patch and I'm only trying to get to the bottom of things.

Emilee: Rocky patch? That's one way to put it. LOL. Skyler and I started talking at the beginning of summer. Everything was fine until he met my mother at a bar one night. They started dating while we were dating. Awksauce.

Taylor:	You do know I've been dating him for over a year now right?
Emilee:	He seems real interested in you hunny. We've known about you, my mother and I. He says he's single but neither of us really care either way.
Taylor:	So you and your mom think it's normal to share the same guy?
Emilee:	Did I say it was normal? No. But it's fucking interesting. That's what keeps him coming back to us. Not you. Us! Our favorite thing to do is to get him drunk and give him the threesome he craves. Something that you've never given him. He tells us how selfish you are. He talks like he hates you. I ride his face while he fucks my mother and then we rotate. Learn how to keep your man on a leash.

That feeling was back. The feeling of being pushed from a cliff only to land straight on your back as your breath is yanked into the sky. I was angry. I think. The audacity of this fifteen year old tramp! This was like, *incest*. But I was hurt. He was sharing all of the private parts of himself with the world, and I, as faithful as ever, had been royally betrayed. I sent Skyler a screenshot of my conversation with Emilee followed by a brief, heartless breakup text:

All you'll ever be is a lonely liar. I am positive of that. I'm done.
He never denied Emilee's words. He never picked up the phone to beg for my forgiveness. He never apologized.

He never let me hear his voice during such a paralyzing time. Instead I received a chain of text messages; another hand-crafted, heavily detailed, bullshit excuse of a fairytale. *Our love is rare. Don't you see that? People are jealous of our happiness and they want to destroy us. We can't let them!*

I drove. It was one of those murky drives where you're suddenly seconds from home and wondering how the hell you made it because you don't remember seeing the road once. I ignored Skyler for as long as I could that day, giving myself some serious time to reflect. As a woman of closure, it was a challenge to leave his messages unanswered. I thought about the broken marriages I'd seen during my short time in the baseball world, how wives effortlessly hid such chilling secrets, and how I could have easily become one of them. I was already doing what they were doing, hiding, I just didn't have a marriage license to intensify the situation.

I promised Sam on a beach chair in Florida that I'd live my life according to the way I wanted to live. After foregoing auditions for the Boston Bruins Ice Girls last summer to spend the off-season in Georgia, I intended to create a life of my own. While ignoring Skyler's outrageous attempts to prove his innocence, I submitted an online application for the team and started back in with my college courses. I could either sink or swim in this very moment and I decided to swim for the first time in a long time. Curling up into a ball in my bedroom wouldn't make me a better human. I needed to stop feeling sorry for myself. I needed to begin the change.

Ignoring Skyler was easiest when he was on a road trip. Knowing I couldn't physically see him if I wanted to made for attainable restraint. Within twenty-four hours, I found a congratulatory letter from the Boston Bruins in my email. *Congratulations! You have been selected as a candidate for the first round of Boston Bruins Ice Girl auditions.* Cloud nine. I got a taste of what it felt like to be Taylor again and I owe most of that courage to Sam. I worked hard to prepare for the audition. I skated constantly and brushed up on my knowledge of the hockey team. I wanted it so bad. I had hope that making this team would free me of all things Skyler. That it would occupy so much of my time that nothing he did would entertain my thoughts. My life, my serenity was riding on these auditions. I was outcome dependent. I pictured myself making it to finals, I pictured the coach announcing my name as the newest member of the rookie squad, I pictured myself on the ice at TD Garden wearing the black and gold uniform, I pictured a confident, clear minded individual. It was mine. *It had to be.*

Skyler was away when I submitted my audition paperwork and seven days later, he'd still be away as I auditioned for the team. It was purely a sign from the universe. I still question whether or not I would have auditioned if Skyler was home persuading me with his bullshit.

On-ice skating drills, photoshoots, testing, physical fitness testing, trivia, a ticket to final auditions, and multiple rounds of interviews in front of a panel until I heard alas: *Number eighty-three, Taylor Higgins.* I did it.

I had also convinced one of my best friends to audition at the last minute with me. *Number eighty-four, Victoria Reid.* My best freakin' friend made the team by my side! We were psyched. Good things come to those who… are brave enough to let the poison drown? Skyler would shit himself if he knew.

After all he'd put me through, I was still determined to fix his warped perception of a healthy relationship. I knew he was ill. I wanted to heal him. I wanted him to know that our love could move mountains if only he'd move them with me. I wanted to know why he was the way he was. What caused his actions? His childhood? His parents were controlling and manipulative and demanding and expectant. Had this caused a form of post traumatic stress? Having no control over himself at home had led him to control others, especially those who are easy to control. Controlling women was where he thrived. The platform of a baseball player; the prominent job title. It was easy to prey on women who gave into his control and status. Everyone looked at him with googly eyes thinking he was a famous superstar, and this gave him a high. But when he could control their actions and thoughts with just the tone in his voice, was when he actually came alive. He was powerful for the first time in his life and this was intoxicating. Like his addiction to prescription pills, sleep aids, the state of intoxication, and innocent women, he became dependent on this feeling of power. He was devoted to weak minded strangers. He was dedicated to everyone but those who deeply loved him. He was a slave to all things that had the ability to alter who he truly was. He needed saving.

I didn't tell my mother about Emilee Wood because Skyler was already on thin ice with my parents and if my mother decides you're no good for me, you're no good for me ever again. The disgusting truth is that I missed him and I still pictured growing old with him. He just needed gentle patience and boy, did I have that. I expressed interest in going to his first home game after a two week road trip and to my surprise, my parents jumped on the bandwagon. *The seasons almost over! We have to see him play one last time! His family never comes to watch him! We feel so bad for him!* If they only knew the extent of what I was dealing with.

It was a scorcher of a day. A day where your ass practically rides the plastic seat in the stands like a waterslide. A day when black clothing was an absolute must when dealing with this abundance of swass. I entered the stadium with my parents and immediately noticed a familiar face at the wine stand. *Leslie Finn.* She looked even older in person. Leslie was wearing a white, spaghetti-strapped tank with daisy dukes and a pair of espadrille wedges. Her bare legs were perfectly lathered in oil. She wasn't here for a baseball game; she wanted to be noticed. My adrenaline, the shakes, the boiling blood— she sparked all sorts of emotions inside me. *You lonely witch! Why are you here?* I listened as the voice inside my head held an imaginary confrontation with the malicious woman from my nightmares.

My parents and I found our seats in the empty family section. They made small talk as I continuously scanned the stadium for Leslie. I needed to know where she'd be sitting. Three young girls, young as in high schoolers, found seats directly in front of us in the family section. When new faces enter the family section, you are obligated to find out which player they belong to. I eavesdropped on their conversations to the best of my ability as they discussed different dating apps and giggled. They were quiet for the most part, that is until one of the team's top prospects emerged from the dugout. A well known, highly thought of, *married* prospect. I'd met his wife a few times during spring training but she wasn't ready to leave her full-time job in Kentucky to commit to the baseball life quite yet. One of the young girls pointed directly at the man that made her giggle in the first place and yelled, "There he is!"

"He *is* cute!" said another one of the girls.

"I know! Can you believe we met on a dating app?" said the first girl.

My heart automatically went into defense mode for his wife. *How could he do this! She's at home! She's working so you can still live your dream!* I hated it. I couldn't believe what I was hearing. Even worse, I didn't know his wife well enough to bring this to her attention. Skyler would kill me if his teammates knew I was the one that tattled on him too. I was forced into a silence when I knew it was wrong. Then suddenly, I found Leslie in the crowd with her two daughters. They were sitting behind home plate in the front row. I now monitored her every move. The tan, crinkly skin that spilled from the sides of her tank top drove me mad. The white, sheer, braless tank. The outline of her stimulated nipples. The creasing in her cleavage. The sag. This is Double A baseball asshole, tuck your milk wagons into your shorts and relax. My gut told me something was very wrong.

After the national anthem, the visiting team was introduced. Leslie was calm, cool, and collected during this time. I watched her. Halfway through the introduction of the home team, Leslie was still unamused. *"Number twenty-six... Your centerfielder... Skyler Williams!"* Leslie Finn went fucking bananas. She jumped up from her seat; screaming, whistling, clapping, and bouncing up and down. Her daughters sat still in their seats with heads still glued to their phones. Leslie was testing the limits on the skinny straps of her tank with each bounce she made.

Skyler started in centerfield. Seconds into the game, he just so happened to make an unbelievable diving catch to get the first out of the day. Most people stuck with the golf clap, but not Leslie. Yet again she leaped from her seat, screaming and jumping.

"GO SKYLER!" She was making a scene.

"I guess Skyler has a fan," my father laughed.

"You have no idea," I replied.

Three outs later, Skyler was the leadoff batter. As he loosened his body, stretching and taking practice swings before entering the batter's box, Leslie fixedly gazed at him. She was yelling for him but he didn't dare look over to her. When he was introduced at the plate, as expected, Leslie went berserk. Her and her grapefruits. Something inside of me snapped. There were a few empty seats behind Leslie

Finn and I headed straight for them. I was tired of being stepped on, and I especially wasn't about to let a woman who was eligible for retirement rub salt in my wounds.

I planted myself behind her with sunglasses shielding my eyes. I listened to her conversing with her daughters for a minute while searching for the words I wanted to use. I waited until Skyler was due up at the plate for a second time so she could cheer him on. When he was finally introduced again, Leslie held nothing back when it came to showing her support. Her behavior fed my confidence. When she sat back down, I leaned forward to tap her on the shoulder.

"Scuse me. I couldn't help but notice how you selectively cheer for one player and one player only out of the nine rostered players here today. I find it extra disturbing to know you have interest in conducting conversations with men half your age. I've seen you in his direct messages and I don't appreciate that. I don't know what your obsession is with minor league athletes, but I will not be caught in the experimental phase of masking the damage your failed marriage has caused you. If you're looking for someone to dust the cobwebs from your pussy lips, join a bowling league."

Skyler singled to first base as I released my anger that could have so easily been avoided had he handled her differently. Leslie was quiet for the first time all afternoon, as were her daughters. I returned to my seat with my parents. The internet made dating such a fearful task nowadays, and if Skyler wasn't willing to stand up for me, I'd have to dig my own motes, build my own walls, and defend my own heart.

Leslie Finn was a mute for the remainder of the game. She sipped her wine carefully without making any other movements before leaving. Watching her salami udders dance down the exit ramp made me one happy camper. I was sure her name would never be an issue again.

Skyler and I shared a quick hello and goodbye in the player parking lot with my parents before embarking on a silent drive to the host family's house.

"I saw you talking to that woman at the game today." Skyler broke the soundlessness of our car ride.

"And?"

"What were you saying?"

"She seemed pretty excited to be cheering you on and I wanted her to know how disturbing it was."

"Fans are so crazy."

I turned to look out the window so I could roll my eyes without hearing his reaction. *Whatever helps you sleep at night, kid.*

"Tyler Caufield is a terrible human by the way," I said.

"What makes you say that?"

"He had a girl he met online in the family section today with two friends and she couldn't stop bragging about it. He's fucking married!" I added to my rage.

"His wife is pregnant."

"Are you serious?"

"Yeah. He just told everyone. You know it's not our place to get involved in their business. We can't get caught up in other people's decisions. There's an unwritten rule in baseball where you just have to turn your head and pretend you don't see certain things sometimes."

"I couldn't imagine living that kind of life. I refuse to. He deserves to be exposed. Anyone that does wrong should be exposed."

"Don't go saying anything to his wife, Taylor. You could ruin a marriage. The locker room would be so awkward. Worry about us. You know we'll never have those types of problems."

"I do worry about us. We do have those problems. That is why we broke up. Did you forget?"

"You came to my game. You don't want this to be over."

I had three choices. I could reach out to his wife and potentially ruin a marriage and disturb the upbringing of their unborn child, I could allow my voice to make my boyfriend become the outcast of the clubhouse, or I could neglect the truth and forever live with the guilt of knowing about a person's unfaithfulness. Skyler received a text message from my mother:

Mrs. Higgins: This game will never be a fair game. Don't let it get the best of you. We know how hard you work and if anyone deserves a chance, it's you. We enjoyed watching you today. Great game!

"Are you tearing up?" I said as I glanced into his watery eyes.

"That message meant a lot to me. I don't get that kind of support from my parents. Your family is my family and I don't know what I would do without y'all"

"You have us, don't worry."

Skyler's next series took place in Manchester, New Hampshire. The stadium was only forty minutes from my house but I always chose to stay with him at the team hotel. Actually this consisted of me begging my mom for money as I cried in my car in a random parking lot. *You have to pay for the hotel! I have to stay! I won't sleep tonight! I'm scared! I don't know what he will do if I don't stay!* I would rock back and forth in fear as I waited for saving from the only person that knew how to rescue me— *Mom.* I had zero dollars to my name. I emptied the change compartments in both of my parents' cars frequently and rummaged through bags and purses to fill ziplock bags with as many coins as I could. CoinStar saved me one too many times. Balancing my priorities had turned into throwing in the towel on who Taylor was and who Taylor wanted to be simply to follow Skyler and his dreams around in order to keep myself relatively sane. In order for me to feel calm, I'd have to put myself in random cities, random hotel rooms, all to have some sort of peace in my life. Holding a job was out of the question. I wouldn't be able to travel in the baseball life if I had a job. My schedule had to be wide open and flexible so I could be anywhere at any time. I convinced myself that this was normal. That I was doing the right thing. That *I* was the definition of the ultimate sacrifice. He'd never find better than me. Like a robot, or rather a mistreated female, I was programmed. Nobody could relate, nobody could save me, and nobody could change my thought process. I was responsible for my own changes; my own saving. And I knew change meant excruciating pain.

The next series took us back to Binghamton, New York. Skyler was all too familiar with Binghamton and its people, but for me, this was my first time. It was one giant baseball game— my life. I love him and he loves this game so who am I to not drive around the country like an idiot to support him? Besides, the last time he came to Binghamton he tried to have sex with another girl. My car needed an oil change so my already hesitant mother insisted I drive Skyler's truck six hours to Binghamton instead of my own car. Since it was mandatory each player ride the team bus, I was forced to make the drive alone. It would be the longest I'd ever driven before and I was doing it on my own and without a phone charger. Stupid, I know. I drove and I drove, only stopping for gas once on those long, lonely roads until parking at a gas station across the street from the baseball stadium for five dollars. I made it just in time for the game. Feeling genuinely afraid for my safety as well as the truck's safety, I made sure the doors were locked several times before hustling into the stadium. Guess what? The stadium was empty. Granted it had rained all day but not a single person was seated in that stadium by the time the first pitch was thrown. I was the only fool that showed up.

By the third inning or so, two girls seated themselves in the row in front of me. Assuming they were Binghamton

WAG's, I introduced myself. You will always learn from strangers.

I leaned forward to grab their attention. "Hey there! My name is Taylor."

The two girls turned to each other to make eye contact.

"My boyfriend plays for the Sea Dogs. Are you here for the home team?" I asked.

They both spun around to face me.

"Marissa," one of the girls said as she offered her hand for a greeting.

"Hi I'm Ana!" followed the second girl.

"I actually met one of the Sea Dogs' trainers on Bumble a few months ago and now he messages me whenever he's in town. His name is Marcus. We don't know anyone that plays for Binghamton," said Marissa.

"And I met one of the players online a few months ago and we've been talking since. Blare Belfort. You must know him well," said Ana.

"I'm definitely familiar with both of those names." I said.

"We are best friends. We attend college together right up the street. Nothing good ever happens around here so we get excited when different teams come to town," said Ana.

I sat back in my seat cringing at the rising popularity of social media dates and random girls the internet so easily allowed into the baseball world.

"Which number is your boyfriend?" asked Marissa.

"Twenty-six. He wears number twenty-six now."

Expecting an *oh shit* facial expression or bad news to seep from their lips, I held my breath. I wasn't proud to announce my affiliation with Skyler anymore. In fact, it was embarrassing. Scary. *They definitely know someone whose had sex with him. They totally think he's a dirtbag. They know more than I will ever know. How can I live like this?!*

"Aw, nice. Well I hope he has a great game tonight," Ana said.

Phew.

The beautiful sight of a completed scoreboard meant I didn't have to freeze in the stands any longer. I found my way out of the stadium, across the street, and back to the gas station where I'd left the truck. The streets were pitch black and gross men shook spare change cups at me and grumbled provocative words as I passed by.

I drove around to the back of the stadium to pick Skyler up at the clubhouse doors. We shared a kiss, he asked about the drive, and I told him I hated Binghamton. I thought about Brianna the entire time. We ordered takeout from iHop on our way back to the team hotel. The thought of hotel pillows and condensation-drenched scrambled eggs in a styrofoam container made me happy. This was our life. Soggy pancakes, chewy bacon, and moist toast in bed. This was *our* paradise.

I was chased straight out of Binghamton on my way home. No, seriously. After driving a few short miles on the interstate, I noticed a black truck following close behind me. Being in the fast lane, I put my directional on and moved over so the alpha male could pass. Practically riding my bumper, he followed me into the middle lane. The windows were tinted but I could see a driver and a passenger. I drove faster. At ninety miles per hour the truck clung to my tail lights. Exits were miles and miles apart; I had no choice but to keep moving. If I slowed down, he would line his truck up alongside mine and ride steadily at the exact same speed. I didn't know if this was a sick game to him or if he actually wanted to run me off the road. I started video recording to have a visual description of his truck, his license plate, and footage of his antics. Then, terrified for my life after twenty minutes of being chased, I called Skyler.

"Someone is literally trying to run me off the road. I don't know what to do!"

"What? Seriously? Call the police! Why are you calling me!"

"I don't know what to do I'm so scared!"

"I'm calling the police."

He hung up. I regained focus on keeping a reasonable distance from the black truck. My knuckles were white around the leather steering wheel; my hands shaking with sweat. After one hour of highway harassment, the road came to a split by a toll booth. The black truck exited right as I continued onward through the tolls. In my rearview mirror I noticed a state police cruiser bombing up the freeway with lights flashing and sirens singing. He went in the same direction as the black truck. Meanwhile Skyler proceeded to call me over and over again.

"Finally you answered! Did the police come?" said Skyler.

"They went after the black truck. Did you call?"

"Of course I called after your stubborn ass said you weren't going to do it."

I sighed. "My adrenaline was going. I was afraid. I wasn't thinking correctly."

"You know better than that."

My cramped, stiff limbs unfolded in my driveway once again. Cracking and stretching, I was home for a short while until I'd have to leave again. In my bedroom sat a vase of assorted flowers on my bureau. Attached read the note:

My Beautiful Future Wife—
Thank you so much for spending a long weekend in Binghamton with me. If it were up to me, I would have you with me every second of every day.

— Skyler

There he goes again. He kept me believing in him; us. Just when I'd start to think our hourglass was running out of sand again, he'd find a way to flip it back upside down.

Two days after returning from Binghamton, I drove up to Maine. Skyler and I had dinner in Portland during a monsoon after his game was rained out. Unexpected date nights are the best. His phone rang at the table.

"This is him. Yessir. Yessir. Tonight? Yessir. Thank you sir."

The conversation was short and vague. Skyler's facial expression hadn't changed a bit.

"Andrew Jones got hurt today. He plays center in Pawtucket. I'm being promoted to Triple A again."

"This is your time!" I said with excitement.

"I don't know how bad he's hurt, or when he'll return. This probably won't be a permanent promotion either. They just need an extra body up there."

"Have a little faith, sheeesh! They can't send you back down if you're giving them what they want."

"We have to drive to your house tonight."

We returned to the host family's house, put the lids on Skyler's plastic traveling bins, and headed for Massachusetts in our pajamas once more.

The following evening, Skyler came marching out of the Triple A clubhouse after his first game back in Pawtucket with a shit eating grin across his face. He held a container of food and two forks in his hands.

"Couple big leaguers are rehabbing in Pawtucket. They bought the dinner spread! Look, I got us lobster tails, scallops, steak tips, and shrimp. It's from Capital Grille! I wonder how much it cost them."

I stabbed a cold, buttery scallop with my plastic fork.

"That was really nice of them."

"Yeah, I guess it's like a courtesy thing. Big leaguers always buy a spread for the team. I don't hate it."

"You did great tonight, babe."

"I'll be back in Portland before you know it."

The season was coming to a close. Skyler's mother, though completely distant from us, aggressively inquired about his living quarters for the upcoming off-season.

When will you be home? Daddy needs his hunting partner. Your brother wants you to coach his baseball team.

Unbeknownst to her, Skyler had agreed to spend the entire off-season in Massachusetts this year. We had a lot to work on in our relationship, and we decided that traveling more than baseball had required us to do would be detrimental to our happiness. Distance was one of the very last ingredients we needed to juggle at the moment. I'd sacrificed my social life, my everyday life, and my pageant life all for a game. The least Skyler could do for me was spend the off-season at my house.

His mother's persistence was taking a toll on our relationship because he didn't know how to say *no* to his parents, and I got the brunt of his frustrations. It was a delightful pattern that wore heavily on me. Then I became the devil in his parent's eyes. The one who'd steal their beloved son away forever. It was when Doreen called me selfish that I felt the need to confront the situation at last.

Taylor: Hi. Was wondering if you had a minute to talk on the phone?

Doreen: I'm at the ballpark. You can text me.

Taylor: I just wanted to discuss the whole off-season dilemma. I can sense the tension and I'd like to resolve things with you.

Doreen: Skyler needs to come home for the off-season.

Taylor: And why do you feel that's your decision to make? I follow Skyler around nine months out of the year making sure he's happy and healthy and all of his needs are met. But now I'm the bad guy for wanting a semi-normal life for myself during the months that baseball doesn't control us.

Doreen: Nobody asked you to follow him around. He's a grown ass man. He can take care of his daggum self. He don't need no help. Live your life up there. Skyler can come home and do the same. He wants to come home, Taylor. Just let him go. He hates Boston. And he hates stayin' at your house. Let him go. Quit bein' selfish.

Taylor: I don't know why you refuse to be happy for us and the decisions we make together. We spent the last off-season sneaking in the back door of his gym because he couldn't afford a gym membership. He has a job up here at a baseball facility and there is a gym there he's allowed to use for free. This is good for his career. He wants this.

Doreen: I want my son home and that's that. If it wasn't for you there'd be no problem. You are the problem. You don't want him around us. You want him all to your dang self. You want to control his life and his decisions because you're spoiled. But you ain't winning this time. He's comin' home.

Taylor: Clearly this conversation is going nowhere. It's unfortunate I wasted my time trying to resolve this issue. You don't care about his well being.

The only thing you've latched onto is the slightest potential of success he might bring to the Williams' name. You are the farthest thing from a mother I've ever come to know. Skyler gives you bragging rights in your tiny town and that thrills you. So when you're sitting next to your husband on the sidelines of a junior varsity high school baseball game, not to watch your second born son because you've already squashed his confidence (enough to make him quit sports altogether), but to watch other locals and make small talk with other parents all while already feeling like the world's best mom because your son "made it". You're always too busy, Doreen. Baseball consumes you. Ever think of skipping a game to learn how to prepare a meal? Your sons aren't playing in half the games you attend and Dairy Queen's chicken tenders aren't a sufficient meal to offer every night. But no. I get it. You'd rather sit in those JV bleachers, slurping down every last bit of your jumbo Mr. Pibb. People bombard you with questions about Skyler— *the professional baseball player.* You'll answer with pride in your eyes and a smile across your face because this is the only topic in your world that makes you feel important. *Relevant.* Imagine living vicariously through your child; riding on his coat tails in case he finds his way to fame and fortune. Imagine? I've tried to be nice. I've tried to be fair. But you are a mean woman and I'll never be able to fix your bitter self. So instead of scolding Skyler for having a bad game, because bad games equal zero promotions and zero promotions equal small salaries when *you* have major debts he's expected to pay off, why don't you focus on yourself. Stop micromanaging his life, our relationship, and his bank account. Take your coupon binder down to Kroger, introduce yourself to some fresh, green produce that is bound to make a crunch when you bite into it, and be a real mother.

She never responded. If Skyler had the bean bags to be honest with his parents, this could have all been avoided. I mean, she is a lousy mother. Was it my place to tell her? Well, no. Probably not. I was raised to always respect my elders and I always did. Except today. Today I stood up for what I believed in and I hope to god I shocked the oatmeal cream pies right out of her.

14

His season ended in early September, as did his grandfather's life. His father's father passed away at the age of seventy-two of lung cancer. My initial reaction to his passing? *Shit, he has to go home by himself for the funeral.* Skyler cried tears of guilt as I suffered panic attacks over the thought of him returning to Georgia alone. His greatly desired trip home to hunt quickly turned into a week to mourn with his family. Mamaw put him on a flight almost immediately. I feared for our relationship. I was afraid of our destiny. We, no, *he* was not capable of loving me from far away. Funerals; *death.* These subjects bring people out of the woodwork. Exes, unwanted females, *exes.* And while I do not wish loss or sadness amongst anyone, I felt defeated by this tragedy. *Why now! We aren't ready to be separated yet!* I feared the condolences he'd receive; I feared the small talk. The talk that followed the, "Thank you I'm doing alright." I feared the recaps he'd have with people from his past; the quick summary of the years since they'd last seen each other. Will they reminiscence? Will they meet up for a drink that I'll never know about for old times' sake? I would never know.

My mother had a flower arrangement sent to the funeral home and I was careful with the blatant resentment I held towards his parents. The only circumstance that forced me to be civil was death. The days were a fog if I'm being completely honest. I was existing in a hostile state of anxiety. I worried, excessively, and my compulsive nail biting habit was at an all time high. I'd lost all concentration on even the simplest of tasks. I isolated myself, ignored people, and began to fear life outside of my house again. I was right back at square one, the basement of my rock bottom, and nobody was sending me a ladder to help me climb out.

But it was when Skyler told me he was comforting his parents around this death that made my insides burn with rage. *Comforting others when I need fucking comfort myself?! Look how you've damaged me!* I knew my morals had been tampered with. I did not like the person I was becoming but I had no way of stopping it. I received a text from Skyler:

Skyler: Tay, I feel like you'd want to know about this.

This was the caption to a screenshot of another text message. A picture of a message from Melanie, his almost first wife.

Melanie: I heard about your grandfather. I am so sorry. Please let me know if there is anything I can do for you or the family. You'll be in my prayers.

Melanie, elsewhere with your sympathy messages. I hate when people say *let me know if there is anything I can do for you*. Like, what can your ex- fiancé do for you at this very moment? And why is her name still in your phone? I thought I deleted it, damn it. The flood gates for random communication had been opened. I told you this would happen. I was being bitter, you say? This is death we are dealing with! How could you be so cold? Ha, well darling, you've never been betrayed by someone you've given the world to.

I had my first appearance as an Ice Girl while Skyler was gone. Thank Christ because I still hadn't found a way to tell him I made the team. *Hey babe, remember that road trip you went on, yeah well I tried out for the Ice Girl's behind your back and I made the team. What are the fucking odds of that!* Yup, not easy. Anyway, the appearance was in Boston at a supermarket. I got to hand out raffles with my teammates. Invigorating! The best part of my night, though, was when my mother showed up unexpectedly with my eighty-eight year old grandfather. He lived in an assisted living community and was legally blind but he is my biggest fan in the world. It meant everything and more to have Papa present on my first night in uniform.

Skyler was expected to return on a Tuesday. I spent Monday morning doing his laundry and reorganizing the one closet in my house he got to call *his*. It was in the office. I did these things to make him feel welcome and taken care of. He had been seemingly happy and overly descriptive with his days while home (except for the day he said he was hunting until he sent me a picture of himself at the Georgia Bulldogs game). His excuse? *If I told you the truth we would have argued all day.* While cleaning his closet, I noticed his ancient laptop laying perfectly on the floor. For a split second I thought, no way will I find anything on that old thing. He only uses his iPad! But for whatever reason, my curiosity got the best of me and I picked it up. I closed the office door and sat down on the floor. His laptop was fully charged and required no password. It was *too* easy. Some sort of web chat appeared on the screen when I opened the computer. I hadn't clicked a thing and it practically brought me where I needed to be; what I needed to see. He had about a thousand friends on Skype. All females. I scrolled and I scrolled.

LauraLynch27
KrystalKate46
BigTittyBabes_
DiamondEyedLover9887
LilacTurner
MaevConnell7
RitaRayJones8
TristyRaker00
RyleyCarter
MonicaSherez_72

Porno_Live247
LateNiteLonelys
BigGirlsOrBust96
124_skvjgsg_4785
RussianActivities1001
BaseballFinatics112
HannahAriel
TaylorHiggins26

Then there was a section for his most popular contacts.

LauraDevins
LeslieFinn99
MelanieBurke_
BaseballBabeX4
MargJohnson674
MilitaryWife111
BigBlackBeautiful32
BriannaMonique90
CanadienQueen45
SandraPeters002
MRS_WOOD
JulieKane1990

I was alone in my own mistakes, unable to breathe; unable to process. I'd been empty and I'd been broken, but this feeling was far worse than anything I'd dealt with before. One by one I opened each chat. I was entering the territory of a predatory creature who was able to exploit numerous women simultaneously. Skyler had a second life, a second personality, and a beautifully organized online sexual agenda. I had been duped. This man never loved me. But our sex has always been good! When it was consensual at least. It's not like he fucks me with stares as cold as ice and no concern for my pleasure. What was he missing?

Laura Devins. She was morbidly obese with pale skin, brown hair, and glasses. I know this because each chat came with a recorded copy of the woman on camera. This sick fuck, my boyfriend, recorded them. I scrolled up to the beginning of their conversation.

Skyler: You gonna let me watch today?
Laura: Idk. I'm nervous.
Skyler: Wtf… You made me a promise.
Laura: I don't feel comfortable doing this. I feel stupid!
Skyler: Whatever bye.
Laura: Wait! Fine. Ugh. I'll do it.
Skyler: Fine.
Skyler: I'm waiting.
Laura: Can we do this tonight? I have to pick up my niece from school soon.
Skyler: No. Coaching baseball tonight. Now or never.

I pressed play on the video. I watched as Laura slowly and shamefully undressed herself on camera for my Skyler. She was shy and she made it obvious. She was uncomfortable and she was disgusted with herself, or maybe just her body, but she continued on anyway. She undressed until she was left in nothing but a cream, lace bra that held, kind of, tits that sat in her lap, and matching cream panties. Her skin matched her undergarments. She looked like a glass of milk. She adjusted her glasses nervously.

"Do you like what you see?" she asked him.

Skyler's video was smaller and in the corner like it was on most webcams. He refused to show his face, he just spoke in a dark room.

"Take off your bra," he demanded.

I lowered the volume on the computer. Jesus, someone is going to think I'm watching porn in here.

His camera angle shifted to his penis. His screen gave off just enough light to see the veiny shaft of his manhood. He stroked it slowly.

"Will I ever get to see your face?" she asked.

"You're not allowed to ask questions. I want you naked now."

Laura continued to strip her milky-white skin of materials. Skyler's breathing increased as the jerking of his cock grew harder and faster. The veins in his wrist were now noticeable too. His pecker was glowing with lubricant.

"Happy now?" she asked.

"Play with yourself. Play with your damn tits," he demanded again.

I watched this timid woman, Laura, with no sense of self-worth, fondle her breasts with a pout on her face. *Wait.* Who am I to talk about self-worth? I haven't discovered mine yet either. Moving on…

Laura couldn't even look into the camera. It was painful to watch; pre-recorded and alone at my house. For whatever reason, Laura complied with his every order. Is this what sexual dominance and submission was like? I don't know, but I believe Skyler made Laura feel needed.

Skyler yanked his penis even harder. He couldn't last long; I knew he was about to blow.

"Lick them," he barked.

Laura lifted her boob where her tongue met her bumpy nipple. Watching a stranger lick her headlights for the man you love was indeed troubling.

"Lean back in your chair," he said. "I want to see you play with your pussy."

"I don't know if I can do that today," she confessed.

"Don't you want me to cum?"

She nodded. Laura leaned back to insert a few fingers into her unshaved vagina. Skyler moaned and moaned, and he moaned again. There it was. The finish line. The journey's end. He shut his camera off.

Laura: Where did you go? Why did you shut it off?
Skyler: I just busted. I'm done.
Laura: Do you want to see more later?
Skyler: Nah.
Laura: Did I do something wrong?
Laura: Hello?
Laura: So you're never going to talk to me again?

After digesting that splendid performance, I mustered up the courage to open another chat. On deck was Leslie Finn, a name I was all too familiar with. I was intrigued. I was upset. I was curious about Doctor Finn's online performance.

Leslie: You'll never be bored on your road trips again. Nobody has to know.
Skyler: I need you.
Leslie: You can have me whenever you want me.

A large, nude photo of Leslie appeared on the screen. She was holding a dildo inside her rotten excuse of a beaver. A sixty-something year old surgeon with children, she too was living a double life. I opened the next chat. I wanted to scroll through as many as I could before my mom caught me on his laptop. If she even sensed I was upset, I'd never hear the end of it. She would force the truth out of me and I didn't want that. The engaged and pregnant Melanie Burke was next. *She's pregnant.* Please, no videos from the ex.

Skyler: I want to see you again.
Melanie: Skyler I'm getting married.
Skyler: We should be getting married. My ring should still be on your finger. You should be pregnant with my child!
Melanie: We can't change the past. I'm happy, I am. You've moved on too.

Skyler: Turn your camera on. I need to see you.

Melanie: Davis will be home soon. I don't want him to hear me.

Skyler: Just for a second, Mel.

Melanie sent a picture of herself. No belly, just face and boobs (in a bra). Her fingers were near her face in the photograph. Another man's diamond glistened in the sunlight from her bedroom window, *their* bedroom window. This world, man. In the background sat a bassinet awaiting the arrival of the child she would share with someone else. Davis, I presume. I stared at the picture of his ex-fiancé. She did look like me. Blonde, almond shaped eyes with big pearly whites. Her smile cut through me like a dozen knives. Laura Devins and Leslie Finn hurt, but this was a different type of ouch.

I moved onto 'baseball lover' who was later identified as a girl named Macy.

Macy: Thanks for leaving me tickets. Your girlfriend is in the stands. You told me she wasn't coming? I have a gift for you. Gonna try to beat her to your truck after the game so I can slip it in the back.

Macy: Games over. I'm right behind her walking out of the stadium. Looks like she might beat me there.

Macy: She has your keys? I watched her get into the driver's seat of your truck. How does she have your keys?

Macy: Guess I won't be able to give you your gift today.
Macy: Next time.
Macy: She got out to talk to someone and I put it in the
           bed of your truck without her noticing!
Skyler: You're the best.

These messages were sent during his last home stand of the season. To now know that a stranger followed me into the parking lot behind the stadium and watched me get into his truck was totally invasive. My privacy had been violated, and my safety as far as I was concerned, and I had no idea. I was followed, watched, monitored, and stalked in a public place where I spent most of my time. This chat rattled me more than the woman licking her pizza pie nipples. Tears piled up in my eyes and quickly spilled onto my cheeks. I wiped them, hoping to remain discreet in case my mom walked in.

Margaret Johnson was next and her profile came with a biography.

Fifty-six year old mother of two pugs — Happily married — Southern Maine

Skyler: My bus gets in at five this morning. You still
             want me to come over?
Margaret: My husband will already be at work by the
             time you get here. That's perfect.
Skyler: Where did you say you lived again?
Margaret: Ogunquit.

Skyler:	That's a forty-five minute drive for me from Portland. We've been driving through the night. I'm exhausted.
Margaret:	It will be worth your time.
Skyler:	Yeah? How so? I want you to blow me.
Margaret:	I want that too.
Margaret:	Please come. 55 Daile St. Come around to the back porch when you get here so my dogs don't bark.
Skyler:	(5:03 A.M.) We just got back. Heading your way now.
Skyler:	(5:52 A.M.) I'm here.
Skyler:	(7:04 A.M.) Wow. Does your husband know you can suck dick like that? Wow.
Margaret:	Hope to see you again soon.

Watch porn, Skyler. Watch tons of it, I don't care. Masturbate to live videos, I don't care. Subscribe to a porn channel, I don't care. I won't be offended the same way you are when you accuse me of cheating after I tell you I'm using my vibrator while you're on the road. But when you have physical contact with another person with zero regard for the safety and health of your partner, that is where I lose all respect for you. I matched the dates of the last chat with his whereabouts on his baseball schedule. It was a Friday. I skipped my cleaning at the dentist to see him because he had been away for a week and a half. I arrived around eleven that morning and we started our day with wild sex because *it'd been so long*. Little did I know a fifty-six year old married woman had already blown his brains out that very morning. Did he shower? The memory of him naked on top of me that morning replayed in my mind over and over. He looked me dead in the eye every time we made love and he said, "I love you. Do you know how much I love you?" He had passion and love and beautiful intent in his eyes whenever he said that.

Heartbroken, obviously, I continued on. I couldn't stop breaking my own heart. It was addicting. My body was a wooden statue, but my insides felt like Skyler's bare hands had pried my lungs open in order to get to my heart, only to detach it from my body and leave it out in the cold to die. I see good in everyone, I truly do. I give second chances. And third and fourth if they need them. I'll let people break my heart if they can admit they were wrong afterwards. We all have lessons to learn. I don't mind being the subject of your errors as long as you understand how to be better the second time around. I believe people act out if they are lacking in another department in their life. Instead of yelling at you, I will just ask *why*. But people like him can't understand people like me. People with no soul will never understand those with loving hearts.

Next, a military wife. Could this get any more disappointing? The profile picture included a middle-aged mother surrounded by four young children. Her name— Dresden from Iowa.

Dresden: Hey! My husband is deployed overseas. I am bored and looking to have fun while he is serving. Does my situation interest you?

Skyler: YES! Would your husband be mad if he knew about me?

Dresden: Oh yes. He would be very mad.

Skyler: I love it!! What are you going to do for me?

Dresden: How about I get these clothes off and we hop on the video chat?

I pressed play. The homely mother and wife pulled a gray t-shirt with wet pit stains over her head. She wasn't wearing any undergarments. Behind her sat a bed with an American flag fastened to the wall above it.

"One time my husband came home early and surprised our family. Imagine if he walked in on us?" she giggled.

"What would he do? Tell me what he would do." Skyler gripped his penis and began stroking it.

"He would be very angry with us. I think he'd want to hurt you."

She stood up to unbutton her jeans. She slid them to the floor with her ass facing the camera. She laid down on the California King.

"Yeah? He would be mad if he saw me fucking his wife? The mother of his children?" he said.

Skyler's breathing was out of control. The more fucked up these scenarios were, the more he got off. It was twisted. She began touching herself; appreciating the way she could excite her own body.

"I think so," she whispered. "But that's a risk I'd be willing to take."

Stroking and touching. Stroking and touching. Moaning. Deep breathing. She reached for the drawer on her night stand and pulled out a silicone penis.

My mother walked in. Holy fucking pause button. I was kneeling on the floor next to a pile of unfolded t-shirts, staring at his laptop, with my mouth wide open and in shock.

"Taylor would you mind vacuuming the—." She paused mid sentence. "Everything good in here?" she asked.

"I'm fine," I chuckled.

"Whenever you say you're fine, you're usually not fine. I know you. What's going on?"

"I promise I'm fine. I'm good. Please shut the door. I'm so good."

My mother backed out of the room in suspicion. She knew I wasn't telling the truth. I was in no shape or form to disclose my current findings. I wasn't even sure I'd *ever* be ready to share these things with her. I resumed the military video.

"This is a mold of my husband's cock. He had it made for me because he's away so much." Dresden was speaking in her sexy voice. You know, the voice used in the porn industry, the baby voice.

She shoved the fake penis into her mouth and savored the way it felt between her lips.

"Do you like watching me suck my husband's cock?" she asked.

"Fuck yes!"

"I wish it was your cock instead. Come to Iowa."

"Tell me how you'd suck my cock."

The demands, the orders!

"Well sweetie, first, I'd lay you down on the bed to unzip your pants, unleashing the one thing I crave between my thighs more than anything. I would stare deep into your eyes as my tongue unraveled down the sides of your stick. This is where I'd allow you to cup my breasts. Feel them before you taste them. Arouse my nipple. Prepare to suck it like my youngest son still does. He depends on me; as will you. I'd use both of my hands to stimulate your cock before aligning it with the entrance of my pussy. Then it will be your turn. I want you to fuck me. Fuck me harder than my husband ever will. Fuck me in our bed. Fuck me in the same place we conceived our children. You can finish wherever you want, I don't mind. My chest, my face, my mouth. And when we are sweaty and tired and our crotches are covered in a clear mess of mucus, I'll still have you in my mouth. I will still taste you on my tongue, trickling down my throat. I want you *weak*. Can we make that happen?"

Skyler's penis exploded on his stomach in the dark room. The screen went black. He shut his camera off. He did the same thing to every woman. He faked desire and intimacy only to use them for his own personal benefit.

Dresden: Bad internet connection? Where did my handsome man go?

Skyler: I finished.

Dresden: Are you going to take care of me so I can finish?
Skyler: No lol I don't care if you finish or not.
Skyler: Take care of it yourself.

Harsh. Big, black, and beautiful was next. No chats, just a video. She had short, spiked dreadlocks. I braced myself but it only ended up being a video of her talking. I guess you had to pay her if you wanted her clothes to come off and we all know Skyler is a cheap bastard.

Onto Brianna from Binghamton. Oh Brianna, if you haven't destroyed my life enough already. This conversation had taken place exactly two weeks prior.

Skyler: I wish our last series of the season was in Binghamton.
Brianna: I know. Would love to see you again.
Skyler: Figured this was the best way to contact you. Taylor is a head case.
Brianna: Haha! Hey, that's never stopped us before.

I read conversations with girls from Canada and girls from Europe. And then the internet introduced me to Sandra Peters, my final straw.

Skyler: How old are you?
Sandra: I'm 74. I love the Red Sox. Go Sox!
Skyler: I bet you have grandchildren.
Sandra: Yes. Six. Would you like to have some fun?

Skyler: Sure. Do you have a husband?
Sandra: He passed years back.
Skyler: Yum. Well let's get you naked.

Sandra, like all of the others, stripped down to her bare, unshaven skin. I focused on the varicose veins on her heavy, swollen legs. Gnarled, developed veins. It was the most unforgiving sight I'd seen. Sandra was a **victim** of Skyler Williams, as was I, as were most of the others. Or were we all just a bunch of broken people drawn to one another to make our existences here on this planet more bearable for the time being. We are all broken from someone or something. We are all products of our bangs, bumps, chips and damages. We must allow our jaggedness, our scars and the corrugations along our faces, to serve as a sign of knowledge. We are not defective individuals; we carry centuries of wisdom inside our core. These troubles have faced us because we are powerful. The universe knew all along we'd never allow these hardships to win. We will shout about evil. We will expose their wickedness. Dishonesty mustn't prevail.

I'd watched my conniving, unscrupulous *soulmate* unload himself to the sight of granny the fossil's ancient, unused bologna cave. I'd watched him recline himself in his chair to the sight of a fifteen-year-old girl from Maine undressing herself. Enticed by her young body, her undeveloped breasts, her stick skinny figure, and her belly button ring, he broke boundaries that even the law would disapprove of. I'd seen it all, honestly. Obese, underage, elderly, foreign, married. My boyfriend, my confidant, was one crooked motherfucker.

Because I couldn't live with myself if I didn't explore every inch of this computer, I opened the photo gallery. It may have well been a pornographic website. I recognized a disturbing number of familiar faces, including my own, and many remained strangers in this shady example of love. I saw a woman remove gelatin beads from her anal cavity, a striptease from one of the promotional managers of Hadlock Field, squirting, and Skyler's proposal to his ex during a college basketball game. I also witnessed a team photographer pour soap across her breasts in her bath tub for a slippery massage. The team photographer didn't surprise me though, I'd heard she had a few different run-ins with some married men on the team already.

Ah, the images. The videos. *The women.* They were all so entrancingly engraved into my memory. Lacking sensation, I closed his laptop. The aroma of his cologne spilled from the closet and met my nostrils. I bought him that cologne for his birthday last year. I wondered how many of these women had smelt it too. A once sensitive, overly understanding young woman— I felt nothing. I was not sorry or heartsick. I was not overflowing jealousy. Each beat inside my chest felt like a chore. I sat on the floor with the laptop in my hands and wondered, "How do I approach him about this one?"

I went outside to call a friend. One of the only friends I had left since getting into this relationship. I only called her when Skyler made me cry and I saw her, well, never. Victoria, or as I called her, Tori. Skyler never liked her but I blame it on the fact that she didn't have a filter. What pathological narcissist likes an honest person that is willing to pop a hole in their inflated sense of self-importance? Pathological narcissist, yes that is my opinion. In tears, I told Tori about my findings. She made me promise not to let him board the plane back to Boston. She told me I had to leave him.

"He needs serious help," she said. "Like this is some mental institution shit. Like, padded walls and straitjacket shit!"

"I know, Tori. That's the worst part. *I know.*"

I went inside and against my better judgment, I told my mom. I told her what I had just told Tori and I literally watched vitality escape from her eyes.

"You know Taylor," my mother started. "This doesn't surprise me. I've always been unsure of him. I've always liked him, but I've always been unsure. I have to tell you something that I've been keeping from you."

My heart stopped.

Eyes wide I screamed, *"What!"*

"The other night when you, Sean, and Skyler went to the driving range, um, well, he left his phone charging on your nightstand. Skyler did. I picked it up and realized he didn't have a password on it. So I did some exploring. His texts were clean: Mom, Dad, Future Wife, Mrs. Higgins, Sean. His photos were clean too. Nothing out of the ordinary there. I felt ridiculous after finding no evidence to back up my unsure feelings about him. Then I checked his call logs. There were a ton of incoming and outgoing phone calls at three, four in the morning one night in late August when his team was in Virginia Beach. I entered this particular number into the search bar on Facebook. Sure enough, Peyton Massey from Virginia Beach popped up. She had bleach blonde hair just like you, blue eyes, and a beautiful smile. She looked exactly like you actually, only heavier."

"And," I said. I knew my mother had taken the investigation into her own hands.

"I was so disturbed that I reached out to Peyton myself… using my work phone… and pretending to be you."

"You what!" I yelled.

"I told her I found her number in my boyfriend's phone and was simply looking for an answer. She was so kind. She told me they met on some app when he was in town. She said he went by the name of Jason on the app. She said he begged her to come to his games and to visit with him at the hotel every night."

"Did they have sex?" I questioned.

"She said she went to the hotel on his last night in town, got into bed with him, they started kissing, and his roommate walked in on them. Skyler apparently asked him to leave for a few minutes but she decided to leave instead. She said she thought he was single."

"How long have you known about this?"

"Not long. Not even a week. I wanted to tell you. I've been trying to find the right way to break your heart and it hasn't been easy. I know you're in a really low place right now because of him and the thought of letting you down again scared me to death. I want my daughter back, T. Look at you! He's destroyed you. It's summer and your skin is white, green practically. You're flesh and bones. Your hair is falling out. You don't eat. You don't talk to people. You don't work. You aren't doing school work. You're a young girl! You should have so much more energy than you do. I'm so thankful you have the Ice Girls. I don't know where you'd be if you didn't have that. But you need more in your life than just the Ice Girls."

My mother broke down in tears. What's more devastating than watching your parents cry? Not much. Not much at all.

"Mom." I fought back tears. "I'll survive." The crack in my voice made her that much more emotional.

"I don't want you to just survive, Taylor. I want you to be alive again. I want you to be in love with the life you lead. You have to find yourself again Taylor. *Let him go.*"

That was the first time my mom had ever told me to let him go. She'd known about our problems in the past but she never once tried to persuade me on what to do. My decisions were my decisions and she'd always respected that. Knowing the damage he'd done to me, my parents never kicked him out of my life in fear that I would follow him anywhere and they would lose both of us. They were probably right. I was at my absolute bottom, but my mother met *her* record low today.

15

Against everyone's wishes, I allowed Skyler to board his flight from Atlanta to Boston under the impression that I was excited to see him. Bare with me, I had a plan. I wanted him to waste money on the return flight that he booked himself only to greet him at the front door with his laptop in my hands. He had to get his truck anyway. I fantasized about watching his tearful academy award winning performance; how he'd shift the blame onto somebody else while defending his ability to be faithful on his hands and knees. I couldn't wait to tell him I'd already tapped out.

I told Skyler I had an appointment and couldn't pick him up at the airport. Pissed, he asked an acquaintance from work to get him. I sat on my bed instead, laptop open, waiting for him to arrive home. Forty-three minutes after his flight landed, I listened to him struggle his suitcase through my front door.

"Helloooo?!" he called out for me. I sat in silence while my finger rested on the button that would play the undressing of Laura Devins at my touch. Up the stairs he came.

"Tay?" he called again. My life would change drastically in a matter of seconds. I was afraid. Surely I couldn't live with these secrets; my only option was to confront him. But I was so afraid. He neared my bedroom doorway and my finger slipped across the keyboard. He turned the corner with a smile, wide as ever, and we locked eyes for a second. I remembered all over again why I loved him to begin with. *What have I done? What have I started? He's going to be so mad.* The happiness in his expression quickly turned to betrayal and disgust as his brain processed what he was witnessing on his very own computer screen. With flesh whiter than a ghost, he charged at the laptop to slam it shut. I cowered thinking he was coming for me. I know he wanted to.

"What the fuck is wrong with you!" he hissed. His nastiness was brewing; he was about to transform into a different man. I was ready for it.

"What? I thought you enjoyed watching strangers play with themselves?"

My sarcasm only made things worse, I knew that, but I did it anyway.

"Why do you have *my* laptop. It's *mine.* Meaning you have no right to touch it. Holy shit you're a fucking weirdo. What did I get myself into! You're crazy, you know that? I can't believe I came back here for you."

He paced back and forth in my room. Thankfully we were home alone.

"You need help Skyler. You need to talk to someone about your problems. This is immoral. I think you have an addiction to sex and fragile women. You need to get professional help."

I watched the anger build and build at the sound of my voice. The accuracy of my words annihilated him. I was hitting the nail on the fucking head and he hated me for it. I had intruded on his secret life, his second identity, and this exposure made him uncomfortable.

Confrontation, check. Self-victimizing, check. Now began the denial phase of his production.

"If you must know, because you're this fucking insane, my brother was using my iPad all week at home. It must have been Shia."

"Skyler, you talked about road trips, baseball games, and baseball lessons. This wasn't your brother. I know your voice. I know your hands. I know your wordage. And I know your cock. You did this."

And *waterworks*. No remorse. No instinctual apologies. I would have even settled for a, "I fucked up". Nothing but Niagara Falls from his eyes.

"Can't believe you made me fly here for this bullshit. I didn't even want to come back. I told you if you didn't learn to trust me you'd ruin our relationship. *You* ruined it. *You* did this. Not me. *You*. You get that? *You*. So good job. I hope you feel really good about yourself. You ruined something special. Congrats Taylor."

I shook my head and laughed at such uncanniness. His deranged, unbalanced mind was doing what it did best: Defend and Flee.

Skyler rushed into the office and opened his closet. He began packing his belongings. I watched as he ripped open drawers and squished items into the first bag he could find.

"My daddy was right. Ain't nothin' but a waste of time comin' back up here for your ass. I'm fixin' to get the hell on with my life." His southern accent got so sloppy when he was mad.

"I feel sad for your parents Skyler. Their son is very sick, a pervert if you will, but they'll never be able to admit it because they don't know you well enough. They know you for baseball. They know you for your games. But they don't know *you* for the deviant you are. The warped, atypical species that you are."

"You better shut your fucking mouth," he demanded.

"But when you're raised by narrow-minded, mean-spirited individuals with unimaginative brains who destroy the property of others, cheat, steal, and shun those who spend money on experience, you're bound to be a spawn of such creatures. You are the way you are because they are lousy people. It all starts somewhere. We are all broken from *something*. They are your something. They are the reason you lack interpersonal skills, social skills, and avoid coping mechanisms at all costs. You are a walking disaster and you have them to thank for it."

He dropped the shirts he'd been packing with violence in his eyes to approach me; to attack. Me, his prey, smaller and much weaker, shrunk into my shell as he neared. My undefended self feared his unwelcome hands that were sure to be cruel, and even more so the deplorable actions that were about to take place. *Him*, my protection. He used to make me feel guarded. I was his worst enemy right now. I was not free from danger anymore. In my home, my family's home, my childhood home. Who would have thought these walls would see such ugly things?

I put my hands out in front of me. "Please Skyler. Stop!"

"What the fuck did you just call me?" I turned my head sideways as his slobber landed on my face in a rainstorm. He was outraged. I couldn't redeem myself even if I tried.

"Look at me when I'm talking to you, you piece of shit!" He slammed his fist against the wall next to my head. *"Look at me dammit!"* Drywall crumbled to the floor. His knuckles; white and chalky.

Crying, I turned my head back to face him.

"Are you scared?" he asked. "You weren't scared a few minutes ago when you were talking about my family. Why are you scared now?" he sung. *Slam!* He hit the wall again. I cowered thinking it would be me getting hit this time. He laughed at me. I was pinned against the wall. He grabbed my chin and cranked my neck to face him once more.

"I said fucking look at me!" he screamed. His voice echoed throughout my house. My cat ran to find hiding. I wish I could find a place to hide too. I wish someone would hear him. My adrenaline came alive. If I didn't react

now, I wasn't sure what would happen. Out of absolutely nowhere, I wound up my fist and clocked him on the side of his face. I'd never punched anyone before; he was the first. It hurt like a bitch. I clipped the edge of his eye. I thought, *holy shitballs!* He immediately spit in my face. Like, on my actual face. As I absorbed the massive loogie into my eyes, I noticed for a single second that our pupils met again. We were alone in that moment. Together. Me and the man I loved. *Hi baby, it's me. It's Tay. Please don't hurt me.* I thought he might sense the fear in my bones and stop. *BAM!* Our foreheads collided. Skyler head butted me so hard that my skull bounced off the wall behind me. The impact brought me to the ground. My world went black.

"*Bitch,*" he said, as I stared at him from the floor.

I hoped I was hallucinating. The pain in my nose assured me I wasn't delusional. I swore it was broken. I reached for my profile to see if its shape had been maintained or if blood had shed. It was intact, but I was bleeding heavily. In fact I was covered in my own vital fluids. My mind was disabled. *What do I do? Where do we go from here? What will my parents say about the hole in the wall? How can I hide this from them? Did this really happen? What did I do to deserve this? Why aren't I angry?* I sat against the wall and cried in deep agony. My nose was throbbing and Skyler didn't care. Of course he didn't care, he did this! He returned to packing as I hemorrhaged before him.

"I fucking hate you," I whispered through the froth in my mouth. Without saying a word he came for me a second time, this time taking his shoe to my rib cage. He kicked me as hard as he could. He released every bit of animosity he held within on me; the bag of bones that I was. I cried out for help with the little fire I had left inside. When finished, Skyler picked up his bags, stepped over my oozing body, and headed for the front door.

"Quit cryin'," he said. "Nobody can hear you."

His right eye socket looked as if it had taken a ninety-mile an hour fastball. He had robbed me of my integrity, it was the least I could do. My pain was severe. The house was empty. The police still couldn't save me. On my stomach, I dragged myself to the bathroom floor. The tile was cold against my torrid skin. I lay there to catch my breath until, *blah!* I puked. And I puked. And I puked; blood. I puked until I had nothing left. I let the dry heaving exhaust me as I lay in my own vomit. I couldn't stand even if I wanted to. He left me to rot.

Let's talk about dark places. Your final destination on your inescapable journey to everlasting punishment. I was injected with the atrocious feeling of gloom many times before, but now— a record low. The depths of my soul were stone cold and concrete; my blood vessels carried nothing but glaciers of envy. I induced myself with over the counter sleep aids in order to spend my hours in a state of unconsciousness. I hindered my minds awareness as often as humanly possible. Alcohol, marijuana, and prescription sedatives were never my cup of tea. I didn't plan to create new, harmful habits over this asinine critter either. I'd commit to paper, writing with a locked grip of anger around my pen and a clamped jaw, only to end my suffering.

I thought about death often. I had been pushed to many breaking points and in those moments of weakness, I thought death would be an easier, less painful version of the present. People would come to grieve my corpse at an open casket viewing. Rosary beads would be woven between the fingers of my folded hands. People would stare at my Ferrari red nail polish; my acrylics. They would be reminded all over again of my youth and how unfortunate this goodbye actually was. At one-hundred and six pounds, I was thinner and more feeble than ever. I found love by mere happenstance and I was sure it would cost me my life. I was sick and I was tired. Tired of making lists because I couldn't remember anything, lists that I could never complete. Sick of riding next to him in the car when he'd stretch his arm out fast, as if going to hit me in the face, only to have me wince and rest his hand upon my headrest. He'd snicker knowing I feared his hands. Our love had become nothing short of an occupation used for Skyler's amusement. He loved to torture me, I just loved him. He hated me; the music I listened to, the way I stirred my coffee, the way flowers brought me joy, and the way I cooked eggs. Blonde hair made me an attention seeking whore and my neon workout attire made me desperate for male praise. I must always be wearing my ring, and if I was ever not, he'd tell me it was a waste of money. He'd analyze photographs of me to make sure I was wearing the ring. He hated Massachusetts and he hated when I wore makeup. *Why do you need it? Who are you trying to look good for? I don't like makeup, so why are you wearing it?*

He hated any friends that trickled into my life, my hobbies and interests, and he hated the noise a plastic water bottle made when I drank from it too quickly. He hated when I'd bite my nails, when I got excited, and the way I brushed my teeth. He hated that I didn't make money, he hated that we weren't in Georgia, and he hated when I was visibly happy. He hated my expectations and my routine use of a battery operated orgasm. He hated my dreams and he hated my fears. He hated me.

Sleeping next to him throughout our relationship at night was both terrifying and necessary. I was afraid of him, yet his body made me feel calm. I relied on him. I'd climb into bed wearing one of his dirty t-shirts and cuddle up on his shoulder no matter how bad our day was. If he was on his phone, he'd usually accuse me of eavesdropping. He'd say, "You only want to lay on my shoulder so you can get a look at my messages." I'd flip over in tears. If my cold hands or feet touched his body at all during this time he'd let me know. He'd push me away as fast as he could, usually into the wall, and yell at me. I'd squish myself up against the wall leaving him the entire bed so he wouldn't complain about being uncomfortable on my queen sized mattress. I would have woken up with a stiff neck and knots in my back for the rest of my life if that meant starting our day on the right foot. If he was horny, he would take what he wanted from me. You all know this by now. I'd cry silently as he used my body. He'd finish and roll over. I'd lay wide awake; completely violated and saturated in his cum. My wet eyelashes would drag across my pillowcase. He always knew when I was awake because he'd listen for blinking.

"What's wrong now?" he'd whine to me.

"I can't sleep," I'd respond with a stuffy nose and a raspy voice. He'd sigh.

He was a stalker and his hunting tendencies made for the perfect analogy of our life together. He listened well. He was overly observant. He had unparalleled vision. And he preyed on those weaker than him. He could hear me blink, he could hear me smile. He knew when I was looking at him even when his eyes were closed. I stopped using my phone in the stands at his games because he would literally notice from the outfield that I was texting. *Who is more important than me? Why don't you care about my game?* He crept up on me, always. And not in a cute, playful manner. He would sneak up on me while making a sandwich in the kitchen. He would hide in closets just to spook me. *Everything* was a problem. When I was 1000% alone, I still felt him near me. I felt him watching; somehow, someway. I was never alone. Even when I was, I had an undeniable feeling of company. I developed a fear of the dark. Believe me when I say the dark had never fazed me, but now. Oh, I was uncomfortable in the dark. The pitch blackness of my room each night made ghastly scenarios flood my brain. I thought. And I heard. I became so afraid of the dark that I couldn't leave my bed. For water. To pee. Nothing. I absolutely could not get up. My hair had thinned. My personality was gone. My confidence— well that had been taken a long time ago. I was irritable, short-tempered, and easily frustrated. I suffered recurring outbursts of anger. I became a recluse. I couldn't get out of my own way and that in itself pissed me off. All while the world thought Skyler was charming and handsome and talented. His status joined by his good looks made him the perfect man— externally. But to me, he made me jumpy and uncertain. He made my spirit cry out for help. The power always remained in his hands. He was my puppet master and he knew how to make me dance. This incredibly sensitive, judgmental prick of an emotional abuser knew how to manipulate me better than anyone. And every so often when I'd decide to gain a pair of balls and confront him, he'd flee the scene because *I* was crazy.

The truth is, breaking points are simply unfounded theories. We imagine the end of ourselves because it is easier to spread ourselves thin than it is to admit the infinite beginnings we have to offer this world while our hearts are impaired. *I will never find my purpose in this world. I have been overstrained. I am not worthy of greatness.* A breaking point is just a figure of speech. It sounds better than a "coping method" at least. A breaking point is a fork in the road; *your* road. You can continue on with fear, or you can make a change. You will know when changes are needed when you're ready to accept them. You have to be ready to surrender.

After the physical altercation at my house, Skyler swore he was Georgia bound. Three days later I found out he had crashed at a (male) co-workers house. I told my parents that the hole in the wall was an accident and they bought it. On the fourth day, he was of course sorry. He showed up at my house to have a conversation. I of course gave him the time of day. I never said broken hearts were practical.

"Thanks for coming outside. Tay, I fucked up big time," he started. We sat together in his truck in front of my house. My arms were folded across my chest. I said nothing.

"Where do I begin? Um, I messed up. I know that. I crossed the line and I know you'll never forget about what happened, but I'm so sorry that I hurt you. I don't know who that person was."

"I don't know what hurts more, Skyler. Being head-butted, kicked in the rib cage, or finding out your boy-friend has had sex with random people when you thought he was asleep."

"Look I know you're mad. And you should be. You are the greatest thing that's ever happened to me and I cher-ish what we have together. You make me a better man."

"I don't think I'm doing a very good job."

"With what?"

"Making you a better man."

"Tay I'm scared. I've spent our entire relationship brac-ing myself for the day you tell me you're leaving me. That we can't be together anymore. That you don't love me like you used to and you don't know why. You're too good for me. I don't deserve you, Tay. I know you'll find someone better than me someday. Someone younger. Someone that works a normal nine to five and will come home to you every night. Someone that will give you the time you deserve. He'll have more money than I do. He'll be able to take you to dinner and do nice things for you. I don't deserve you. I get that."

"I know you majored in psychology but don't you start pulling that reverse shit on me right now. You are *not* the victim here."

"The things I've done to you, I'm not proud of. I would love to call you my wife someday. But my mind is all over the place, especially during the season. My manager is telling me they want to try someone new in centerfield. I play center seven days a week and they want to put a second baseman in center! And my agent is telling me he can't get me a discount on the brand of bat that makes me most comfortable at the plate, that I have to pay full price because I'm a nobody, and when my bank account is overdrawn and my parents are in my ear about making it big so I can take care of them, I'm just lost. I'm so fucking lost. I don't even know who I am anymore. This game is killing me," he cried aloud.

"I understand your struggles within the game," I started. "But this isn't about baseball right now. This is about you and I."

"Baseball makes me someone I don't want to be and I don't know how to make it stop. I just can't lose you Tay. I will do anything to save this. I'll change my phone number again. I'll get a new email address. Tell me what you want and I'll do it."

The lousy truth is that I still wanted to be with him. I wanted to believe him. I wanted him to prove me wrong. I wanted him to fill me with genuine sincerity and reason. I wanted him to leave me speechless. I just wanted him. I'd invested so much into this relationship already. People expected us to be happy. I couldn't give up now. But I absolutely had to give up. I had to let him go. I had to continue on alone.

"I appreciate your words," I said. "But you can't pretend to love me for one more day."

I pulled on the door handle and the interior lights lit up his face. I had to say goodbye to my forever plan because he didn't know how to love me.

"I can fix this Taylor! Just let me. I swear I can fix this. Oh god, let me fix this."

"Bye Skyler."

The next morning and without my asking, Skyler texted me from a brand new phone number. I told him I needed space. I dodged his calls, texts, flower arrangements, notes in the mailbox, and gifts on my car. This carried on for *months.* He was free to return to Georgia, something he wanted all along, yet he chose to stay in Massachusetts. I took full advantage of my new life without pain. My mind was free and it was ready to take on the world. I became a licensed realtor and started my own business, all while documenting the story of Skyler and I in writing. If I could save anyone with my story, even just one person, that was good enough for me.

The problem with my new life without pain, is that I was still in pain. I missed him, the kind version of him, and I'd do anything to travel back in time just to spend a little bit longer with the man I first met. He was endearing, even more so now that I was resisting him, and I was giving into it. I didn't want to live without him.

Skyler came clean about his erratic behavior, specifically his fantasy world on his computer. He admitted he needed help. He told me he was afraid of himself, that he didn't know what he was capable of. I offered to stand by his side once more during his quest for self-love. My heart couldn't beat without him.

But first, I'd have to tell him about my new job. I prepared a speech for Skyler. It took me weeks to concoct my announcement about the Ice Girls. *This was a goal of mine, like baseball is for you, and I made the team. I did it for the friendships.*

"Can we talk for a sec?" I asked him. He was watching the hunting channel. I had to convince my parents he was safe to allow back into the house. Luckily, they barely knew half of the truth.

"Imagine if we had our own hunting show? That would be a dream come true. I think I'd like that more than playing in the majors."

I smiled. I smile when I feel awkward. My nerves were nervous. We were together and happy again and I was about to ruin it.

"Remember how I said I always wanted to be a Boston Bruins Ice Girl?"

His eyes squinted. I had his full attention now.

"Well I actually auditioned and I made the team. I auditioned when we were in a very bad place. I had to do this for me. I hope you can understand."

"You made the team? You're on the team? When did you audition?"

"Over the summer when that whole Binghamton thing made a mess of us. Yes, I am on the team."

Skyler shook his head. He looked disappointed.

"I want the experience Skyler. It was a bucket list goal."

I leaned in to wrap my arms around him. He refused to be cradled.

"I can't. I'm sorry. I just can't. I can't have you running around in a slutty uniform while I'm trying to focus on my career. You did this to meet players didn't you? I know you did. I can't do this. I'm done Taylor, I'm done. I need to leave, holy fuck, I need to go home. What have I done? Oh no. I need to go home!"

Skyler put his shoes on and headed for the door.

"Skyler please. It's not a big deal. It's a great opportunity," I pleaded.

"Opportunity? How much they payin' you for this garbage? Are you paying bills with that money? Is this going to be your career? No. You're getting paid pennies to be a whore. Why don't you find a real job that pays you real money. Good luck to you. I'm out."

His truck started, the sound of it filling the neighborhood per usual, and disappeared into nightfall. I let him be. I didn't call him or text him like I normally would.

His belongings were at my house so I knew he wouldn't go far. His girlfriend became an Ice Girl and he needed some time to cry it out. That was all.

He returned about an hour later.

"You good?" I asked him from bed as he entered my room.

"I don't wanna talk about it."

I got up to grab him and tell him it was going to be alright.

"Come here," I demanded. "Kiss me."

Chomping on a wad of mint gum, he leaned in for a peck. I caught wind of the slightest scent of cigarettes and booze.

"Where did you go?" I asked. "A bar?"

"Just drove around to clear my head."

"I see," I said. "You smell like cigarettes and alcohol."

After dating for well over a year, I'd not once smelled smoke on his clothing or random alcohol on his breath.

"*No!* What the fuck."

"Let me smell your breath."

He breathed on me. The wad of gum in his mouth was the size of a ping pong ball. Minty freshness.

"Let me smell your fingers. Your wrist," I said.

I grabbed his forearm and pulled his wrist up to my nose. Tobacco.

"You liar! You were ripping butts and downing beer this whole time. This is pathetic. All because I made the fucking Ice Girls. Unreal!"

I grabbed the keys to his truck and raced outside. It reeked of fresh brews and smokes. I dug around for the carton of cancer. I looked everywhere until, under the backseat, I found a carton of Marlboro Reds. I slammed them on the ground and stomped on them. Skyler was in bed by the time I got back inside.

"Not a good start Skyler. Not a good start."

"Everything is a fight with you."

16

I worked Bruins' games at least twice a week. Game days came with a guaranteed argument with Skyler. My mother would drive me into town so I wouldn't have to pay to park. Then I'd really be cutting into my lofty Ice Girl salary of fifty dollars per game. I showered, spent two hours in front of a mirror doing hair and makeup, and headed to TD Garden. My mother dropped me at the fancy *Employees Only* entrance on the side of the building. I proudly made my way to the door wearing my Bruins gear. I earned a spot on that team and I was proud to represent the black and yellow. I scanned my employee ID card and the door to security opened where the usual security guy would check my bags. I'd then climb three flights of stairs because the service elevators were always crowded with caterers and other employees. Winded, I'd reach the ice level. I'd pass the entrance to the ice on my way to the Ice Girls' locker room. The Bruins' locker room was right around the corner from ours and upon arrival, you could usually see them warming up with a soccer ball or doing stretches in the hallway. After helping my teammates tease their hair because, who better than a beauty school dropout to give you big hair, we were summoned in groups to hand out game night rosters to fans entering the building for the game. Socializing with people who were hyped and honored to be in such a legendary building really set the tone for the game. Boston fans never disappoint. I'm sure you've heard by now: Boston sports fans are the greatest sports fans on the planet. The roar from the crowd when a puck slipped into the visitors net and the vibration of the building when the goal horn sounded and KernKraft 400 took over the speakers, you just can't beat it. I checked my phone when I returned to the locker room after rosters.

Skyler: I can't sit at your house while you whore yourself around a Bruins game all night. I'm going crazy. I'm going to the DogPound to hit some balls and let off some steam. It's closed but I have a key. Maybe I'll get a second workout in. I'll come home when I'm ready to come home. I don't want to see you in that slutty uniform anyway so make sure you shower and change as soon as you get home. You should be ashamed of yourself. Look at what you're doing to me; to us. You cause so many problems for us. You keep embarrassing your unborn children. Someday they will see pictures of you on the internet and realize their mother had no consideration for them. We can never have children because you decided to become an Ice Girl and do pageants.

I swallowed a glob of spit in my mouth. I came back to him to be abused all over again. Looking down at my ring finger, I spun the silver band he had given me. I was surrounded by many people, thousands and thousands actually, but my world was still and I was alone. Paranoia set it. *Why does he do this to me? Everyone must notice my sadness. I have no personality. They could fire me over this sadness. What if I don't make the team next year? I swear I am better than this.* My job at TD Garden was to excite; to ensure a good time. I visited sick children with cancer, military homecoming heroes, and tossed burrito-like wrapped t-shirts into a crowd of over seventeen thousand. I *had* to be happy. But I wasn't.

When the game ended, I met my mother in front of the Garden for a ride home. I made sure I told Skyler I was on my way. My mother wore an uncomfortable disposition.

"How was the game?" she asked. She forced small talk. She had something bigger to tell me.

"Good. It was good. Bruins won."

"I heard. Yes. Good. Good."

We both went silent. My heart sensed trouble. I was scared before having a reason to be scared. There goes my oxygen again.

"Taylor I have to tell you something."

My frame was tense; everything was still. My heart danced loud and fast. I felt the world escaping me once more.

"What did he do this time?" I asked.

"You know… he gets so upset when you work these games. He was watching TV in your room. I went in to offer him dinner. He said he was too disgusted to eat. He asked to be left alone. He was so angry. Minutes later, he walked out the front door with his baseball bag."

"Yeah. He told me he was going to hit to blow off some steam. He always acts like this. I'm used to it by now."

My muscles became less rigid thinking his rudeness was the extent of the issue.

"I decided to pack him dinner and bring it to him at the facility. I wanted to calm him down. I wanted him to know that these games are harmless and he has nothing to worry about. I knew he had to be hungry."

My throat clenched; my soul cringed at the words my mother's lips were about to deliver.

"I drove to the baseball facility. His truck was strangely parked snug up against the building in the dark, empty parking lot. Just as I was about to enter the lot, I noticed a woman appear from a smaller car parked behind his truck. If I didn't see her I wouldn't have noticed her car. It was barely visible from the street. I panicked when I saw her little, navy sedan Taylor. I didn't know what to do. I circled the building, thinking, wondering, and trying to get a view of the inside. I couldn't see anything. I should have barged in on them. I wasn't thinking straight. So I called Skyler. I parked my car across the street from the facility and called Skyler. I asked him who the girl was when he answered the phone and seconds later she came rushing out of the building. She peeled out of the parking lot and that's when I noticed her car had Maine license plates. Skyler peaked his face through the blinds. He couldn't see me but I could see him. Maybe I brought him dinner because I needed to witness that. Maybe this was the push you needed to let him go. The place was closed Taylor. She had Maine plates! He's a cheater!"

"Did he tell you who the woman was?"

"He said she was a potential customer from Lowell inquiring about private lessons for her nephew... at nine o'clock at night. Are you shitting me?! And Lowell? His baseball career started in Lowell with the Lowell Spinners. A Lowell resident with Maine plates doesn't just "stop by" a baseball facility in Reading. It's too out of the way. And it was closed! To me that says it was one of the only towns he could think to name at the time. You have to get rid of him Taylor. He is scum."

Completely unsurprised and unable to feel any more broken than I already had been, I reclined in the passenger seat and let out a deep, aggressive *UGGGGHHHH!*

If you are wondering why I continue to allow Skyler Williams in my life after he consistently proves his behavior to be monstrous, my answer to you is *I don't know.* I'm bluffing. I do know. I know he is severely unwell and I know that he is bad for me. I know that we are supposed to release the things that break our spirits in order to reach pure bliss. I know I can identify his lies and continue on as if they'd never happened. I know I cannot last a lifetime with a being like him. I know that if I don't end us, he will end me.

"Just leave him!" They would say. My family. The few friends that knew our truth. Strangers. They all told me to kick him to the curb. I knew his lies would asphyxiate him eventually. They would recognize him as danger and snatch every last bit of his oxygen. He would be remembered for not baseball, but a burglar to women and their purity. For now, challenging the legitimacy of his statements was easier than letting him go, leaving him free to fuck anyone without my repercussions. The thing is, he never received any consequences for fornication. I just wanted to own his control no matter what.

I made my mom drive me directly to the DogPound. The building was dim and his truck was still hugging its perimeter. I told my mother to wait in the car as I mentally prepared myself for his tears and a cleverly-crafted lie that would be spoken with utmost sincerity. I approached the building wearing my Bruins uniform knowing another woman, another gutless weakling, walked these same steps with sexual intentions in this grimy warehouse. Snow was starting to fall. Enough to create a crunch under your shoe blanketed the pavement. The noiseless flakes made the thoughts in my head seem louder than usual.

The door was locked. I knocked on the glass panel beside the entryway. Skyler came from the darkness and pushed the door open just as he had done for the girl from Maine. The lobby was partially lit by street lights. Skyler retreated to a chair in the corner where occasional head-lights from passing cars would expose his troubled face. He knew why I was there.

"Let me explain," he pleaded.

"Please do."

"I've been sitting in bed all night thinking about you at the game. I kept thinking about all the guys that must hit on you. As the game went on, I thought about how drunk guys must get, and how they must hit on you more as the night goes on. I was so angry. I had to occupy my mind. I came to hit a few buckets of balls. While I was hitting I saw headlights out front. A lady, middle-aged mother, was at the front door. I told her we were closed and she apologized but said she saw the truck and wanted to see if anyone was here. She said she was in the area and wanted to sign her son up for baseball lessons. I invited her inside while I dug up the brochure with coaching and pricing options. Next thing I know, your mother is calling me. That's all it was Taylor."

My arms were folded across my chest. I stood as he sat. His flimsy, impuissant stories worsened and worsened with his declining sense of reality.

"She had Maine plates Skyler. Who was she?"

"I don't know, Taylor."

"Show me one of the brochures you gave her. I've never seen a brochure for this place."

"I couldn't find any."

"Of course you couldn't."

I demanded he exposed her identity. I stood there, as still as a statue, glaring at the one human that could ignite happiness or shatter my walls with his words.

Skyler's voice became shaky as he pleaded for mercy. He stood, dragging his body towards mine, and resting his head on my shoulder.

"Please don't touch me," I said.

He wept into my chest, soaking my cleavage and the Bruins logo on my uniform. My arms were still folded, his— draped around my body. I refused to comfort him as he collapsed over me. This brought me the feeling of power. Cold hearts are very real. Mine, however, had frostbite.

Motionless, I repeated myself. "I said don't touch me."

Skyler broke into a wailing cry. He scurried back to the chair in the corner like a dog with its tail tucked between its legs. His manic outbursts were meaningless charades. When his fabricated stories failed him, he would resort to an emotional fit. It was all he had left, well besides the truth, but that was hardly an option for him.

I watched him shake back and forth, occasionally walloping his head against a nearby wall. He wasn't verbally remorseful in any way, but these performances were his way of begging for forgiveness.

"I asked you to handle each situation as if I were standing next to you. Would you do something if I could see what was going on? If you think it would upset me, you're probably right. I can't even repeat myself anymore.

I'm sick of hearing my own words. I'm ready for bed," I said totally exhausted.

Skyler nodded. "I don't want to hurt you. Ever."

I drove home with my mother. Skyler rode behind us. She asked me how it went. I told her I didn't believe him but I also didn't know how to tell him to pound sand. I wasn't ready to let him go, it was as simple as that. My heart wasn't fucking ready. Especially when he acted like the things he'd done never happened. It confused my run-down heart. I wasn't ready. My mother was beside herself. She wanted him gone. *I'm. Not. Ready.*

Skyler apologized to my mother via text message for the trouble he'd caused. She didn't like him anymore but she accepted the fact that my heart still clung to the love that occasionally surfaced. Christmas came and went. Skyler got me a dozen roses and reminded me a dozen more times how much he hated spending money on things that died. I made him a scrapbook of our journey together. Photos, baseball game tickets from around the country, hotel room keys, movie ticket receipts, and much more. One week later we packed our lives into bins and bags once again in preparation for our departure to Georgia. The plan was to drive to Skyler's parents' house, spend a week with his family, and then venture down to Florida for our second spring training together— his sixth or seventh. I don't even know anymore. I stopped counting. I barely wanted to go. This spring training we would be staying with the host family because neither of us could afford our own place and my parents had lost all interest in helping this relationship. We accepted our invitation to stay with a college acquaintance of Skyler's. The family with four children and three dogs, yes.

"I'd like to leave early tomorrow morning for Georgia," Skyler barked as he covered his bins in masking tape. He was anxious to get on the road for reasons that did not exist.

"We are getting a blizzard tomorrow into Saturday. We should plan to leave to Sunday instead. The roads will be fine on Sunday."

Anything to prolong our departure. This snow was a gift from above.

"Then we will leave tonight instead. We will beat the snow."

"I'm hardly packed!" I cried.

"Get to packin' then."

He popped an Adderall and washed it down with a glass of chocolate milk.

"This'll keep me going all night."

I looked at him with repugnance.

"Don't worry about me, worry about gettin' your bags packed. Hell, I'll leave withoutcha."

"You're an asshole," I grieved.

"Let's keep it to one suitcase this year. We don't have room for all of your nonsense."

"This is ridiculous. You're rushing out of here so we can go punch the time clock with your parents. You're so rude to me. Your wonderful parents always seem to bring out the best in you."

"Yup! Spending the weekend with them because they will be at work all week. They have a real job, unlike you."

"God forbid they take time off to see you. I'm so glad we came back to this, Skyler. This really seems to be working well for us."

Fuming, Skyler grabbed some bins and began loading the truck. I grabbed my notebook and knelt down on my bedroom floor to write a letter in hopes it would calm me down. Writing was my crutch, always.

My love for Skyler was just about spent. Something inside me kept me from leaving, though I hadn't yet deciphered what it was. The wick that once lit our love had burned down. I don't know why he held on either. He looked at me like I was his enemy, he spoke to me as if I was irrelevant, and he used my body for emotionless sex. He was just the stranger that fucked me. I was his ghost. My preferences, opinions, and desires meant nothing to him. He led me to believe that I would be no good on my own. I was afraid to be alone. That's the truth. I was afraid of a muted world. A phone that would not ring. A room with nobody but myself in it. That is fear. I was going to Fort Myers because I was not brave enough to say goodbye to what was breaking me. He couldn't be trusted on his own. I must be present. I must hunt as much truth as I can. If I do not go, I will ache. I will starve and I will spend every waking second of my days prowling truth. I will go mad. I fear that kind of pain.

The snow had started. Skyler cursed as he hurled bags of baseball equipment into the bed of his truck. I went outside to discuss the current forecast with my disgruntled boyfriend.

"You ready? We have to leave now. It's snowing bad. We gotta go."

"Skyler we can't drive in this. We'll get there when we get there."

"We're leaving now. Or at least I am."

"Damnit Skyler we can leave Sunday. All this aggravation just to spend an extra two days in Georgia. We aren't driving through a blizzard. What for? To sit at your parents' house all week eating cereal and binge watching trashy TV shows *alone*. This is insane! Invite them to visit you during the season. I will lose my *shit* if I spend a full week with those selfish people!"

The light in my neighbor's bedroom window had turned on and a shadow appeared near the shades. My screams were deafening. I didn't care who heard me. I wasn't driving to Georgia tonight. Skyler dropped his final bag on the pavement in my driveway and turned all of his attention towards me.

"What the fuck did you just call my parents?"

His gaze was toxic. I took a step back, leaving ample room between us for my protection. My breath traveled through the freezing air in front of me as I panted. My hands had tremors and I shivered uncontrollably. Not because I was cold, because I wasn't at all, but because I was livid. In nothing but sweatpants, a t-shirt, and ankle socks, I didn't feel winter at all.

Skyler picked up the bag. "I'm leaving without you."

I dove for the bag, pulling it backwards so he couldn't load it into the truck. My heart was beating right out of my chest. I was asking for trouble at this point. I wanted him to hurt me.

"Stop! Please! Stop! Just fucking stop!" I screamed. I screamed so much I started to lose my voice. I was crying. I was rampant. I was out of control. I was pushing and yanking and pulling and unloading the things from the truck bed whenever I had an opportunity.

"Get the fuck away from me, Taylor! You fucking nut! I'm leaving!"

I latched onto the hood of his Portland Sea Dogs sweatshirt, the one I usually wore to bed while he was on the road, and attempted to pull him away from the truck. I sobbed. My vision was unclear. I looked like a wacko, I'll admit it, but my actions were caused out of extreme passion.

"I said get the *fuck* away from me!" he yelled in my face. He grabbed both of my forearms, digging his fingernails deep into my flesh until there was blood. His grip was so tight making the pain unbearable. I begged him to stop. I told him it hurt.

"How does that feel?" he asked.

I cried for help through a flood of tears. Tears that had fallen from anger were now tears of actual pain. The more I begged, the tighter his grip became on my arms.

Then, suddenly, he used all of the strength baseball had given him to send me spiraling down onto the frozen ground. My body skidded across the frosty remnants of dead grass and barrel rolled through ice and dirt. It didn't hurt at the time, but wow did I feel worthless. Messy, relentless me brought myself to my feet. Skyler was repacking the items I'd taken out, completely unaware of my wounds. I cried my way back up to the driveway in my muddy socks. My arms were bleeding, as were my shins. Blood stained my clothes. I limped through the snow like the zombie I was. I limped right back to him.

"The two of you! Inside now!" My mother's voice echoed from the front door. Skyler entered the house first and sat down on my bed— eyes closed and all. I followed. My mother gasped when she saw me in the light.

"Taylor! What happened!" I continued to my bedroom without saying a word. I couldn't speak. I had no words. My breath was abnormally rapid when my knees met the floor in the center of my room. I was used to begging for help from the floor. I was inches from Skyler. He gripped his keys and lay there with his eyes closed as I panted for dear life. I prayed aloud for help. Shaking, I begged the man above to save me. *Please! Somebody! Anybody! Help me! Take me away! I can't do this! Why is this happening? I don't know what to do anymore! I can't handle this pain anymore! I'm not strong enough! Make it stop!*

"Taylor," My mom was standing in the doorway. "What's going on?"

I pointed at Skyler and erupted. *"Him! It's fucking him!"*

I jumped to my feet and grabbed the first object in sight. My large [sharp] makeup container. I fired the whole damn thing at him. Lipsticks and eyeshadow pallets went flying as he dodged the massive box.

"Taylor!" my mother screamed. She called for my dad who was in the kitchen. It was too late. Nobody could save this; me. I was already gone. My mind that is— it was fucking gone. I snapped. I turned back to my bureau grabbing glass picture frames that held photos of us at different ballparks and discharged them at his face. They were square with razor-sharp edges. I intended to damage him. The frames hit walls leaving gashes in the paint and shattered glass covered the bed where he had been laying.

My dad arrived at the sound of disaster. Skyler stood in place next to my mess.

"What the hell is going on in here?" my dad questioned.

"I fucking hate his parents! That's all he cares about! He doesn't care about me! I can't live like this I really can't! I hate him!" I bawled through my words.

"Then let him go Taylor! Just let him go!" yelled my dad.

"Alright. I'm done with this bullshit," Skyler announced as he pushed by my parents. His reaction was normal. He always left me when there was a problem. Nobody stopped him. The house shook when the front door slammed and all was silent for a moment. I listened to the bubbling of the exhaust when the truck started. I listened as the noise disappeared down the road. He'll be back. He always came back. My suitcase sat open on the floor spilling with clothes made for warmer weather. I was calm when he left. I regained human consciousness and found my breath amidst the mess I had made. My parents were stunned. I sat on the foot of my bed across from my vanity so I'd be able to stare at my reflection in the mirror. I wore a pink, marbled sadness across my flush skin's surface. A permanent frown; a pout. Inflamed eyelids that matched in color to a goblet of Merlot with eyes greener than the fresh cut grass in centerfield on a July morning. My sweet reflection, we met again in the loneliest of times. I promised my counterpart in the glass that we would find our composure shortly. I waited for his return.

An hour passed. And then two. I called Skyler from my bed. No answer. I called again. No answer. I called him three more times. Nothing. *Did this fucker actually leave without me?* I called again.

"Stop calling me Taylor. You're messing with my GPS."

"*Skyler!*" I was surprised he answered. "Where are you?"

"Uh, I don't know. New York I think. Hard to tell. The snow is pretty bad. I gotta go."

"You seriously left without me?"

"Yes. I couldn't deal with you anymore. I had to get on the road."

"Are you kidding me? You're just going to leave me here like this. Skyler come back."

"Taylor I've been driving for over two hours. I'm long gone. You had your chance. You can fly to Florida next week. You should be happy. You got what you wanted. Now you don't have to see my family."

He hung up. I called him back. No answer. I called him another seventeen times as I drenched myself in tears. I cried aloud. I didn't care who heard me. I just wanted to talk to him. I continued to stare at myself in the mirror.

My chapped lips held chattering teeth. I could not refrain from staring at the unfortunate sucker looking back at me with a cell phone pressed against her face. *You sad fucking thing, you.* I hated myself. I called him again anyway.

Skyler got a week at home in Georgia with his family. I got a Pomeranian puppy. Yup, you read that correctly. I was at war with severe anxiety, depression, and self-destructive thoughts. My presence here on earth was lessening and I prayed to anyone that would listen: *How can I take my life back?* I spent hours on the internet researching Skyler's behavioral traits. Certainly I wasn't the only one facing these challenges with a partner. Skyler, very much an introvert, held zero friendships and avoided public conversation. He was private and secretive and lacked basic social skills. A narcissist, someone who was all about thyself, matched Skyler's qualities like no other. He was unable to enter civilization until his hair was gelled to perfection, used every curse word in the book if his cowlick was misbehaving, and allowed bacon neck to ruin his day. What's bacon neck, you ask? The wrinkly neckline of a stretched out t-shirt otherwise resembling a slice of cooked bacon.

And then an eight-week-old blue Pomeranian was delivered to my house. I've told every boyfriend I've ever had that my dream pup was a Pomeranian. One of my exes even bought his new girlfriend a Pomeranian. *You're welcome.* Pom's were *my* thing! And here she was. Smelling like dry pee and dog food, my saving grace had arrived. All three pounds of her. I just didn't think Skyler would be the son of a bitch who would answer my prayers. My mom handed me an envelope during the dog's arrival at my house. I opened the card:

Taylor, we have been through too much to let our love go to waste. You are my everything. Here is a little something you've always wanted. I'm sure she will keep you company down here in Florida. Can't wait to see you and meet our little girl. Cheers to starting a family of our own. I love you more than anything. — Skyler

"I can't believe he bought me a Pomeranian," I said to my mother.

"I bought her. He didn't want his mother to see the transaction in his bank account so he gave me the money and I bought her. He knew she'd be upset if he spent big money on a dog. Especially a dog for you. I paid for her shipping too." She was bitter. She didn't want me to go to Florida. I told her it was imperative I go, for my well being of course. She listened. Against her judgment and against her will, she let me go. Knowing there were a million other things I could have been doing to better myself, she let me go. Knowing I hadn't finished school, she let me go. Knowing I barely had any money, she let me go. Knowing he wasn't the one for me, she let me go. I wonder what it was like to watch your broken child, your baby, crawl back to the man who was killing her. My poor mother. I knelt down on the ground to see my new ball of fuzz. I am not a bias dog mom, but she was the most beautiful angel in the world.

"What should I call you?" I whispered to her sweet, stinky face.

She popped a squat on the carpet and peed. The stain was the size of a quarter. It was the cutest thing I'd ever seen.

"How about... hm... I'm trying to think of baseball related names. Sox, Louisville, Chandler, Nike, Homer, Cleat, Stitch, Fenway. They all sound so masculine. I don't know."

"Don't name her anything that has to do with baseball," my mother said sternly.

"Why not?"

"Because how terrible will it be to have a dog with a baseball oriented name after you guys break up? Explain that to your next boyfriend or future husband."

"Mom."

"Just saying. Awkward."

17

*B*lu. I named her Blu. Blu the blue Pomeranian. And today I learned that baby Blu is not a fan of airport security. She clung to the insides of her carrier like there was no tomorrow as impatient travelers huffed and puffed behind me. The line, a complete halt, all because of us. Talk about sweaty armpits. New mom traveling alone here, excuse us. All the excitement at TSA knocked her out and she slept her way to Fort Myers, Florida.

My heart was ready to see Skyler. I missed him. I also couldn't wait to introduce him to our Blu, our muffin cakes. She was incredibly aware, highly intelligent, and ridiculously funny. An unmatched personality for sure. Also, I'm positive she understood the English language but I'll get into that another time.

Touching down in Fort Myers was bittersweet. The tropical climate filled the aircraft on the tarmac. Inevitably I was escaping New England's worst winter to date. But

I was actually just escaping reality, the reality of facing much needed change. Sure my parched, flaking skin could use some Vitamin D, but I didn't belong here. My mind knew that much. When I think of Fort Myers I think of unsolved truths and emotional pain. But here I am, in a sundress, promenading down the same path and expecting a different outcome.

"My girls!" I heard Skyler's voice from afar. He was tan and muscular, wearing sunglasses and a backwards hat. His arms made the sleeves of his t-shirt beg for dear life. His ass, ready to split his shorts in half at the seem. He looked delicious.

"Hey babe," he said as he greeted me with an embrace. "I missed you."

"Bluuuuu! I finally get to meet my Blu bear." He tapped on her carrier.

"She's going to love the weather down here. I'm excited to get her outside," I said.

Having a dog in the baseball world was a necessity. Everyone had a dog and some had a dog and a baby. It's a lonely journey for us baseball girls. The more company the merrier. I'm not sure if Skyler bought Blu as a necessity to make it appear that all was well in our relationship or if he actually wanted to fulfill my ultimate puppy dream. Either way, I wasn't complaining.

Little Blu stretched her chicken legs and walked her way through the airport on the leash. When the automatic doors opened to the outside world and the balmy, Florida breeze found my face, I was met with energized hope.

There was something about the grass in Southern Florida; thick and durable. The birds; noisier than anything, practically inviting you into their humid habitat. Blu found new sounds everywhere.

My family of three boarded Big Red in the parking lot and we drove ten minutes down the road to the host family's house. They lived minutes from training camp at JetBlue Park, not to mention it was free. The family of six and three dogs lived in a private community. We settled into their home while the parents were at work and the children were at school. The bedroom we were given belonged to the eldest daughter. She was eight. Her lime green walls were covered in mermaids and her bed, a stuffed animal sanctuary. Skyler set up a pen at the foot of the bed for Blu and we placed her inside for a snooze.

"I need to put shorts on," I said.

Skyler pushed me backwards onto the bed.

"No need," he said as he crawled onto the mattress to join me. "Take this dress off."

I hurriedly slipped myself out of the sundress. I lay there in nothing but my thong and sticky boobs.

"Take this off," he said as he tugged at my bra.

I obeyed. Just like every other girl had obeyed him once before. The inhalation and exhalation of his breath grew deep and heavy. He had me pinned on my back.

"I missed you," he whispered through his panting.

"I missed you too."

His fingers pushed my undies to one side leaving my vagina susceptible to receive whatever he chose to give me. His finger of choice manipulated my figure with each stroke of my clitoris. My body was his possession.

I grabbed handfuls of the little girl's starfish-covered comforter. I knocked our fictitious audience of sea creatures off the bed with each pulsate. Down he went. I shut my eyes to fully appreciate the way his tongue felt against my inside walls. I didn't get this as often as I'd like.

He tasted me. Periodically inserting a finger or two, my build would spasm, sending me into a frenzy of enlightenment. Ecstasy. Euphoria. Everlasting paradise. Call it what you wish. Nipping, caressing, swallowing. He missed me alright. My figure would elongate to find heaven and then it would release itself in the form of rapids. I refused to be still. All at once, my insides succumbed to him in fluid form. My devotion to him had never been more alive. *Fuck, I love this man.* He sampled a taste of the liquid melting out of my labia before using this velvety lubricant to cart his erection into my body. I didn't know when our relationship would end, but I certainly found ways to enjoy the process.

The host family welcomed us and Blu with arms wide open though their household had its own kind of mayhem. I intended to reconcile our broken bond; our broken hearts. We were broken people coexisting together because the universe refused to stop and wait for lost souls. Broken for different reasons. He, from a distorted sense of love during his upbringing coupled with a seemingly unattainable future. I, a product of his broken pieces. He created this version of me that I am not so proud to share with the world. But here I am— the result of his damaged goods, and together we clash at the mere thought of farewell.

It finally felt like spring training when I had to drive Skyler to the field at the break of dawn with Blu in my lap. The air was chilly and the sky looked like coal. He still chose to be the first one to the field which, for me, meant rolling out of bed at the last second and throwing a sweatshirt over my t-shirt to shelter my pointy, contracted nipples. Day one of spring training meant physical examination day. Height, weight, body fat, peeing in a cup to make sure you're only abusing the legal drugs. The whole nine yards.

I reached across the center console to cup Skyler's balls.

"What are you doing!" he cried. He was still half asleep.

"Cough for me. I'm preparing you for the ballsack exam today. Cough!"

"Taylor. Really?"

"Cough!"

Ahem.

"Feels good to me," I said.

The temperature outside would rise by the time I'd exited the player parking lot, forcing me to part ways with the hoodie. The outline of the soundless ballpark greeted the peach skies at daybreak. I'd purchase a coffee that would be savored on the lanai of our temporary home. It overlooked a pond and it was the finest silence I'd known. I did a lot of thinking out there. After my cup emptied, I'd find sandals and walk Blu before the pavement began to sear. I'd complete laundry, tidy our borrowed bedroom, or familiarize myself with the aisles of the new grocery store.

I had come to Florida on a one way ticket. The Bruins would play five home games this month— February. I attended four games before leaving Boston. I was not scheduled to work the fifth game. The next game I'd have to work was on the third of March. Spring training was over at the end of March. *Should I quit the Ice Girl's and stay for spring training? How will I be without him for a month?*

My mom gave me two-hundred dollars when I left home. She told me to make it last. She said if I ran out of money, it would be my indication to come home.

"How was testing?" I asked as Skyler climbed back into the truck with hair wet from his shower. Baseball life; a bad, echoing chorus to a never ending song.

"Exhausting. I had strength and endurance testing today too. They said I look great."

"So they were happy with your off-season workouts?"

"Yeah. I need a nap."

Spring training brought two things to its trainees: extreme fatigue and harsh t-shirt tans. I knew Skyler was consumed with the mind games this political game brought him. I knew his days would get longer and the sun, hotter as time went on. I knew this wasn't a vacation. But I also knew that in order to patch the gaping cracks in our love, he'd have to be willing to try.

"What do you say we head to the beach this afternoon? Before your days get long. We can introduce Blu to the ocean."

"Taylor. We've talked about this. I hate the beach."

"We don't have to stay long. Please. I'd love to see Blu's reaction to the ocean."

"You've had all day to go without me."

"Please Skyler."

"Whatever. Drive."

We hit traffic on the single bridge that carries you to Fort Myers Beach. I cringed when I saw brake lights knowing the influx of cars would anger him.

"Damnit Taylor. We should have just gone home. I don't wanna sit in this shit."

"It's moving," I assured him.

"It ain't moving."

Alas we made it to white sand. Skyler was quiet; still irritated from the traffic. Blu however, was in her glory. She galloped through the sand. She dug. She buried her face in it. I brought her to the edge of the Gulf of Mexico to wet her paws. She ran from the tide as it swept the shoreline and chased it back out as it returned home. Skyler watched from a towel on the ground.

I craved so badly an interaction that I couldn't find with Skyler. No matter what we did, together or apart, our conversations were dull and obligatory. Sometimes I felt like his roommate. A slave to his needs; a housekeeper for his temper.

I posted pictures on social media against Skyler's wishes. Of us. Of me. Of Blu. He didn't want me in connection with the world. I tagged my location. I continued to lie to my followers about our happiness. My images misrepresented our reality and everyone, *everyone* loved us.

Our housing community had a pool for its members. I'd douse myself in oil after a morning walk with Blu to roast under a powerful sun. The sound of the pools filter and a decent read made me feel like I was far, far away without a single problem to worry about. Skyler came home more exhausted and less enthused about my presence each afternoon. I need money for groceries. *Not my problem, ask your mother. I can't pay for two.* Walk Blu with me. *Do it yourself, you've had all day.* Let's drive out to Sanibel Island. *Are you putting gas in the truck?* I'm going for a run. *You need to gain weight, not lose it.* I'm starving. *Get a job, you'll be here almost a month. Pay your way.*

Why did you wear shorts to my game? Did you curl your hair to get attention? Why did you wear a push-up bra today? Why are you biting your nails? Why did you fold my shirts like this? Why did you touch my phone? Why don't you work? Why did you take your phone into the bathroom when you were showering? Why did you talk to your mom for forty-two minutes today? Why do you take pictures of everything? Why didn't you put gas in the truck? What took you so long to answer my text? Why do you hold your fork like that? Why are you tired? Why did you make the bed like that? Why don't you cut my nails for me anymore? Why are you eating on my side of the bed? Why are you in a good mood?

Each time he cut me down or left me to fend for myself, I felt a little less for him. For too long I had been attacked; pummeled by his careless words and actions.

The easiest way for a spineless wimp to disguise their guilt is by making someone else feel guilty. Try to at least. My ability to feel had frozen over some time ago. I'd been numb for too long but my feet were always planted in the soil amongst the frontline of our battles. I would have fought forever if he'd let me.

Our time together had clearly expired. Our story was dead. It was time I let it perish. I had to close this chapter. I had to. I could not waste away like I had been, hiding out in ballfields like this life was a treasure. I was a grain of sand. I had been pushed around in many directions and I had seen many places. I had touched, and been touched by, beautiful people from all over the world. I was unique, containing many dents, but carrying stories within me that would someday revolutionize the way we give love. This is my flare gun; my SOS. I am not enough for him. I am too whole; too alive. I must jump ship. I will swim through storms until I reach home. Anywhere is safer than here. He was my everything until today. Today, he is nothing. It happened just like that. I refuse to carry this mountain of abuse on my back another day longer. I have been pushed to no return. I have been thrown out of love.

I plotted our goodbye in secrecy. On Valentine's Day, he bought me a luxurious bouquet of roses. I was malnourished but I now had roses. The thought of deserting him made me come alive. I would blindside him; escaping our mess while he was not there to save himself. He doesn't think I'm strong. He doesn't think I'll leave. Watch me.

I kissed him good morning and goodnight each day as I designed my escape. I told him I loved him. I played his game. He couldn't see the end but I could.

I told my mother that Blu and I needed to come home. She asked if I was alright and then found me a flight. There was nothing left for me to explain; she already knew. I was ready to let go. I finally met the day my tired heart decided it couldn't love him anymore. I woke up one day, grated by neglect and damage, and I was done. I wanted to *feel* again.

My flight to Boston was on a Friday. I packed as much as I could into my suitcase on Thursday while Skyler played a doubleheader. I left some things behind for the night so Skyler wouldn't notice how empty the closet was when he got home and then I put the suitcase back where it had always been. Ellie, a fellow Massachusetts native and Red Sox WAG, would drive me to the airport in the morning while the boys were at the field. I'd pack the rest of my belongings into a cardboard box in the morning for Ellie to mail home. Skyler would return to an empty room, if he was able to find a ride home that was.

A Cadillac from 1995 led us in a slow moving line of cars to Skyler's favorite café on the way to the field. Southwestern Florida was heavily populated and full of retired folk and their town cars. There was always traffic. Skyler got an iced coffee, a breakfast sandwich, and a muffin every Friday morning. I've never had anything from the café. He never asked.

"Can I get something today?" I asked shyly.

"I told you I can't support two."

"Right. I know. Sorry."

My belly grumbled. I put my hands on my hip bones that protruded through my clothing. I was so thin. I held back tears as we drove silently into the player parking lot. He thinks he will see me this afternoon. This is the last time we will see each other. He put the truck in park and leaned over for a kiss. My throat was sore with pain.

"Have a good day." I yelled as he headed for the entrance of the minor league clubhouse.

"Love you. See you later," he waved back.

I climbed into the driver's seat like I'd done many times before. Today would be my last. I burst into tears. We had shared our last kiss. Doubt swarmed my mind. *Change can be good. You're due for change. You need this.* I talked to myself as I drove back to the host family's house. I loved him more than I loved myself but he didn't deserve to occupy space in my life anymore. Melancholy descended over my heart. It ached so much I thought it might burst.

I got into our unmade bed with Blu when I returned home. I laid on Skyler's side with my nose pressed against his pillow. I held it tight as if it were him. I would never smell him on the sheets again. I soaked the linens with delicate tears. Blu licked the sadness from my face. Her little toes smelled of pine needles and Fritos.

Two hours later I was standing in the airport. I did it. I was calm and I was terrified but I knew I had to get on this plane. Our mermaid room at the host family's house was near vacant. I was certain he would notice my decision to part as soon as he entered. It rained on our last day of spring training last season and today, my last day, rain again. Like New England hail, this heavy rain made the pavement smell like a long, lost friend. Fort Myers, a temporary home on our list of temporary homes, would always have a piece of me. I peered out the window as my flight left the ground. My stomach had knots and I wanted to cry. I looked down at the roads, the palm trees, and the backyard pools that I could see from the sky. My heart reminisced about the rare journey I had been given. I'm not sure I'll ever see you again, Fort Myers. And into the clouds we went.

When I landed in Boston, I expected to be flooded with messages from Skyler. *Where the fuck are you? How could you leave me? You ruin everything.* But there was none of that.

Skyler: My mom sent me a screenshot of the picture you posted yesterday. Enjoy the creepy dudes who leave comments on your pictures. They can have you. I'm done with you.

Hold up. I was supposed to be dumping *him*. Why didn't he ask about the empty room?

Taylor: Sue me. I posted a selfie. How about the fact that I'm *gone?*

Skyler: Going to bed. Can't deal with this. I don't need this.

Taylor: Don't bullshit me you aren't going to bed.

Skyler: Sleeping. Early morning. Bye.

Taylor: Can you fucking stop?
Skyler: No. You dumped me. Let me sleep.

Blu and I met my parents at baggage claim. I pretended to be happy, for them. I should have just ignored him. Why couldn't I ignore him? In the backseat of my parents car, I texted our host mother whom I'd developed a wonderful bond with.

Taylor: Meg, I'll be up all night if I don't say something. First I wanted to thank you for welcoming me into your home and into your family. I love you all so much. I left Florida today. I wish I could have said goodbye to you all. Skyler and I haven't been doing well and I thought it would be best if I leave. It has been a long time coming. He told me he was home sleeping right now. I'm sure he won't be honest about why I left anyway.

Meg: Hi Taylor. Skyler isn't home— hasn't been all day. I've been in your position before. I totally get it. I applaud you for doing what is best for you. Get out while you can before it's too late. Before you bring children and a house into the picture if you get what I'm saying. Keep in touch. We all love you very much and we support you.

I called Skyler. No answer. I texted him:

Taylor: Meg said you haven't been home all day.

I cried quietly in my bed, but on Skyler's side of my bed. This bed made me feel safe but the escape from my relationship was much harder than I imagined. I woke in the middle of the night to a text message. My phone lay next to my hand in the sheets.

Skyler: I'm home you psycho. I've been sleeping this whole time. Going back to bed now. Night!

Attached was a picture of himself. He was laying on top of the mermaid bedspread, eyes droopy and bloodshot. I was still wondering why he hadn't mentioned the fact that I deserted him?

Taylor: You look really sober. Nice.

18

Like the smoking of a gun, the dangers our love had caused us were over, however I struggled deeply with my decision to part. I loved him out of habit and habits take time to break. Nobody called me. Nobody texted. I was alone as an individual for the first time in a long time and it was frightening. Who would I share my day with? I dabbled with the thought of going back to Fort Myers, that maybe I had made a mistake, that I wasn't ready for this change. The truth is I was vulnerable. I needed to rebuild my strength. I needed to detach myself and I owed myself the time to do so.

The ferocity at which I choose to love is extreme. I love you completely or I'll never love you again. After twenty-one days, my soul would free itself. I was sure of that. My insides determined overnight that I needed to cut any and all ties with him. Don't answer his drunken phone calls. Don't entertain his regretful messages. Send him on his merry way for good. My notebook was now my only companion. My stunning savior. I would write my way out of this darkness.

Twenty-One Days Freed

Day 1: I flew home from Florida today with our puppy. You got mad about a picture I posted. You're lying to me right now. You told me you were in bed. You aren't even home. How drunk are you? My heart is burning. I've only been gone for a few hours. Already? I'll cry myself to sleep tonight and ignore the family I haven't seen in a month.

Day 2: All I can do is cry. My biggest priority is getting on the next flight to Florida so I can be in your presence. So I know you aren't with other women.

Day 3: We are barely speaking. Why do we hold onto something that is so far gone? Our love is nonexistent. Grant me the strength to walk away for good.

Day 4: Your brother and your cousin came to town to visit you today. They are there for the week on spring break. You haven't called once. Don't you miss the sound of my voice? Why don't you miss the sound of my voice? I wonder. That's all I can do. I'm barely eating. I'm so hungry. I touch my bones. I cry harder. I'm not hungry. You make it so hard for me to eat. I need to get on a plane.

Day 5: I wonder what time you've been falling asleep lately. Because I no longer know and that hurts me. I've tried to fix you for so long. Because I believe in helping the broken find their way home. I know you are a good person. And every time you've ever split apart, I was there, telling you we could withstand any storm. I need a plane ticket.

Day 6: I've cried. A lot. I've cried so hard that my mother has cried for me. I cannot speak to another human being without an unfortunate amount of trembling in my voice. My words collide. They don't make sense. You left me all alone. Damaged. Destroyed. Broken. Sadness pours from my expressions. The squint of my forehead. The nightmare in my gaze. It's so obvious. My mom says she's worried about me. I can't eat. I'm shaking and starving but I won't eat. I can't. I'll be sick. I need to get on a plane.

Day 7: I know you don't love me. I've known for a while, but it's clearer than ever right now. I told myself every day that I needed a plane ticket. I never booked one. I couldn't do that to myself. I don't want my head to hurt anymore. My belongings have been mailed home from Florida. I won't have to speak to you again.

Day 8: I don't need a plane ticket today. Or tomorrow; ever. I will not be coming back to you. I don't want to be in Florida. Alone. Watching you play that selfish game that makes a mess of your mind. Begging you for money to eat is degrading. You'd get coffee and a breakfast sandwich on the way to the field. Afraid of your reaction, I'd softly ask you to get me one, too. You would yell at me every time. There was hardly any food at the house. I wanted you to care about me. You showed me you had no interest in that. Why wasn't my love enough to carry both of us?

Day 9: My belongings should be here any day now. You no longer hold any reason to see my face again. I'm so glad I'll never see your face again. Why did I ever want a plane ticket?

Day 10: I said goodbye to you that morning before you went to the field. The man I've loved wholeheartedly for the past two years kissed me goodbye without knowing it. I never thought we'd have our last kiss. You stripped me of everything I once was and now I feel like I am incapable of greatness. You made a fool out of me.

Day 11: I told you I couldn't keep up with our half-assed communication any longer. You didn't fight it. You didn't argue. You didn't even try to change my mind. You did nothing to prevent me from walking out of your life once and for all. You practically held the door open for me. You said "If that's what you want" and then you were gone. I felt free. The knots in my stomach loosened almost immediately. Was I sad? Well, all endings are sad. Passion doesn't disappear overnight. A beautiful lesson built upon lies had finally lost its grip.

Day 12: During the day, I am OK. I promise you this. I keep busy. My mind has to stay occupied. The second I get a moment to myself, though, the truth creeps up on me. *Nights*. Nights are the worst. They seem to get harder and harder every time I lay my head on the pillow. You've spent many nights on this exact pillow. I lose myself in the silence. You chase me down in my dreams. When I lay on my left side and doze off, my body will jolt. For a split second I can feel your warm body laying behind me. You are against me in that moment. You are here. I'm happy. And then I'm awake again. I'm alone in these memories. It makes me cry so hard. I cry out for you. Can you hear me?

Day 13: I'm dying inside. Part of me stayed with you on the day I decided to leave you. I don't think I'll ever get that missing piece back. I wish you could understand what you've done to me. In the mornings, I sip coffee in my bathrobe. My swollen eyes are tired and they would like to go back to sleep. I don't have anything to do today. I might as well go back to sleep. My mother is so worried about me. I can't tell our story without crying. I'm still waiting on the strength I've been praying for.

Day 14: Have you ever cried so hard you received nothing but a splitting headache in return? One that Ibuprofen couldn't even take away? My hands; always shaking. My heart is split open. I am bleeding out, Skyler. I can't breathe out of my nose. Why did you do this to me? I told you I would stay forever. I still would.

Day 15: I started to clean out your closet today. I held one of your dress shirts up to my nose to smell you again. It brought me back to the night I laid my head against your chest and together we slow danced in the night. I began to cry and closed the door. Too soon, I suppose. Each shirt held a certain memory, a restaurant, a city, a promotion, or an argument. My hands are not ready to touch our past.

Day 16: I didn't cry last night. You made a new Twitter account today. I realized it while I was eating dinner. I immediately dropped my fork, had explosive diarrhea, and crawled into my bed. I don't eat when I'm upset. You remember, don't you? You followed all the women you've cheated on me with. You knew I would see. You got what you wanted, Skyler.

Day 17: I'm learning to live without you. My spirit seems to make appearances here and there. You met me when I was just a teen. I was the most confident girl in the world. I was Miss Teen Massachusetts for fucks sake! I don't see my own beauty anymore. Where has that girl gone? Why did you take her from me? Why must this get worse before it gets better?

Day 18: My box of clothes arrived from Florida today. It was a big box. Crazy how much I over pack, right? My brother carried it to my room for me. That box signified the end. The *real* end. I sliced the tape with scissors. A familiar fragrance entered the room. It was the detergent we used. I picked up the first shirt I saw and sat on my bed with it. I used to fish in this shirt at the pond in the backyard. It smells like you. It smells like us. It smells like the time we spent together; our last time together. It smells like Fort Myers. And it reminds me of the last time I saw your face in Cypress Cay Park. There are stones in my throat. Why do I feel like you passed away? I can't unpack my things today.

Day 19: I need to unpack the box. So, I did. With every pair of shorts I tucked away, I was another step closer to my new beginning. I took a shower to stare at my tan lines. I wanted to be alone with my thoughts in case I shed a few more tears. I doused my skin in sugar scrub. I watched suds run down the drain. Your touch washed away in the form of soapy water.

Day 20: I feel you fading with my sunburn. My days no longer feel like I'm carrying burden in my chest. I am not afraid today. I am alive, without you. I will survive.

Day 21: They say it takes twenty-one days to make or break a habit. I was convinced I couldn't live without you. I never wanted to imagine a day without you by my side. But it just required me being away from you long enough to realize you are nothing but waste. Some days are harder than others, of course. But I made it. Thank you for neglecting me so much that I was forced to befriend myself again. Without you Skyler, I will change the world. Watch.

— A Heart That Once Loved You

Operation *Take Back My Life* was in full swing. I finished an incredible season with the Ice Girls, graduated with a degree in criminal justice, and was offered a job as a reporter on New England's number one sporting network. When the end of March finally rolled around, I thought of Skyler. I wondered if he'd finally start a season in Triple A. I knew he'd think of me when he returned to my stomping grounds up north.

On what was the last day of spring training, as I joined my mother in the kitchen for breakfast, my phone rang. It was Skyler.

"I'm not answering it," I said aloud.

"Answer it!" she said. "See what he has to say."

"Hello?" I said apprehensively.

"Well my life couldn't get any worse," he started. He was bawling. I hadn't heard from him in weeks.

"What's wrong?"

"I hurt my leg at the end of spring training. I've been rehabbing for the past week. I was just packing up the things in my locker when one of the managers called me into his office. The Red Sox released me, Taylor. Now I have nothing. I lost you. I lost my job. I lost my dream! I'm not getting any younger Taylor. I live in my parent's basement. I have no education. I refuse to go back to school. How will I make money? Baseball is all I know. How will I pay my bills? My truck payment is due next week. My pills are almost gone! My life is over Taylor. I should have never went to the team doctor. This is why you can't be honest about injuries. You become baggage. I'm so stupid!"

Skyler was beside himself. The Red Sox gave him reason to belong. They made him feel comfortable and safe. They had been all he's known for so long. Now, with no backup plan, his life had been turned upside down. Nobody said facing the unknown was easy. I heard pain and I heard fear through the phone. I imagined this is what I sounded like to him many times before. How he shut me out when I called crying for help. I had no words to give Skyler. I supported his dream since the day we first met but today, I did not care about his troubles.

"I don't know what to say Skyler. I'm sorry. Another team could pick you up. I wish you the best," I said before hanging up.

I took a deep breath.

"Everything alright?" my curious mother questioned.

"They released him."

"Are you serious?" she asked.

"Yep. I was the first person he called. If we thought he was bad before, this will definitely take him to new levels. He will crash and burn for sure now. God bless anyone that crosses his path."

Skyler was forced to drive home to Georgia the day he was released while his teammates and friends traveled to their new homes for the season. For the next two consecutive days, he called me over and over again sobbing; begging me to press the reset button on our relationship. He would gag on the tears in his throat as I listened. I never ignored him but I never had much to say. I was just there. *Please let me come see you. I just want to talk. I can make this right. I'll drive to you right now. I don't want to be in Georgia.* He'd leave me voicemails at all hours of the night. No words; just him crying into the phone.

On the third day there was silence. I didn't hear from him at all. His excessive sob sessions vanished into thin air. I didn't ask him where he'd gone. I figured he'd moved on. That he met someone on social media to occupy his needs. He wasn't my problem anymore. I wasn't even worried about him.

That was until a big, red Silverado appeared in front of my house. I heard his truck before I could see him. The prick drove here all the way from Georgia. He never liked New England and its cold climates but today, on this bitter March day, he found reason to be here. I was mortified. My family gave me the *Who invited this guy?* look. I didn't think he would ever drive here, but it was now my responsibility to handle him.

I approached the truck with Georgia tags on the passenger side. For a moment in my mind we were happy, leaving a late night horror flick in Portland, discussing how shitty the ending was. Flashbacks are the worst.

"I'm sorry Taylor. I can't live without you. I'm sorry. I had to see you. I don't want to live if I can't have you," he said softly.

He spoke as if he were ashamed of himself for driving eighteen hours to share an encounter with me. He was determined to restart a life of our own without the pressure of baseball.

"Skyler you can't stay here."

He looked like shit. Like he had been crying through many sleepless nights. I used to photograph the way he made me look after a long night of crying to remind myself of the person I was dealing with.

"I know. I already talked to some of the guys at the DogPound. I'm staying with Craig until I can get a place of my own. I already got my job back too. I start tomorrow. Baseball made me someone I am not. I want to be the best man I can be for you. Now we can build a life together. The life you've always wanted for us."

Skyler had broken my heart a million times before but now it was my turn to break his. I didn't feel for him the way I once did. His words meant nothing to me. They just made me annoyed.

"This is... this is *crazy* that you're here," I began.

"I know. I know this is surprising and overwhelming and I can understand if you want some time to think things over. But I'll be ten minutes away whenever you're ready to talk about this. We can fix this Tay."

"I don't think time can fix this Skyler. I don't love you like I once did. It's too late."

"Just think about it. Call me when you're ready. I love you. I want this."

"Skyler."

"Yeah, babe?"

"Don't do that."

"Do what?"

"The whole babe thing."

As I climbed out of the truck, I noticed he hadn't even unpacked his clothing and equipment from spring training. His parents must really *love* me now.

From my understanding, Skyler's agent, who could never find him a deal on bats, worked tirelessly to find him a spot on an independent league baseball team. Independent ball was considered a professional organization that had no affiliation to major league or minor league ball. Playing independent ball would hopefully help him find placement in another minor league organization. Skyler taught baseball lessons eight minutes from my house. A month had passed since his release from the Red Sox and there were zero baseball opportunities on the forefront. Rosters were full, players were healthy and hungry, and I was sure his baseball career was over.

We spoke. Often. I didn't love him anymore but I felt responsible for his happiness, especially after he told me he was willing to shoot himself in the head over this.

I felt like I was the only thing keeping him alive. I asked him why he hurt me and he said he didn't know. I told him I couldn't be with him and he said he wouldn't have been able to live the rest of his days if he didn't come up here and at least try to make things right.

"I've felt like a microscopic piece of shit for the past five years. *Lost* in the minor leagues, just trying to earn a chance at a chance at a chance. The attention from the random women on the road reassured me. They made me feel important. I can't explain it."

Those were his words. The truth was that my love for him was never enough. He always needed something new; something more. And now he had nothing. I prayed every day that a baseball contract would present itself and the game would swallow him up far, far away once more. Skyler's time in Massachusetts was temporary; we both knew it deep inside our hearts. He would leave to chase a new dream with hopes I would follow. When the time of his departure came, I would tell him we would never see each other again. That we must travel down separate roads and pursue new hearts. That we are not meant for a love that only paralyzes ourselves. He will cry, and I might too, but our story will end there. The chapters prior to now will be so proud. They will clap for me and they will sing out with joy. I am determined to make magic out of my past.

Unbeknownst to Skyler I started dating again. I met a beautiful man that worked at a prison as a correctional officer who told me he wasn't looking for anything serious.

In fact, he barely had the decency to answer my text messages. Obviously I pursued him. I even got ready for our "dates" in Skyler's old baseball tees. I invested all of my time into the sheriff. He was my escape. He made me excited about life again. I wasn't necessarily looking for something serious either, but the chase occupied my broken heart.

Nearly two months after his release, Skyler was offered a position on an independent league team in St. Paul, Minnesota. He told me he would only accept the offer if I would move out there with him which forced this exact conversation.

"Skyler I can't love you anymore. I can't continue to take part in your journey. But I need you to go. I will never stand to be the reason you walked away from something you've wanted since you were a little boy. *Go.*"

"I can't do this without you," he said as he began to cry. "I'm so scared."

"A new beginning is exactly what you need. We both do."

"The distance will ruin whatever is left of us."

"If it is meant for us it will find us."

I lied through my teeth. I gave him false hope so he would move to Minnesota. Three days later, after some deep thought, Skyler signed with the St. Paul Saints in Minnesota. He was relieved that his baseball career had not completely folded. I was relieved that he would be moving far away from the state of Massachusetts.

My shaken heart was preoccupied with a man who had no intention of mending its bloody channels. Sheriff didn't know about my battle scars and surely he wouldn't care either. Sheriff was a personal retreat; a reason to pluck my brows and keep a well groomed pussy. I could leave reality behind when I was with him. I could live a false life.

On Skyler's last night in town before leaving for St. Paul, sheriff, who identifies as Matthew, purchased front row seats to a Red Sox game for the two of us. I was growing on Matt. I knew it because regardless of his words, he chose to spend the majority of his time with me. I escaped to the game that once brought me so much misery, but tonight, brought me internal happiness. I shut my phone off, indulged in too much alcohol, and spent the night at Matt's apartment. Nobody knew where I was except for Matt. I'm not good at goodbyes, alright? I hide from them. Maybe I didn't want to watch the man I pictured to be my husband go down in flames before me all over again. I buried my head in the sand and hid from the one thing I couldn't gather myself to do; to formally say goodbye.

With a dead phone and a fierce hangover, I drove home from Matt's the next day. I knew in my gut Skyler was gone. I knew he would no longer consume my energy, right after the scolding I was about to get from my parents of course.

"Where have you been!" my mother screamed as I closed the front door behind me.

"Good morning to you," I said. Her screams sounded the alarms in my scalp. My head rang.

"I thought something happened to you Taylor. I was about ready to call the police."

"I was with the police."

"You were *what?*"

"I went on a date. He works in law enforcement. He took me to the Sox game."

"Well Taylor I'm so glad you enjoyed your night. I didn't know where you were. Skyler came to the house in tears. He cried into Blu's fur all night before saying a goodbye. He thanked me for all we have done for him and for creating such a lovely blessing in his life. You. You were his blessing. It was sad, honestly."

"Damn," I blurted out. I could still taste beer in my burps.

"You should text him. You know, make sure he got to Minnesota safely. He was in really bad shape when he left."

"Not sure why you care. He's been nothing but a prick to me."

"I don't care, Taylor. I just thought it would be the right thing to do. You can still be kind."

I never texted him. I could go the rest of my life without contacting Skyler Williams again. He didn't care about me when I was in rare form and this angered me now. I carried so much anger within my body. Everything I did, I did with anger. Within a week I heard from Skyler as if nothing had even transpired.

Skyler: St. Paul is a beautiful city! You will love it here. There is a huge shopping mall close by. I hope you decide to make the trip out here soon. I miss you already!

His outlook on our current status of the relationship was psychotic. He was delusional at best. He completely disregarded the fact that I had blown him off. I ignored him and continued developing my "situationship" with Matthew. One week later, another message.

Skyler: I went shopping today! I bought gray, black, and white bedding, towels, and rugs to help furnish my condo. I know that is your favorite color scheme for a house. Hopefully that will make you feel right at home when you visit, even though I have three roommates. Come visit me soon, my beautiful wife! I love you! Muah!

His behavior only got stranger and yet I couldn't look away. I could have blocked him but he was so amusing. I thought our story ended in Fort Myers but every day he continued to re-write our ending and I wasn't mad about it. The harder I ignored his endearing messages, the calmer and nicer he was. He was so patient. I assumed he had every dating app up and running before leaving the state of Massachusetts. He didn't need *me* to be there; he just needed someone; anyone.

Skyler excelled in independent ball. He was batting above .200 for the first time in a long time and after finding his rhythm in an organization with less talented players, he was picked up by the Minnesota Twins organization. He was sent right back down to Double A ball, this time in Chattanooga, Tennessee. This would be Skyler's sixth season in minor league baseball, his fourth consecutive stuck on a Double A roster.

My situationship with Matt bloomed that summer. I wasn't searching for serious romance and he definitely wasn't either, but it happened anyway. I eventually confided in him about my severed heart. I told him I started writing about such loss. I told him I wanted to publish the story of Skyler Williams and Taylor Higgins. I told him I wanted to relate to others who had faced great loss and together, we would heal each other. He encouraged my wishes. He listened as I spoke about the past without judgment or irritation. He told me I was brilliant; a genius rather. He told me I could do anything I put my mind to. He told me I would save the world. I believed him. I believed in my message. And my heart began to believe in sincere people again.

Skyler spent that same summer begging I come to Chattanooga. He offered to buy flights and pay for any expense the trip would cost me. He promised me he would never love again if he wasn't loving me. He went from playing five games per week to one or two. He was a washed-up, pine riding benchwarmer. But my plane ticket to Tennessee always remained an option.

On my birthday that July, Sam and Kyle gave birth to an adorable baby boy. It was the most magnificent news. Skyler got a DUI and was arrested that same night. He was caught drunk driving from Georgia to Tennessee. The Twins organization released him shortly after his arrest. His baseball career had finally concluded, as did his attempts to see me, and he was forced back to Georgia to live in his parents' basement with his new mugshot boogying around the internet. He told me he drank a bottle of whiskey every night since I'd been gone. He also told me he was addicted to the way moonshine made him feel. He told me if I came to see him he would quit drinking forever. He told me he spent more time at the liquor store than he did anywhere else. For once, I think he was telling the truth. I never blocked him, but I hardly responded. I just took note of his behavior.

One Friday morning in August, I received a message on Facebook from a girl named Emery Grace. She told me my name was saved in her boyfriend Skyler's phone as *Future Wife* and she needed to know who I was. She confessed in her plea for help that she and Skyler had been dating for a few weeks but she had a hunch he wasn't being completely truthful with her. I offered her my number in return. Seconds later, an unknown Georgia number appeared on my screen.

"Hi Taylor, this is Emery."

She had the sweetest, most gentle southern accent.

"I don't know where to begin Emery."

"Well how do you know Skyler?" she asked.

"He is my ex."

"I met him online a few weeks ago and I'm sure he is *the one*. I have two daughters with two separate father's and it don't bother him one bit. I mean I think I love him already. I love his family. His parents told my girls they will be their grandparents. It's so hard to meet people out where I live, out in the middle of nowheres land, and Skyler asked me to get a place together so we could raise the girls as a family. We are going ring shopping this week too. I just need to know why y'all two were texting? He's moved on, you know. It ain't his fault you couldn't keep up with the baseball lifestyle."

The innocent Georgia peach had turned into a brainwashed fool by the time she finished speaking. Congrats, you found a father and a set of grandparents for your daughters in a matter of two weeks via the internet. I was pissed yet I wanted to laugh in her face. *You idiot! Do you hear yourself?* I chomped on my nails as my body began to shake. My adrenaline took over.

"Hopefully he hasn't financed that engagement ring yet," I said.

"Scuse' me?"

"I said, if I ever accepted his weekly invitation to Tennessee, you wouldn't even be in the picture. Actually, he's that shitty, you'd probably still be in the picture."

There was silence on the other end of the call.

"But I denied his offer to move to Georgia after he was arrested and fired from his job. He offered to rent a condo for us. I told him I was in love with somebody else. He told me he would never love again after me. So you are his next victim, Emery Grace Lendell from Gwinnett County Georgia. And I see he has already given you the speech! *You're the one for me. I love you already. Let's move in together. Let's get a ring. Let's start a family. I can't wait to call you my wife.* Sound familiar? He's a liar. He's a cheat.

He's a phony. You still listening, Emery? He told me that the girls he dated before me couldn't handle the baseball life. That it was *too much* for them and they left him. And that's exactly what he told you. Another lie. I went to every game and supported every fucking emotion that sport brought him. What I chose not to "handle", Emery, was his infidelity. *That* is why we are no longer together. Your charming, fill in of a want-to-be father will fuck anything with a beat in its chest. Run. While you still can."

"Skyler was right. You do just want to ruin our happiness."

She hung up. Skyler's enticing words had already eaten her sense of reality. There was no saving her now. Emery would learn the hard way, just like I did, maybe just a diamond and a divorce attorney later.

19

Today I had lunch with an old friend, a fellow minor league WAG from Kansas. Joslynn's husband was recently promoted to the Red Sox but today, Sunday, the Sox were in Texas. We met over avocado salads in Boston's Seaport and caught up as the sun slipped into the ocean for the night.

"We bought a house in Fort Myers to escape our tiny hometown," she chuckled.

"I'm jealous. I love The Fort."

"How are *you*? I heard about the whole Skyler thing."

"I'm good actually," I continued the small talk. "I'm dating someone new."

"Good, good. As long as you're happy," Joslynn grinned.

The sound of lettuce crunched in our teeth as we decided who would speak next. She had something to tell me, but she didn't know how to.

"I'm writing a book about baseball and my relationship with Skyler," I said.

Joslynn gulped down the food in her mouth, rested her fork against the plate, and reached for her glass of chardonnay.

"What is it about?" she questioned.

"Being in a relationship with an athlete; cheating, heartbreak. You know, the basics."

She paused for a moment.

"Um," she froze. Her eyes filled with tears. "Excuse me I don't mean to cry. I'm so sorry."

"I didn't mean to make you cry!"

"It's just... um." Her voice cracked. She cleared her throat. "Um... The real reason why Luca and I bought the house in Fort Myers was to start over. To create a new beginning for our relationship. I think your book will be a huge hit. Baseball sucks. Baseball *life* sucks. Anyone who tells you differently is a liar."

By now Joslynn had pushed her plate far out in front of her to work on the wine by itself.

"Why are you upset? Can you relate to my story?" I pried for information.

She twisted the massive boulder on her boney ring finger. The type of ring that suggested her husband was a prospect and was signed for a good chunk of change.

"I never wanted to marry Luca," she admitted. "I was in love with somebody else. I didn't love Luca the day I married him. I almost called the wedding off right before I walked down the aisle."

"What stopped you?" I asked.

"My family is very religious. The wedding was expensive. I was scared. There were several factors. But I married him anyway. I was still in love with my high school sweetheart and I married someone I didn't love. Can you believe that?"

"But why?"

"I don't know honestly. Since then it has been terrible. I teach high school in Kansas so I can't visit him often during the season. We got married the year he started in Portland. We barely spoke and I got really good at spying on him. I found him on Tinder and Craigslist. He used his actual name on both. He would post advertisements on Craigslist looking for sex and blowjobs. His email, his Twitter, all of his inboxes were filled with disgusting girls. He gave out his number. He invited them to hotels. He even took a fan out to dinner to say "thanks" for the support. She was fat, Taylor!"

"Jesus," I said. I knew I wasn't alone in this experience.

Her David Yurman bracelets clanked against the table as her expressions and hand gestures grew more and more theatrical. She came from money.

"We tried counseling. Divorce is hardly an option. Our families would shun us. The problem with counseling is that Luca didn't speak. And then he stopped coming with me. So I stopped going eventually, too. I kill myself to check on him every second of every day. I'm trying to catch him in a lie and even when I do, I don't leave him. It is so sick."

She bawled at our table. I ached for her because I was too familiar with the type of pain she was experiencing, only I wasn't married to it.

"Look at me. I'm a mess," she said, investing in comic relief.

"I'm so sorry you are carrying this weight around with you. It's not easy. I know what it feels like."

"His parents hate me. We should just divorce. I told him I'd only take what's mine. I don't care about his money. But he doesn't want me to leave for some fucked up reason. He told me he's never physically cheated, that he has only talked to other women. Does he think I'm stupid? He must think I'm stupid. Wanna know something?"

"Sure, yeah of course," I said.

"I had sex with a co-worker of mine in our bed at our house in Kansas. I told Luca about it when I saw his ads on Craigslist."

"Oh my... holy shit. Wow. Alright. Wow."

"Yup. Ever since then I receive blackmail and death threats to my house. His parents even follow me home from work sometimes. It's a disaster. Which is why we bought in Fort Myers."

Our server appeared to check on us.

"We'll do another round of drinks," Joslynn demanded.

"Thank you," I added to the end of her order. "Look, Joslynn, it sounds like you're in a very unhealthy situation. I'm sure your parents would understand the reasoning behind your divorce if you were honest with them."

"I have hope. Divorce is a hassle. Besides, I've been putting antidepressants into his smoothies in the morning and it seems to make him more mellow than usual. His stupid ass doesn't even taste the difference."

Liquid truth serum was in full swing tonight. The more chardonnay Joslynn consumed, the more freely she spoke of her troubles with Luca.

"All I'm saying is I would try to get out if I were you" I suggested one last time.

"I came off birth control. We are going to start trying to have a baby when he comes home. Maybe that will soften him up. I want a girl so bad."

I made eye contact with our waiter.

"Check please!"

In October, Skyler moved into Emery's brother's house with her, her brother, and the two girls. He found a part-time job teaching baseball lessons. How do I know this? Not even a month into the relationship, Emery sent me a message saying I was right. The poor thing caught him having sex with her daughter's tee-ball coach. In his truck. In Emery's brother's driveway. After he had put a deposit down on an engagement ring! He was big deposit guy when it came to engagement rings. God forbid he save up enough money first.

Matt and I spent a long weekend in Dallas, Texas to see a New England Patriots game. And a Dallas Stars game. And a Texas Rangers game. Go sports. He told me he wanted to spend the rest of his life with me on a roller coaster at Six Flags while we were down there. I told him he was stuck with me for life.

That same month, as I conducted a personal journey in self-growth and inner happiness, a certain someone forced me to become enthralled with the idea of studying the wrongful behavior of others. Oh, Ron Samson, you've inspired me so. Your actions will write the ending of my story.

Ronny Samson, a teammate of Skyler's in Portland, spent a lifetime in minor league ball as a pitcher. He was recently called up to the big leagues, starting on the west coast and making his home field debut this past weekend in Boston. He poked me on Facebook as soon as he arrived to town. He had a girlfriend, I knew this. An aspiring social influencer with, in my opinion, sub-par blogging abilities and overused content. Reading her poorly combined mixture of sarcasm and attempted inspiration made her lack of originality shine bright like a diamond. Over the weekend, this particular WAG hopped on a cross country flight to Beantown to see her happily ever after make his first appearance on the bump at Fenway. Her mother flew in to join her. They were so proud of him. Ugh! They posted pictures and they bragged to the social media universe. *Ron is so deserving of this opportunity. You have worked your whole life for this moment. You made it, babe.* I cringed at the words they shared. If only you knew what I knew, toots. As Ron's lady was lost in the clouds, forty-thousand feet above civilization, he was poking me on the book. To test him, I poked back. Since returning his poke, I've included our exchange of Facebook messages:

Ron Samson: Hi there. Just checking in. Wanted to see how you were doing.

Taylor Higgins: I'm doing well thanks for asking. Congrats on the promotion. How are things?

Ron Samson: Awesome!!! Thank you!!! Things are amazing!!!

Taylor Higgins: So crazy seeing all the guys I've watched play in random cities over the years play so close to my house at Fenway.

Ron Samson: How far do you live???

Taylor Higgins: About twenty minutes from Fenway.

Ron Samson: Oh damn. I didn't know that.

Ron Samson: You still talk or hangout with any of these guys??

Taylor Higgins: No I do not.

Ron Samson: Oh nice!!

Taylor Higgins: I guess so. Well it was nice to hear from you.

Ron Samson: Was it??

Taylor Higgins: Sure. Twas' a nice surprise.

Ron Samson: You're a nice surprise....

Ron Samson: See you around soon??

Taylor Higgins: How is your girlfriend?

Ron Samson: She's great!! When can I see you?

Ron Samson: Add me on Snapchat. soxofthered01

Taylor Higgins:	You want to see me?
Ron Samson:	It's probably not a good idea but only if you and I knew about it then we could do something.
Ron Samson:	Snapppppp meeeeeeee!

I did exactly what he asked for. I played along. I even told Matt about my plan to expose his behavior to his lover. Maybe then she could write about something pure. Ron was a reflection of Skyler and I was finally going to witness their game as the starry-eyed fan girl on the other end of the phone.

Ron's behavior on Snapchat was aggressive. He implied sexual desires he held as fantasies that he would like to see carried out with me. How clever he was. I watched his girlfriend explore Boston in pictures; riding the swan boats and allowing our local coffee shops to capture her heart. *If only she knew.* I would make sure she knew.

Sunday— I was outside walking Blu in my neighborhood when my phone rang. It was Ron, on video chat, shirtless in bed. He was at a hotel. I knew this because the white sheets on his bed were crisp and neat. Sunday— the day his girlfriend would return home to the west coast.

"What can I do for you my friend?" I shouted into the camera through the morning breeze.

"Just wanted to see your face," he said with an awful grin.

I struggled to host a conversation with one of the most unattractive males I'd ever laid eyes on. He was goofy and cocky in the worst way possible and his entire vibe made me want to humble him so quickly.

"Where's Cailey?" I asked.

"She went to take a spin class before her flight. Do you want me to show you what's under these covers?"

He hung up before he had the chance to expose himself. Not that I wanted him to. Gross, please no. He followed up with a message on Snapchat.

SoxOfTheRed01: Sorry. My girlfriend just got home from her spin class.

Attached to his message was a picture of his penis he had previously taken but saved for a desperate time such as this. Times when your girlfriend cramps your style and sabotages your morning wood with her return. I knew this particular nude was old because it was photographed in a bathroom stall while wearing baseball pants and cleats. He was in the locker room at the field. This picture was originally meant for someone else. Maybe it belonged to Cailey. Maybe it didn't. But today this hand-me-down dick picture was used to entice me. To lure me in. *Oh, Ron. The shrubbery escaping your pants beneath your petite third leg has me weak in the knees!* No. Just no.

I gathered my findings in screenshots and carefully typed a message to his girlfriend Cailey on Instagram. I even included the picture of his penis. I was on a mission to expose the unfaithful. Cailey opened my message and without responding, she blocked me. She posted more about her man and less about anything else after seeing my message. How they were so happy and in love. How baseball life answered all of her prayers. How distance made them a powerhouse of a couple. Cailey knew she had an audience waiting to see her relationship fail. She had too much pride to let him go. Besides, she'd already told her following on social media about him. She was in too deep. Two weeks later, Ron proposed to Cailey. They would marry during the off-season. It was like she gave him an ultimatum or something.

Skyler Williams continued his quest for completion. I watched from afar with a massive bucket of popcorn. Pushing thirty years of age with a second DUI, Skyler's downward spiral seemed to be operating at an expedited pace. He found new love with Harley Johnson, a twenty-four year old nursing student from Georgia. They signed a lease on an apartment and picked out an engagement ring within the first two months. I know this because she eventually found me on Facebook and asked for *my* phone number. Together we shared a tearful conversation about our experiences with the same maniac. Each time I was given an opportunity to speak about him, my body would sweat and shake. My heart would race and the saliva inside my mouth would dry up like a desert. I had so much to say. My lips moved like a motor. I needed water and chapstick just to talk about him and even still I'd pace all over. His behavior drove me mad. Harley became one of my favorite people, once she dumped him of course. And then along came my biggest fear. Skyler's final victim in the story I was forced to share.

Blakely Morse and her four-year-old daughter, Brynn, would submit a deathblow of an ending to prove that some people don't ever change. Skyler and I remained friends on Facebook. The way he plowed through relationships brought me great entertainment. He was in love, he was living with someone, and then he was single. It was fascinating, truly. It also reassured me and my sanity, that I'd dodged a huge bullet. He was the problem all along and his actions were a constant reminder to me that he was not well.

Blakely tagged Skyler in a picture on Facebook. It was a picture of him in centerfield wearing a Sea Dogs' uniform in Portland. I had taken the photo. *I love this man. I can't wait to call him my husband!* read her post. Out of his hysteric rotation of naive girlfriends, Blakely had to have been the most clueless of all. Blakely had brown hair with a faded, orange ombré and pale skin begging for a decent moisturizer and some blush. She was the type of girl who liked her own pictures just to have sixty-two likes instead of sixty-one. She was proud of her ex-minor league ball playing boyfriend. She couldn't refrain from posting pictures that I had previously taken of him during his time in the Red Sox organization. He was small town famous and she was psyched to be attached to his false glories.

I commented on the picture she posted. It was completely out of my character to stoop to their level, but then again, he had ruined so much for me.

"Yikes. This keeps getting worse and worse," I commented on the picture. Blakely, his flavor of the week, messaged me instantly.

Blakely Morse:	He warned me about you. How jealous you are. Just let us be happy.
Taylor Higgins:	Let me guess. He told you I couldn't handle the baseball life?
Blakely Morse:	He said you came from a rich family and that he couldn't keep up with your expectations. That you couldn't accept him for who he was.
Taylor Higgins:	Well, I chose not to accept him for who he was. He got part of it right. I dated him when he was dirt poor. I left him because he's addicted to having sex with strangers. He will be the biggest mistake you'll ever make. Mark my words. xo

Two months after meeting at Skyler's new place of work; Skyler selling solar panels and Blakely a receptionist, Skyler proposed using the ring Harley had chosen for herself. The ring was financed at a chain jewelry store at the local mall. Blakely was his second official fiancé. But could she make it to *wife?* Harley and I spoke often, usually to place bets on how long they would last or poke fun at the fact that they broke up every other day, even changing their relationship status on Facebook each time. It was a joke.

Worst of all, Blakely had a daughter and two ex-husbands dragging behind her.

On the day of Blakely's bridal shower, she asked me for my phone number. She wanted to talk. I went outside to take her call hoping to knock some sense into her. Why didn't I just let her drown? Mostly because I was just that kind. I saw photos of her shower online before taking her call. A bowl of skittles, a neat arrangement of Hostess cupcakes, miniature corn muffins, and chips and salsa. She really outdid her brunch-themed soirée. I circled my yard, crouching to pull at grass or bending branches on trees to keep my body physically occupied as I listened to her concerns.

"We just signed a rental agreement on our house. My ex was a perfectly decent guy and I left him for Skyler, and I don't know, I feel like he is cheating on me," she expressed.

"He probably is cheating on you. Wait, you left your husband for Skyler?"

"Yes. I cheated on him with Skyler. Our divorce will be finalized on Thursday," she said.

"So technically you're married and engaged at the same time. That is interesting. Is this your daughter's father that you are divorcing?"

"No. She belongs to my first husband."

"Oh. Right on."

"I just don't know what to do Taylor. I was hoping you would have some advice. My daughter Brynn calls Skyler her daddy already. I can't take that away from her. He just bought her a blue french bulldog."

"*Blue* did you say?"

"I know you have a blue dog too. He told me it's a small, little thing and it was expensive as ever. Never mind the dogs. Can you describe your relationship with Skyler?"

I winced as she tried to sweep my fur child under the rug before proceeding into the rundown of our time together. I told her he was a relationship supervisor. That he dominated every thought and desire that entered my skull. He regulated my whereabouts. He made decisions for me. He was a piece of shit, basically. A cheater, a liar; a monster. We all know the deal.

She concluded that her divorce from hubby number two might have been a mistake. I told her to be honest about her mistakes to hubby number two and maybe he'd take her back, but please, whatever she did, do not marry Skyler. She told me she wouldn't. She *couldn't*. Her gut told her not to.

Two weeks before Christmas they eloped on a mountainside, Skyler and Blakely. Not a family member nor friend sat in attendance during this matrimony, not even her daughter Brynn. Ironically, Ron Samson married Cailey that same weekend somewhere on a beach. I listened as Ron recited handwritten vows to Cailey in a video on the internet and while he professed his love for her, all I could really hear was him begging *me* to take my clothes off. I didn't know which nuptial pairing was more unfortunate. I deemed them both a slow leaking ship.

I kept to myself. I had a lot of rebuilding still to do. I inched back to friendships I previously relinquished. I hoped they would understand the real reasons why I withdrew myself from society; I hoped they would accept me back. I started thinking about what I wanted my life to look like.

I knew which artificial marriages would turn to soot with time. Wildfires can only burn out of control for so long until they must rest in a smokey residue. Infidelity, much like scorching flames, cannot hide itself, which is why forged love will always be cremated.

Matt and I spent New Years together in Miami, Florida. We had our first argument there because I accidentally booked the wrong flight home for us. He was yelling, I was yelling; it was late at night. He got out of bed to spend the night on the couch and I jumped up to stop him. To tell him he was overreacting. When he walked towards me to exit the bedroom, I no longer saw him as Matt. It was Skyler who was with me in that bedroom, charging at me to knock me to the floor. I protected my head and cowered with excessive apologies. I begged him not to hurt me. I begged him over and over again as I braced myself for impact. Matt brushed by me. I didn't feel any pain. He didn't touch me and he never intended to. I was still standing. That was when I knew my recovery from Skyler was going to be more difficult than I imagined.

20

One month post eloping, Blakely contacted me to tell me everything I said about Skyler was true. I reminded her I had no motive to lie to her to begin with. That same day she posted a happy family photo of her, Skyler, and Brynn on Facebook. She couldn't decide if she could withstand his storms anymore but how humiliating would it be if she let everyone who warned her win. They were *friends* on Facebook, to *single* on Facebook, to *married* on Facebook, to not friends on Facebook. I couldn't keep up with them, nor did I care anymore. Harley remained a close friend of mine through all of this. I will always be thankful for her.

On March 10, 2018, as I indulged in the waffle bar at my cousin's bridal shower brunch, I received a call from Blakely. I held my phone up at the table of family members who had just finished asking me about the status of my book and laughingly said, "Skyler's wife is calling right now!" *Answer it, answer it, answer it!* We'd all thought their marriage was bogus from the beginning, anyway. I excused myself from the function room and found silence in the hallway.

"Hello?" I answered.

In tears she cried, "Taylor you were right all along! I'm leaving him for good this time. He's been cheating, I know he has. Most nights he doesn't come home until four in the morning. I never know where he is. He's so angry with me, always, even when I have nothing to say he is angry. He punches holes in the walls of our house. He destroys my things. He is the worst!"

"Where is he now?" I interrupted her confessions.

"Fishing with his dad. So he says. He just bought a boat. And a brand new truck. He took all of the money out of our bank account and put it in one of his personal accounts. I don't have any money! I can't even put gas in my car! He's going to kick me out. I know he's going to kick us out. He wouldn't give a damn if Brynn and I were homeless. This house is a rental and his name is on the lease. He's going to kick us out."

"Why don't you just leave now while he isn't home? Can you stay at your parents' house for the time being? I'm sure they would help you get out of this mess."

"He took my computer! He took my credit cards! Brynn's birthday party is today! How am I supposed to pay for her party? It's at a trampoline park! How does he expect me to pay for that?"

"I take it that he's not planning to attend the party?" I said.

"He already said he wasn't coming. I don't know what to do Taylor. I need to get out. I can't live like this. I need my life back."

"So just grab whatever belongs to you and Brynn and walk out the door. You have the ability to change your life right this second."

"I have to wait until April. If I move again before my custody battle, I'll lose my daughter for sure."

At that moment, I knew she wasn't ready to leave him. She was upset and desperate and needed a voice that would be willing to listen and understand. She knew I would answer her call. I decided that communicating with her was not healthy. I'd carried Skyler's issues with me for too long and four years later, it wasn't my job anymore.

"I have to go," I said into the phone.

"Oh. Alright. Thank you Taylor. For everything you've done for me. I can't wait to read your book. I'll tell you anything you want to know if you'd ever like to write another book. About how Skyler hasn't changed a bit. Let me know. I owe you. You're going to help so many people."

"Goodbye Blakely."

Later that same day, Grayson West messaged me on Facebook. A name I'd never heard before:

Miss Taylor,

You don't know me but I've been told you once knew Skyler Williams. He is my daughter Brynn's step-father now and I was wondering if you'd be willing to tell me a little bit about him.

My name is Grayson West. I was Blakely's first husband. We are currently fighting for custody of Brynn. We will go to trial in April. I'm reaching out to you because all of Georgia knows you've been writing a book about Skyler, and well, this is my final chance to gain custody of my daughter. I fear that her care isn't what it should be and that her well-being is not a priority to either Blakely nor Skyler. Brynn is constantly sick and her teachers have expressed concerns about her behavior. She lashes out, uses vulgar language, talks back, ignores, and has even pinched and bitten some of her classmates. She is tardy to school almost every day and she has lost all interest in her after school activities. I am very concerned. Anything you say could help my case at this point.

Thank you,
Grayson

I responded to his cry for help by offering my phone number. I'm addicted to saving people if I know I can, especially a child. What harm could a single phone call cause?

"Taylor thank you so much for your willingness to speak to me. I honestly thought you might tell me to screw myself after that message. You're a true blessin'," he started in his country boy tone. He was straight out of hick town; I could hear it in his slow sentences. He must have lived closed to Skyler with an accent as strong as his.

355

"Of course. I am pretty passionate when it comes to talking about shitty people."

"You must be, sure, I believe it. I was at a bar the other night with Calvin, Blakely's second husband. We're friends now, he's a good dude, anyway, we were gettin' some wings and beer and I overheard these girls talking about your book. Musta' been cause they seen me and Calvin but everyone down here sure knows about it. I think it's great you chose to write about your experiences and for the record, I don't think anyone should have to go through hard times like you did."

"I appreciate that. Yeah, it was tough. So how did you find me?" I asked.

"Blakely's shown up at my front door time and time again after having a blow out with Skyler. She's told me a lot about you so I just figured you might be the best one to talk to."

"So what is your ultimate goal here? What do you hope will change after speaking to me? Like, what are you looking for me to do?"

"Best case scenario Taylor, is you agree to talk to my lawyer and they subpoena you to court down here in Georgia. I'd like you to testify against Skyler in front of the judge. In front of Blakely, too. I need you to simply describe him as a person."

Holy shit. The saga never ends. Subpoena? Court? Character witness? Testify! My mind went in a million different directions. I'd have to go buy a new suit. The *I'm here to verbally assassinate my ex-boyfriend's character with the truth* type of suit. What would Matt think of this? Matt will be pissed, who am I kidding. I can't go to Georgia. But there's a child involved! And this would be the final nail in the coffin for Skyler. After all he's done to me and to others, his fate was now in my hands. *Karma!* Imagine? I'd lock eyes with his sorry self from the witness stand in a courtroom as I ripped him to shreds. He'd be standing next to his wife, the one he married to prove to the world he was capable of marriage, to hide his true self. I'd introduce myself to Blakely, someone I'd never dreamed of meeting, and I'd thank her for ingesting Skyler's lies. These confessions she so easily handed to me would once again prove my sanity. I snapped out of the fantasy in my head.

"I'm willing to speak to your attorney," I said into the phone.

"Great. Taylor, thank you. I'll have him contact you in the morning."

I immersed myself with thoughts of waltzing into a courtroom looking like his biggest regret and giving Skyler the ending he so much deserved. I didn't want to go, but I did. I didn't want to be involved in a stranger's custody battle, I mean, I don't know Grayson and who am I to say he's fit to be the caretaker of a child either, but I wasn't going to fight for Brynn's primary residence. I couldn't. I would go to describe my personal relationship with Skyler Williams. *That* excited the shit out of me. A call from Georgia came in around nine the next morning, just like Grayson said it would.

"May I please speak to Miss Taylor Higgins?" a man's voice asked me.

"This is she."

"Taylor my name is Chestler Briggs. I represent Grayson West as his attorney. He gave me your contact information. I was wondering if I could put you on speaker phone so myself along with my superior could ask you some questions. You will be recorded."

I sat down in the chair in my mother's office. I faced what was Skyler's old closet.

"That's fine."

"OK. Miss Higgins can you tell me how long you and Skyler Williams were together?"

"About two years."

"And how old are you now, Miss Higgins?"

"I'm twenty-two."

"So you were about seventeen, eighteen when you met Mr. Williams?

"That's correct. I was Miss Teen Massachusetts at the time."

"Wow. OK. Miss Higgins were you engaged to Mr. Williams?"

"No. Never."

"Do y'all share any children together?"

"No we do not. Thank god," I chuckled. I spun around in circles in the office chair as two men fired questions at me. They didn't laugh along with me.

"Are you married now, Miss Higgins?

"No."

"But you're in a relationship?

"Yes I'm in a serious relationship. Yes."

"Do you have any children of your own, Miss Higgins?"

"No I do not.

"How did y'all meet, Miss Higgins? Yourself and Mr. Williams."

"We met during an event in Portland, Maine."

"And what were some of the issues y'all faced during the relationship?"

"Um, excessive lying and infidelity. Substance abuse. Emotional abuse. Controlling behavior. Verbal abuse. Physical abuse. Mind games. Manipulative desires."

"He was physically abusive, Miss Higgins?"

"On several different occasions, yes."

I could hear their pens scribbling faster as they acknowledged my words. They hit the jackpot with me. Skyler's bats, four of them, were resting in the corner of the room I was in. I had recently used them during the filming of a short screenplay I wrote to provide a visual description of my book. In essence, I wanted to hype up my story in the form of a trailer. I stared at the dents in the bats.

"Miss Higgins, we believe your presence in the courtroom could make or break Mr. West's case. Would you be willing to fly down here in roughly fifteen days? We haven't been given an exact date for the trial yet but you will be one of the first to know when it's received. We would obviously pay for any expense. Your boyfriend is welcome to come as well."

"At the very least I would be willing to leave a statement that could be used in court. Let me think about making the trip down there. I will get back to you as soon as possible."

I thought long and hard about returning to Georgia for a reason I'd never anticipated. Matt had been accepting of my broken past since day one, but he also believed the past was behind us for a reason and for that, it should stay there. I don't disagree. Part of me felt like I was a necessity to this ending. That these individuals found me for separate reasons. But a bigger part of me knew I'd suffered enough through my own story, the story of Skyler and I.

My suffering was over because I decided it would be and I'd be a fool to board a plane directly back to the one thing that destroyed me. What is meant to be will be, and it will be without me.

I sat down with my pen and paper to prepare a statement for the attorney. I couldn't find words. I scribbled in the margin; outlining stars and practicing my signature. I dropped my pen to decide whether this was the right thing to do or not, to help a child, to validate his character in front of a courtroom. I capped my pen. I save people who don't belong to me all the time, but this wasn't my ending to write.

TAYLOR REVISED

I write to you in May of 2018. I've orbited around the existence of this book for the past three years. My Massachusetts hands wrote this story with purpose. To hold this awfulness in black and white offers me an everlasting sense of resilience. I've allowed you beyond the front cover of myself. I've invited you inside to thumb through my pages, to judge, to learn, all while traveling through my secrets and relating through my dealings.

If I've completed my mission, you yourself should feel you have endured and survived the tragedies that I own. You will have spent nights with your back pressed against your headboard, circling, highlighting, or folding corners on content that files the rough, uneven edges of your heart. All damages of another's carelessness but in my words, you were someplace safe again.

We build our lives around people that end up as memories. We cling onto mediocre bursts of happiness and ache for people who never really existed in the first place. We become comfortable in a controlled state of misery because we fear change. We are a society of cold, metal computers, surviving because we must. We live lives that weren't meant for us because of our polluted sense of devotion.

The truth is you should never have to demonstrate the proper way to love you to somebody who already claims to love you. Love is worth a billion battles, as long as the other person is willing match your fight. If such battle has left you empty, you are galaxies away from actual love. Love will never ask you to deduct bits and pieces of your character until you no longer recognize yourself. It will simply greet you and all of your journeys with a warm embrace and say, "I've been waiting all this time for you." Below, I've included my personal guide to outlasting heartbreak:

1. Accepting

That feeling of inescapable trauma is all too familiar. You carry boulders on your chest, longing for one person to save you. You bargain with him and you beg. He doesn't deserve to save you. Eighty proof saves him; a bottle has never saved me. I shake at the thought of us; the thought of him stepping on my feet and pushing me over. Who will he sleep with next? I'll never find this kind of love again. I hate being alone. What does he do with his days?

You cry out for a love that can't respond. The weeks are intimidating; you don't know how long he will make you wait until you hear from him. Everything is always on his terms. You avoid meals until your shaking body allows a morsel of food to enter, only to reject it soon after in the toilet from one end or the other. You call in sick to work, you back out of plans using elaborate excuses, and you bite chunks out of your polished fingers. Your mind relies on his words to operate and now, you just don't want to operate. Keeping busy is necessary, but every time you pause you crave him. Disappointment eventually turns to frustration and frustration to anger, and somewhere in those emotions you begin to resent him. Once you are able to acknowledge his behavior is not up to your standards, you will begin to heal. Because being sick and tired all of the time is exhausting and you now know you deserve better. Lounge in those painful minutes. Overpay your dues in such torture. *I've suffered enough. It should be he who suffers!* Yes, but *time* will take you where you need to be when you are ready— when you are willing to accept reality with a clear mind.

2. Healing

The decisions we make are imperative for our growth, which is why I refuse to criticize those who are stuck where they no longer belong. The universe is strengthening your weakest qualities. You can overload someone with truths they are fully aware of already, but hopeful hearts will only leave when they feel it is time to. Nothing will change that.

The most unfortunate part about heartbreak, though, is that life goes on. We know this. We've lived this. Your heart can be severed but you are still required to function. To walk into an office, to feed yourself, to continue.

You must, for once, choose yourself over the empathy of others. You must search for beauty, a lesson rather, when you find yourself a mess on the floor. When you can no longer look at your reflection in the mirror, know this is part of your reincarnation. This crumbling will launch you directly where you need to be. It hurts, it fucking hurts. But trust me and trust time.

Be gentle with yourself. Time heals most, but you're essentially loving yourself back to normality all alone and that can be uncomfortable. Remember, you are adapting to a new way of life. Mourn the loss of the person who foreclosed your heart. Detach yourself, stay busy, find a rebound, find friends who are willing to stop their world to help reignite your flame, write a nonfiction; whatever helps. Locate your vice, but be willing to embrace new beginnings. They will come sooner than you expect. Let that door close and then lock it shut. Something great will then come your way, I promise.

There is no remedy to mending a heart that has faced catastrophe. Introduce yourself to bravery, stay kind always, and love the shit out of everyone and everything. Those who have wronged you will notice the gaping hole you left in their life and they will spend the rest of their days trying to **stitch** it. Stay amongst the crowd of faithful hearts and let it lead you to the love you deserve. Receive heartache as a blessing and become your own best friend. But always love with pure, unfiltered intentions. The universe will take care of the rest.

3. Rebuilding

One, random day you will wake and everything will be better. You will notice the sound of lawnmowers again; dogs barking; children playing. You will have energy and you will be calm. You will smile at people on the sidewalk as they pass by. You will take care of yourself. You will cringe knowing you gave your all for a creature like him. Demon's only want you when they feel they are losing control of you, but your new mindset is no match for their games. Of course you will have bad days. To this day, I suffer vivid cheating nightmares. It has become one of my biggest fears and these night terrors hound the hell out of me. Imagine waking up next to your smiley boyfriend after watching him have sex with his ex-girlfriend all night? But your new inner strength is only getting stronger. Your drive to be better is unstoppable.

The stillness inside of you: that is recovery. And while you carry stories within you that could lead strangers to their breaking point, your pliable heart has no interest in defeat. Your impactful spirit will serve as a sun to those looking to find their way back to happiness. You will now teach others how to rise again. All scars heal eventually, though they live on us eternally. Be proud of your scars— you are an ambassador for love.

I shared my entire relationship with baseball boy on the internet. When I stopped posting, people started asking questions. The thought of answering to people put me in a state of distress. What was I supposed to tell them?

Oh, he was a narcissistic asshole that suffered an excessive addiction to cheating and thrived on prescription pills, Tennessee whiskey, and insecure women! Our love story was a myth and it broke me to share that but it certainly brought pen to paper and I haven't looked back since. I became infatuated with the idea of being so painfully raw with my truth in hopes of encouraging others to be courageous enough to do the exact same. Being relatable creates a connection, a bond rather, and in that togetherness we are able to empower one another. Sharing our experiences creates spiritual healing. It is a simple reminder that you are not alone. Use your voice even when you're scared. Find what makes every hair on your body stand for an ovation alongside the goosebumps, and stay involved with it. Writing is my ovation. My heart applauds my brain as I create. This is your purpose and it will later stand for how the world remembers you, and we need more passion fueled dreamers that plan to shake up our generation. Thank you for becoming my tragedy within the roots of my writing. One, single voice can change the world. Don't ever underestimate the power of sharing your story.

TO THE MAN WHO MURDERED MY SOUL

IF I COULD SPEAK TO YOU NOW

Skyler—

There are white roses in a vase on my desk that are near death, but in this very moment they are wide and full. Tomorrow the petals should crisp around their pretty edges causing them to plummet. I'm not sure why you ever hated such a delicate flower to begin with. I suppose it is because you cannot appreciate things that do not benefit you. The skies have opened themselves for one last cry beyond my windowsill as I write my final words to you. It is gray outside, this spring day in May. I allow the pattering of the rain to pilot my thoughts.

Nothing ever seems to be as it should, wouldn't you agree? When I think of spring, I think sunshine and blooming agriculture. Today it is about the selfish thundershowers that fall angrily against the wind. Today is anything but spring. The elements know I'm speaking to you. You are a reflection of their performance outside my window.

Love, much like spring, is supposed to be beautiful. We are taught these are beautiful things at a very young age. But beautiful things can only hide their capabilities for so long. And you, Skyler, just like these beautiful things, leave the welcoming stranded. Nothing is built to last anymore.

I'll have you know I cried my way through many chapters of this book. I'd start my days with burnt eyelids; fearing the questions people in this world might ask me. I'd chew the skin around my nails and shake my body into fatigue. My writing, though therapeutic, would haunt me. You remained present in my life far longer than I'd like to admit. Your voice. Your words. Your many scents. I kept you alive so much so that at times I could still feel you against me. You introduced me to true love. Brutally wonderful true love. You, the same person who traded my innocence in for sorrow. You misled me. With a smile on your face, you took me by the hand and guided me straight into deception.

You are a hollow man. Hollow because your emotions have deserted you because they too refuse to lurk in cold, vacant bodies. Your wrongdoings hold you captive inside; you are your own prisoner.

The most unfortunate part about empty people, Skyler, is this. We are all born whole. It is the way we choose to perceive our journey of life that causes the important things to retreat. I used to blame baseball; your parents, for your incompleteness. I taught you about safe havens and second chances. You taught me what it's like to be scared and alone.

You're a predator, Skyler. You search infinitely for an escape from your true self because you don't like your true self. You search in the forms of power, women, medicine, and liquor. You've created an impossible way of life that is hidden beneath your current love affair until she too becomes aware of your dark side. And you, just like much of our generation, refuse to cope naturally. Instead you arrange your own kind of therapy sessions on the internet, making appointments to bury yourself inside foreign bodies. You revert to abuse when you know you're wrong, all while maintaining a phony innocence. When indisputable truths presented themselves in the palms of my hands, you were always faultless. And I never left you. I hardly raised my voice at you. I simply asked *why*. I wanted to understand your actions. You could never tell me why.

You sanded me down to a thin, fragile layer Skyler. You knew you had me even when you didn't want me, but you didn't want me to find somebody that would love me correctly. You cornered me, forcing me to live inside the tiny bubble that only you had access to. Remember how mad you'd get if I socialized?

Tell me, my Skyler, did the virtual sex save you? Did the trolls of the internet give you great intensifications behind your camera that trumped the love I gave to you? I gave you all of me. You gave me just enough to keep me still.

I suffered a great deal after I left you, Skyler. I left you because you couldn't love me the way I loved you. I grew comfortable in the pain you brought me. I turned a blind eye to all signs that led me away from you. I defended you, all while you were busy digging my grave. You killed the only person that loved you. I drowned in your misery. I *died* because I tried to keep you alive.

I can smell the grass today. It has been a long winter. The soil and sod combined reminds me of warmer days. It still has the ability to take me back to a ball field in Portland, Maine. John Fogerty's 'Centerfield' surrounds me as I wait along the first baseline for you to appear from the clubhouse doors. In my yard, the grass takes me some-where where we can be happy together for a moment.

You are gone Skyler, but you are very much alive in these pages. You forced me to make you a stranger but our story will live forever. I must tell you, the hardest part about writing our story was making our readers believe you had good moments. Our love could be compared to roadkill. Intestines and brain matter have painted the pavement yet we unexplainably choose to stare. It's ugly but you look anyway. That was us. We could never turn our backs on our own mess.

Your marriage finally caved. Three whole months, con-gratulations. Your wife called me the day you filed. Your mother must be rattled over the thought of another bitch breaking your heart. You know, my mom once told me she wished you gave me an STD. Not a harmful one of course, but something, just to have a reason to leave you sooner.

Do you still cuss in Spanish? Do you still withhold oral contraceptives from your significant other in fear they will gain weight? Are performance enhancers still a part of your life? Did you know your ex named her son Skyler? Have you heard from Leslie Finn lately, you know, the one with the *cum on me* implants? Does your daddy still give the family dog opioids when he's not feeling himself? Do you still think of me? Do you remember when we were inseparable and in love? Do you remember when we were best friends? Do you still have your ring? Will the sound of my name steal your oxygen? Do you know how much damage you brought to my life? Oh, the wonders I do have.

You are nothing until you own someone, Skyler Williams, and that is the simple truth. With one final fist to my jaw, your hand broke every last piece of me. I spat blood from my mouth and pulled myself out of the ground. I forced you to put the shovel down. Six feet under would have to wait. My time is now. The world deserves to be warned about you.

Forever you will be a red Chevrolet, a sun faded photograph, a bag of sunflower seeds, a tug on my fishing line, an eyeliner note on my mirror, a ticket to a baseball game, the long way home, a love like no other, and my greatest lesson yet. I will never shrink back to comfortable places or people who don't treasure my life ever again because of you, and for that, I am forever grateful.

Thank you heartache, for gifting me
with precious strength.
To baseball, for showing me a new way of life.
To my forever WAG's, for inspiring me, always.
To Katie & Sarah, for being my day one
stadium sisterfriends.
To Emilio, for believing in me from the start.
And to my family & friends, for supporting me
with so much love.
I will never stop writing. This is only the
beginning.
XO

To My Beautiful Mother
For nursing this book to life alongside of me.
Nothing is possible without you. Thank you for believing
in my gift, for being my publicist, my spokesperson,
my Kris Jenner, my courage, and my inspiration.
You are my hero.
I love you.